ELISE PASCOE'S FOUR SEASONS OF FOOD AND WINE

With wine notes by
KEN BIGNILL

M

To my sons Mark and Charles,
whose love for good living
knows no seasons.

First published 1984 by
THE MACMILLAN COMPANY OF AUSTRALIA PTY LTD
107 Moray Street, South Melbourne 3205
6 Clarke Street, Crows Nest 2065

Associated companies in
London and Basingstoke, England
Auckland Dallas Delhi Hong Kong
Johannesburg Lagos Manzini Nairobi
New York Singapore Tokyo Washington Zaria

National Library of Australia
cataloguing in publication data

Pascoe, Elise.
    Elise Pascoe's Four seasons of food and wine.

    Includes index.
    ISBN 0 333 38075 4.

    1. Cookery. 2. Wine and wine making. I. Bignill, Ken.
    II. Title. III. Title: Four seasons of food and wine.

641.5

Designed by Julie Gross
Set in Goudy Old Style by Savage Type Pty Ltd, Brisbane
Printed in Hong Kong

CONTENTS

INTRODUCTORY NOTES
Elise Pascoe

This book evolved out of necessity — demands of living well in this busy world. I was forever running around in ever-increasing circles and most of my friends and colleagues seem to share the same problem — a shortage of time. How to best organize our resources so as to enjoy the best of food and wine? I decided that this was the kind of book that I needed and therefore hoped there would be a host of other people wanting to share the same ideals. I hope it will help all those people.

My original concept was to list a series of seasonally balanced menus and each course was to be married with an appropriate wine or wines.

As the manuscript developed it made sense to put the menus in each chapter in order of dexterity, so that the easiest in each season were at the beginning with the more demanding ones at the end.

In each recipe the ingredients are listed in the order in which they are used in the method, to help you to 'set up' in an orderly and efficient manner.

Wines have been chosen from three major wine growing areas in the world and are listed by a symbol system so that you immediately recognise which are Australian, American and European.

The average times at the end of each recipe are given to assist you when deciding upon a menu, to choose one which you have enough time to carry out. The times do not include cleaning up.

It's good to be able to get ahead knowing that some part of the menu is out of the way to give you that often much needed break from the kitchen. If any forward preparation is detrimental to a dish, then no 'do-ahead' is given. Do remember though that a dish which is already cooked needs only to be heated through — not recooked.

Every recipe is designed to serve six unless stated otherwise.

Menu balancing is commonsense but basically a well orchestrated menu never allows the palates to become bored or tired. It's wise to err on the simple side and often a menu can be balanced by eliminating say, the cream or ice-cream as the accompaniment to the dessert or if you prefer, eliminating the dessert and replacing it with a cheese and/or fresh fruit course.

When planning a menu always keep in mind colours, textures, flavours and presentation.

To cook successfully you should try to have all your five tactile senses alert:

Sight, obviously presentation is very important. Take into account the colour, texture, shape and size.

Taste, tasting as you cook at every step will eliminate that awful moment at the table when you discover that you have put in sugar instead of salt!

Smell, if food smells good, it's as appealing as looking good. Use your nose to guide you when cooking; it will often tell you when something is done.

Touch, for instance, I often say a pastry should be kneaded until it feels like 'chamois leather'.

Hearing, is when I say 'foam the butter', and the butter rises up in the cooking pan, it changes colour to a nutty brown which one instantly smells and sees, and it also stops sizzling as the foaming subsides. So I know even with my back to the pan when the butter is ready because I can hear it and smell it.

When serving fine wines with fine food, try to avoid strongly perfumed flowers on the table. You will notice throughout the recipes that where I have lemon for an accompaniment I stipulate a half lemon. This is because wedges of lemon are often difficult to grasp, with the juice going everywhere except on the food where we want it. And more particularly, most people will pick up the lemon with their master hand which they also use for picking up their wine glass. Once you have lemon on your hand you will smell it when you nose your wine. A half lemon can look very ugly on a plate so I suggest that you decorate the lemon halves with a Van Dyked edge or pare the rind away from the top edge of the lemon three-quarters of the way around and tie a knot in it. This is a half lemon with a twist.

To appreciate good wine it is important that you have the right glasses. They should be stemmed and clear so that you can see the wine. The bowl of the glass should slope in slightly towards the top to capture the bouquet of the wine. A set of tasting glasses is ideal and will take you through every course if you do not want to use the classic shaped glasses. If you are using classic red and white wine glasses the larger glass of the two is for the red wine.

You will notice that not every main course has a vegetable to accompany it. Obviously you must use your own judgement but please cook with vegetables in season.

Australian standard metric cups and measures are used and all measurements are level.

It is important that you understand the difference between the following two measurements: two cups of almonds, finely ground and two cups of finely ground almonds. If you measure the two you will see how different they are.

I have included both Celsius and Fahrenheit oven temperatures because there are still many older ovens with only Fahrenheit readings. I have tested every recipe on a Celsius reading and converted it to the nearest workable Fahrenheit point. Understanding your own oven is very important. You should know which is the hottest part and where the coolest parts are. If you don't, then I suggest you either call the gas or electricity company and ask them to send out one of their home economists or buy an oven thermometer and work it out for yourself. Generally speaking all electric ovens need to be preheated to the temperature stipulated in the recipe. With a gas oven I use a cold start with every recipe except those which need to rise and increase in volume like soufflés.

'Blood temperature' means when the mixture feels neither hot nor cold when you dip your finger into it.

Try not to use aluminium pans for cooking green vegetables. They do tend to spoil the colour. Use stainless steel or enamel for preference. When choosing pans for pies and quiches choose metal rather than ceramic or pyrex. They are much easier to unmould and I think they look far more attractive 'free standing' on a serving plate than in their cooking dish. Metal is also the best material for moulds. Because it is flexible it is easier to release the vacuum whereas with china or pyrex it is very difficult to unmould a 'set' recipe and the mould markings are not usually as sharply defined as with metal.

Always choose heavy based pans for all kinds of stove-top cooking. They are far less likely to catch and usually have a better heat distribution, as well as retaining the temperature, long after removing from the heat.

For the smoothest results for a sauce or soup use a blender rather than a food processor. If a recipe says to mouli it means to pass the result through a mouli-legumes which is a food mill. The alternative is to push the mixture through a sieve. The difference between puréeing in a blender or a food processor and mouli-ing is that with the latter, fibres and seeds are eliminated from the mixture.

When you have pastry left over which has already been rolled it should not be wasted. However it will have to be rolled again and becomes known as 'second roll' pastry and although edible is usually tougher than the 'first roll' pastry.

Pastry brushes are often too small and round ones are hopeless. If you cannot get a professional pastry brush then buy a five-centimetre paint brush.

When making pastry it's important to note that in the winter months or cooler weather you will need a little more liquid, whereas in the summer when it's humid you will need less liquid.

Pastry dough freezes superbly, if packed airtight. The dough should be thawed in the refrigerator, preferably overnight and proceeded with in the usual way the next day.

Puff pastry, once mastered is one of the joys of cooking at home. However, if you are short of time as most of us are it makes sense to make up a double quantity and freeze what you don't need (before rolling of course). Alternatively if you are really stuck buy some from a reputable pastry shop or from the supermarket.

When I talk about a 'roux' it is a mixture of fat and flour, usually butter which must be cooked until it 'cobwebs' the base of the pan. That is when the mixture bubbles and is white and foamy. This is to cook the gluten and explode it in the flour. With a hot roux you must add a cold liquid which should be whisked into the roux over the heat. If you have a hot liquid to add to a roux then it is important that you cool the roux first or you will have a lumpy result.

Beat or whisk to 'ribbon' stage means that when you lift the beaters or whisk above the mixture they leave a ribbon pattern on top of the mixture.

I always use a whisk for sauces, creams and custards, so a word of warning: do not use a whisk in an aluminium pan with a pale sauce, because it will produce a grey result. To test the thickness of a sauce it is still best to dip a wooden spatula into it and run a finger down the spatula. If the two lines do not join together then the mixture is considered to be coating the back of the spoon.

'Reduce' means to cook in an open pan until the mixture is reduced by evaporation. When I talk about a good consistency I mean one which has a syrupy consistency and will coat a spoon.

'Turned' vegetables refers to the classic French method of preparing vegetables to cook in equal time. Each vegetable should be cut into equal lengths and then pared so that it has seven sides. You can buy a special 'turning' knife to do this which is reasonably inexpensive. There is quite a lot of waste preparing vegetables this way so use the trimmings in your stock pot.

Every good kitchen has a stock pot going all the time. You will soon learn what you can put into the stock pot and what you can't. But the main rule is never to let the stock turn rancid. If you boil it up every day, this will kill any organisms. The stock should be refrigerated in between times.

Stocks, like soups and casseroles should be made at least one day ahead. This is to gather flavour and also to allow the fat to settle on the top while refrigerated overnight. Next day, simply lift the congealed fat off the top using a spatula.

Beware of chicken stock in very hot and humid weather. It is more likely to turn rancid than any other stock and I find in hot weather it is best to leave the onion out of chicken stock.

'Parboil' means to cook the ingredients in water brought to the boil and usually the recipe will state for how long the ingredient must be parboiled. It is then drained and ready for the next step in the method.

'Blanch' means to submerge the ingredient in boiling water for however many seconds or minutes stated. It is then drained and used as stipulated in the next part of the method.

To peel an orange without any of the white pith: dip it into boiling water for thirty seconds. To segment an orange without membranes, the best way is to use a very sharp knife and skin the orange removing the pith at the same time. Work over a bowl to catch the juices, cut between the segments removing only the flesh and leave the membranes attached to the core of the orange.

To prepare garlic, remove the cloves and crush with the thick end (held flat) of a large chef's knife. The skin simply falls off. This is a bruised and peeled clove of garlic. It can then either be crushed in a garlic crusher if it's juice you want or if you need the highly prized flavour of the flesh as well, then finely chop the garlic or crush with some cooking salt on a board and the flat tip of a small spatula.

Fresh herbs should always be used when they are in season. The general rule of thumb is, if you cannot get fresh then use half the stipulated amount of dried herbs. I never buy ground herbs, only leaves, because I find they keep much longer. Store dried herbs away from light and keep in airtight containers. They do not last forever so it's better to buy small quantities. Fresh herbs should only be chopped at the time they are used. Within ten minutes they have lost the greatest part of their precious aromatic flavours. 'Fresh bouquet garni' is two pieces of celery tied around a sprig of parsley, a sprig of thyme and a bay leaf.

If you grow your own herbs it's a good idea to let some of each plant 'go to seed' so that they resow themselves. The flowers make excellent garnishes, but more particularly thyme flowers have the most marvellous flavour and should be used in cooking whenever possible.

To seed grapes, hook the seeds out with the eye of a bobby pin through the stalk end.

Some vegetables need to be 'disgorged'. They are egg-plants, cucumbers, and I like to disgorge pumpkin also. This means to liberally salt the exposed cut surfaces of the vegetables and leave for up to thirty minutes. They will weep a certain amount of liquid which you then discard. This process will take away bitter flavours and also make the vegetables more digestible.

To beat egg whites successfully you should use a metal bowl for preference or a glass one. Egg whites are best used at room temperature and of course must have no yellow in them. The bowl and beaters or whisk must also be fat free. Begin to beat slowly by breaking up the egg whites, then beat at a good medium steady pace until soft peak stage. That is when you lift the beaters or whisk and the egg whites still pull through but stand in soft peaks. For the final stage of beating to stiff peaks, you should whisk or beat at an increased speed. Never overbeat egg whites, they must still have a glossy sheen to them. Once beaten, they should be used as soon as possible.

Cold dishes support sharper flavours than hot dishes, so it's important that when making a dish which is going to be cooled and served cold you have a good strong flavour in it at the hot stage.

When you are faced with the proposition of tasting a raw mixture like a liver terrine, drop a small piece about half a teaspoon full into a simmering stock pot or a small pan of simmering water and poach it. Cool slightly and then taste and adjust the seasoning as is necessary.

A word of warning about mixing sour cream, buttermilk, yoghurt, crème fraîche and fromage blanc into a recipe until the time you need them. They will ferment the dish even when it's cold if left for too long.

Vanilla beans should be used where possible and can be used several times over, providing they are properly washed and dried between each use. Split the vanilla bean lengthwise to release the flavour in the tiny seeds inside. This means you will have tiny black specks throughout your mixture but the flavour is well worth it. If using essence then buy only pure vanilla extract.

'Julienne' means to cut into fine matchsticks.

To skin peppers, either hold over a gas flame with a fork and scorch all over until the skin bubbles or cook under a hot griller to gain the same result. Rub the skins off under running cold water.

To rescue a curdled mayonnaise, keep the curdled mixture and begin again with the same basic egg yolks and salt. Beat them until they are very thick and pale and then with the blender or food processor running, slowly ladle the curdled mixture into the new base.

To test the filling inside a pie like a coulibiac or the stuffing in poultry or a galantine or terrine which has a lid with a hole in it, insert a metal skewer into the centre and count exactly thirty seconds. Remove the skewer and place it on the inside of your wrist. If it feels very hot then the mixture is cooked.

Garnishes should not only be attractive and edible but they should also denote what is in the recipe. For instance a black currant food could perhaps be garnished with a few black currants on the top.

Gelatine powder needs to have the granules thoroughly dissolved before using it. Always use gelatine at blood temperature unless the recipe states otherwise. Gelatine mixtures grow leathery as they age, so they are best used as soon as they are set.

To skin kernels: hazelnuts should be cooked in a 200°C (400°F) oven for ten to thirteen minutes or until the skins are crazed. Cool them and then rub a few at a time between your hands removing the skins. If the skins are hard to rub off then either the hazelnuts are stale or they have not spent long enough in the oven. Almonds and pistachios should be blanched in boiling water for approximately thirty seconds, drained, cooked and the skins removed.

To strain pasta successfully, it should never be poured through a colander discarding all the water. Pasta should be caught in a pasta catcher or strainer which means each strand or piece is coated in the cooking water and dropped into a warm serving dish. After saucing the pasta then a little of the pasta cooking water can be ladled into the dish and mixed through if the pasta dish is too dry.

To cook green vegetables successfully, you must retain their colour and texture. They should be cooked over high heat with salt, preferably in stainless steel or enamel. They must not be covered. As soon as they are *al dente* which means literally firm to the tooth then remove from the heat and set aside or, if serving cold refresh either in iced water or in running cold water and drain as soon as they are cold.

To skin and seed tomatoes, either blister the tomatoes on a fork over a high gas flame or blanch in boiling water for thirty seconds until the skins come off easily. Cut the tomatoes in halves horizontally and squeeze out the seeds over a sieve in a jug to catch the juices. The seeds are discarded and the juice can be used either for drinking or cooking.

To seed cucumbers, split them in halves lengthways and scoop out the seeds with a teaspoon.

Successful cooking with chocolate will depend on the quality of the chocolate you use. The very best chocolate available is couverture which is imported and available from good cookware shops and some chocolate shops. Alternatively, use Cadbury's Energy or Small's Club.

Parmesan cheese should be freshly grated each time it is needed. The imported Italian Reggio is the best but the Australian Parmesan bought in the piece and freshly grated at the time of using is acceptable. Prepackaged, grated Parmesan cheese does not have the same flavour.

Eggs come in several sizes but the standard cooking egg is 55 grams. Occasionally I have said use large eggs which means 60s or 65s if you can get them. It is best to cook with eggs at room temperature.

Cream is available in several degrees of richness. The lowest is twenty-five per cent butterfat and is often called thin cream, whipping cream or reduced cream. The thirty-five per cent milkfat cream is the most commonly used and the best for cooking. It is sometimes gelatine thickened. Pure cream is available in some states at forty-eight per cent butterfat but more commonly at forty-five per cent butterfat. It is by far the superior cream to use but since it is difficult to find in some states I suggest you stick with thirty-five per cent butterfat cream for most cooking purposes.

Butchers' twine is the only string to use for tying and sewing. Thin string or cotton will tear flesh and pull through; cheap string will leave hairs on your work and coloured string will stain it.

Oils for cooking: olive oil should be used where stipulated and should be imported preferably from France or Italy and of the finest quality. Remember that you will only get good results from good quality materials. The most commonly used cooking oil is peanut oil and safflower oil is used when I don't want to flavour a dish. 'Sweet' oils like almond, apricot, or hazelnut or walnut are used only when especially stipulated.

Salts: *gros sel* is coarse salt which you can buy from good cookware shops and supermarkets and is used for cooking and salt mills. Cooking salt should be used at the stove and has a more intense salt flavour than table salt which I so often see being used in cooking and definitely discourage. Table salt should be used just for that, at the table. Sea salt which is imported from England has a superior flavour and should be used at the table when necessary. In nearly every recipe I do not stipulate how much salt to use because it is a matter of personal taste.

Zest of citrus fruits should be prepared by paring the zest off the citrus fruit using a potato peeler with a very light pressure so that no pith is on the back of the zest.

There are three ingredients in particular which have confusing names and are often referred to as one and the same thing. The first is shallots which in some states are called spring onions. This is a misnomer and right through this book I have called the elongated white onion with the green top, spring onions.

Shallots (or eschalotes) are the French small brown cluster onions which have a distinctive flavour and are used for sauces and casseroles. They are available in March and April from good greengrocers. But they keep well in a light dry and airy place on a wire rack or in a wire basket. They are very easily grown and multiply rapidly.

English spinach or summer spinach as it is known in some states is not always available, and unless the recipe stipulates to substitute for silverbeet then there is no substitute. Occasionally you can use frozen spinach leaves, in most recipes, the frozen chopped spinach is too wet. If substituting with silverbeet, do make sure that it is young and fresh.

In some states, cantaloupes are often referred to as rockmelons. They are one and the same melon.

I hope these hints will help you make the most of this book and that you get as much enjoyment from cooking the recipes as I did from preparing them.

Elise Pascoe

THE MARRIAGE OF FOOD AND WINE
Ken Bignill

The objective in choosing the wines to accompany Elise's imaginative dishes is to create a true harmony of flavours and palate sensations: a marriage of food and wine. Neither partner should dominate the other; rather the wine should both complement and compliment the food.

If the flavours of the food are too strong for wine, or if the textures and palate sensations of the food would not be enhanced by wine, then no wine will be suggested: the food will be left alone to make its own statement.

In addition, there needs to be a quality balance. The more refined dishes need a more complex wine, while the hearty country-style of dish calls for a more simple and robust style of wine.

GENERAL WINE STYLES

While there is no such thing as a typical wine style for any of the thousands of wine classifications throughout the world, let me attempt to classify and suggest to you a generic grouping of wines by broad flavour characteristics. Reference to the generic style in the choice of wine for individual dishes should then give you both an understanding of the primary reason for the choice of each particular wine and a frame of reference for you to experiment with your own choice of alternative wines.

1. Aromatic Whites

These white wines have fresh, fruity to spicy flavours; they usually have floral aromas.

They include the fruity and floral Rhine Riesling (Johannisberg Riesling in USA), those softer versions of Sauvignon Blanc, Colombard, Crouchen, Verdelho, various muscats (vinified dry), Tokay, grapy Chenin Blanc and spicy, highly aromatic Gewurztraminer (in Australia often labelled Traminer).

Included in this group are the white wines of Germany, Austria and France, as well as the Australian and American whites made from these varieties.

2. Dry Whites with Body

Whites with greater strength of flavour, length and finish.

Very dry Rhine (Johannisberg) Rieslings which have several years' bottle age, especially those from Clare and Eden Valley in Australia, Alsace, and California, may fall into this category. More typically, this group includes Semillon, Marsanne, Chardonnay, herbaceous and crisply acid Sauvignon Blanc (frequently labelled Fume Blanc), Trebbiano (also known as Ugni Blanc, or White Shiraz, or White Hermitage), Chasselas, Blanquette, together with Australian and Californian generically labelled White Burgundy and Chablis.

Among the overseas wines in this group are White Burgundy, Chablis, White Bordeaux (mostly from Graves), White Rhônes such as Hermitage Blanc, Condrieu and Châteauneuf-du-Pape Blanc, some whites from the Loire, such as Muscadet, Sancerre and Pouilly-Fumé, and most Italian, Spanish and Portuguese whites.

Champagne, when not used in its classic role as an aperitif, may be used as an alternative to these wines.

3. Sweet whites

This family ranges in sweetness, lusciousness and intensity.

It includes Spätlese or Late Picked Rhine Riesling, both white and brown muscat under various names (Gordo, Lexia, Muscat of Alexandria, Frontignac, Muscat Canelli, and so on), Chenin Blanc, Semillon, as well as generically labelled Sauternes, and the Rieslings and Semillons affected by *Botrytis cinerea* (Noble Rot), often labelled Auslese, Beerenauslese, or Trockenbeerenauslese, after the German nomenclature.

From overseas, it includes the German and Austrian originals of these classifications, the Alsace Vendage Tardive and Grains Noble grades, the Individual Late Picked Rieslings of California and South Africa, Hungarian Tokay Aszu, Italian sweet whites such as Picolit, from elsewhere in France, the Moelleux whites of the Loire (Vouvray, Anjou, Savennieres, Coteaux du Layon, Quarts de Chaume and Bonnezeaux among the more commonly available), Monbazillac, the great Sauternes and Barsac and lesser Entre-Deux-Mers (Cerons, Ste-Croix-du-Mont and Loupiac) of Bordeaux, the muscats of the south of France, Muscat de Beaumes de Venise, Muscat de Rivesaltes, de Mireval, de Lunel, and Grand Rousillon, as well as muscats from other Mediterranean countries.

Sweet Champagne and Asti Spumante can also be used as a dessert wine.

4. Rosé

This is the transition between white and red wines. There are wide flavour variations between rosés; generally, they are vinified to retain fresh, grapy flavours, often with a touch of residual grape sugar.

5. Light, Fruity Reds

The epitome of this group is French Beaujolais, made from Gamay grapes. In Australia and California, Pinot Noir usually has this character, along with a host of lighter reds made from Carignane, Gamay, Grenache or Shiraz, or blends of these.

Other overseas reds in this category are Italy's Bardolino, Chianti, Lambrusco, Fracia, Pinot Nero and Valpolicella, France's VDQS and Vins de Pays reds, as well as those from the Loire, such as Chinon and Bourgueil, from southern Burgundy, such as Mâcon, and the reds of Germany, such as Spätburgunder.

6. Powerful Reds, full of character

These reds have strong flavours, are tannic, frequently show oak flavours and aromas and usually require bottle age of five to ten years before their flavours integrate. With maturity, they develop great complexity of flavour and bouquet.

In Australia, Shiraz is the most widespread of this group, along with Cabernet Sauvignon (frequently truncated in labelling to Cabernet), blends of Shiraz and Cabernet, Merlot and Malbec (both usually blended with Cabernet), Mataro (mostly blended with Shiraz), Oeillade (also known as Cinsault and Blue Imperial), Zinfandel and Pinot Noir made in the heavier style.

From overseas, reds made from the varieties listed above, plus the great reds of Bordeaux, Burgundy, Rhône, as well as those from the many other French AOC areas such as Bergerac, Cahors, Gaillac, Jurançon, Jura and Bandol, Rioja from Spain, Dão from Portugal, and the Italian reds such as Barbera, Barbaresco, Barolo, Brunello di Montalcino, Chianti Classico, Faro and Taurasi.

7. Fortified Wines

These are both dry and sweet.

They include sherry, Madeira, Marsala, port, Tokay and liqueur muscat, as well as a variety of aperitif fortified wines.

SOME FOODS WHICH CREATE DIFFICULTIES FOR WINE SELECTION

Since balance and harmony between food and wine is our objective, we have tried to avoid the clash of flavours which particular foods create with wine. Some examples of such foods are:

- Strong spices like curry, chilli and paprika — an aromatic white is usually safe, although only if the spice flavours are mild.
- Vinegar — if the serving of a wine is important with a dish containing vinegar (that has not been reduced by cooking or amalgamation with other ingredients), then the alternative of lemon juice should be considered in the recipe, since the lemon flavour will not fight as much with a wine.
- Acidic fruit, particularly citrus — generally cuts across any wine, especially sweet wine; it is frequently more enjoyable to finish the fruit and then drink the sweet wine.
- Chocolate — the bitterness fights sweet whites, although I have discovered that muscats have complementary flavours and marry beautifully with chocolate. This applies especially to those most distinctive of all Australian wines, the Liqueur Muscat of Rutherglen, north-eastern Victoria, and it even applies to the lighter French muscats, including Muscat de Beaumes de Venise.
- Eggs — the sulphur in uncompounded egg dishes masks wine flavours, especially in white wine; try a dry, flor sherry.
- Liqueurs that have not been cooked or flamed — these make a strong enough flavour statement to be left alone.
- Spinach — the strong iron flavour of the vegetable imparts a bitter taste, masking any delicate wine, so if the vegetable is not softened by other ingredients, choose either a sherry or strongly flavoured white with enough fruit to withstand the metallic assault.
- Desserts — these present problems of either acidity or excessive sweetness, both of which may interfere with the glorious wine flavours of the sweet whites usually drunk with them: *botrytis*-affected rieslings, Sauternes and those rich Chenin Blancs from Vouvray and Anjou. If the wine tastes drier when taken with the dessert than when drunk on its own, you always have the eminently logical choice of leaving the wine to be enjoyed on its own after you have completed the dessert. This practice has much to recommend it. Try it yourself.

GUIDELINES FOR CHOOSING WINE

There is only one guideline: drink what you enjoy.

Wine is a remarkably adaptable beverage; there really are no hard and fast rules for wine and food marriage. Within the framework of drinking what you enjoy, experiment with new combinations of wine and food.

Certain 'rules' for the selection of wine with food are frequently proposed and many of these rules are based on common sense, so they may save you some unhappy experiments.

For example, white wine with fish is sound advice, since the iodine and oils in salt water fish may react unpleasantly with the tannin in red wine, whereas the acidity and fruit flavour of white wine are not so affected. As with all such rules, there are exceptions: fresh water fish is sometimes successfully partnered with red wine, as in the case of trout poached in red wine and served with a red.

A sound principle (although somewhat unimaginative) is to begin by matching the colour of food and wine. This will generally yield complementary flavours; when in doubt, it is safe; it is also useful as a point of departure for your more imaginative combinations. It goes like this: white wine with seafood, white meat, poultry and white (e.g. goat) cheese; rosé with ham; red wine with red meats, game and most cheeses. Add to this principle that of using sherry or madeira with soup, sweet wine with, or after, the dessert and port after dinner.

It must be emphasized that this is only a starting point. If you prefer red wine with your chicken, drink it. Also, such 'rules' as these, lead you away from the magic which unusual combinations of wine and food may create: Sauternes with pâté, fish, or caviar; muscat with chocolate; Gewürztztraminer with soup, particularly of puréed vegetables; red wine with strawberries; sparkling burgundy with poultry; port with Stilton; Malmsey Madeira with gâteau.

So, the best advice is to follow your own palate and try different combinations of food and wine.

SUGGESTED WINES

The wines which have been suggested for each dish have been chosen from currently available premium selections. Some are from boutique wineries with very small production, so they may not be generally available. Some Australian wineries in this category are Morilla Estate, Seville Estate, Idyll, Mt Mary, and so on.

Likewise, some of the wines from larger wineries were produced in limited quantities, such as Rosemount Trockenbeerenauslese Riesling.

These difficulties with supply are recognized, so the description of generic wine styles provided in this introduction should enable you to obtain wines of similar flavour characteristics to replace any suggested wines which you may not be able to procure.

Vintages are not given for any of the selections, even though all are vintage wines unless otherwise stated. While vintage variations affect the flavour characteristics of wines from the same vineyard and varieties, generally such variations in Australia are minor and should not negate the appropriateness of the selected wine, even when from a different vintage.

In the case of overseas wines, particularly those from France, the quality of vintage will be suggested, since there is much wider quality and flavour variation among vintages in such cold climate wine areas.

Where it is suggested a light red be served slightly chilled, this advice is intended for Australian readers, as well as those from Southern California and similar climates, not for those from colder climates. The ambient temperature in Summer in Australia is so high that most red wines benefit from being taken to table at cool cellar temperature, or from being chilled to 13°C (55°F) before serving. This temperature may be achieved by placing the bottle in a refrigerator for 30–45 minutes or in ice and water for around 15 minutes. The improvement in bouquet and freshness of fruit flavours on the palate is marked. For intensely fruity, young reds, such as Beaujolais, this practice is common, even in France.

The following codes are used to distinguish the wines of the major geographic areas represented:

A = Australia E = Europe U = USA

Since there is such general availability of European wines in USA, some European wines are also suggested for USA. This does not imply that there is no North American wine of that type. In most cases, I have chosen specific vineyard wines. In doing so, I am not suggesting that this is the best wine of its type that is made (although, frequently, it is), but my choice is made because I am familiar with the particular wine and can, therefore, recommend it with Elise's dish. If you have a preferred vineyard in the general style for which the wine was chosen, or you prefer a different style, you should follow your own judgement.

I know you will enjoy Elise's recipes. I hope your enjoyment is enhanced by the marriage of wine and food and I wish you well in this adventure.

Ken Bignell.

ACKNOWLEDGEMENTS

Though the concept of this book is mine, I could never have written it alone. It has been a grand team effort and I wish to thank those people on the team most warmly and sincerely. In particular:

The Macmillan Company of Australia Pty Ltd, my publishers, for their encouragement, assistance and acceptance of this work; my wine consultant Ken Bignill, whose enthusiasm and expertise is evident throughout these pages — without him there would have been no marriage of food and wine; my right hand and personal assistant Lynette Bignill who supported and ably assisted me through every stage of this book; my typist Lily Panic, for patiently and willingly meeting every deadline on the manuscript; Michael Cook, for beautiful uncluttered self-explanatory photographs; my colleague Joan Campbell, the most stylish of food ladies, for 'staging' the food for photography; all the wine companies and agencies who so generously sent their premium wines at my request; my special friends John, Jill, Lyndal and Kate for their constant support and understanding and for checking and reading the manuscript; and all my catering staff and my students.

I am grateful to Australian Consolidated Press Limited, John Fairfax & Sons Limited, Bernard Leser Publications Pty. Limited, The Herald & Weekly Times Limited, and Bon Appetit Publishing Corporation, for allowing me to reproduce material which I originally contributed to their publications.

ALL
THE YEAR
ROUND

AUTHORS NOTE

Every recipe is designed to serve six unless stated otherwise.

ALL YEAR ROUND

CANAPÉS

◆

The obvious starter to any special menu which has been planned and executed with love and care, is a platter of canapés you have made yourself.

Though demanding and time consuming, much can be done ahead. One or two varieties are enough and they should be chosen to complement the menu they precede.

If serving canapés, you can often get away with deleting either the first or last course.

This selection was part of the repertoire I served in Melbourne board rooms for a decade from the late 1960s. They are excellent for cocktail parties.

Never serve too many canapés before lunch or dinner. They are supposed to encourage appetites, not suppress them!

LEEK AND CHÈVRE TARTLETS
Makes 16 tartlets (7 to 8 cm)

◆

Short Crust:
250 g plain flour
salt
125 g butter, chilled
2 tablespoons lemon juice
2 tablespoons iced water, use extra if necessary

Filling:
30 g butter
2 cups thoroughly-washed leeks (green and
    white parts), finely sliced
salt and freshly ground black pepper to taste
30 g extra butter, softened
200 g Chèvre Pyramid cheese
2 eggs
½ cup thickened cream
1 teaspoon fresh thyme leaves

◆

To make short crust: place flour and salt in a food processor, add butter cut into 12 pieces and process until mixture resembles oatmeal. Add lemon juice and first 2 tablespoons of water and process until mixture resembles fine breadcrumbs or comes together in a single mass. If mixture still resembles breadcrumbs, add a little extra chilled water (about 1 teaspoon). Knead dough on a lightly floured board, flatten to 3 cm and wrap in greaseproof paper. Refrigerate for a minimum of 30 minutes.

Roll dough out to 5 cm coin thickness, stamp out 16 circles to fit tartlet moulds. Butter moulds and press dough into each. Prick thoroughly with a fork, place a piece of foil in each and weigh down with blind baking weights or dried beans. Cook in centre of 200°C (400°F) oven for about 15 minutes or until golden around the edges. Remove blind baking weights and foil.

To make filling: melt butter in a large heavy-based pan, sauté leeks stirring over medium heat until softened. Season to taste.

Beat softened butter with the cheese, eggs, cream and thyme in a food processor. Spoon leeks into bases of prepared pastry cases. Spoon cheese mixture over the top of each but do not overfill. Cook at 200°C (400°F) for 20 to 25 minutes or until set and golden on top.

Serve hot or at room temperature.

Average times Preparation — 35 minutes
        Standing — 2 × 30 minutes
        Cooking — 45 minutes

Do ahead Dough can be made 2 days ahead.
        Pastry cases can be prepared and
        cooked 1 day ahead, completed
        recipe up to ½ day ahead

CROÛTONS

white sliced sandwich bread
butter, melted

To make round croûtons, stamp out 4 × 2½ cm circles, using a scone cutter, from each slice (do 2 slices at once). Place side by side on an oven tray. Paint over with melted butter and cook in centre of 200°C (400°F) oven until crisp and golden — about 20 minutes. Cool on a wire rack and store in airtight containers.

To make square croûtons, trim crusts off bread, do 2 slices of bread at once, using a sharp knife. Cut slices into 4 squares and cook same way as for round croûtons.

As the croûtons dry out in the oven the sides turn up slightly giving them a concave surface. Always use this 'dished' surface as the top.

Do ahead Up to 1 week if stored in airtight
containers

EGG AND ANCHOVY CANAPÉS

butter
small eggs, hard-boiled and shelled

tomato paste, in tube
rolled anchovies with capers, drained

Slice eggs with a wire egg slicer.

To assemble canapés, butter the concave side of the croûtons, place a slice of hard-boiled egg on each, then a squeeze of tomato paste and top with a rolled anchovy.

Make no more than 2 hours before serving. However all the preliminaries can be done ahead of time.

Do ahead Completely assembled, up to 2
hours, but keep well covered with
plastic wrap

CARPACCIO BEEF SAVOURIES WITH OLIVE OIL

fresh brown sandwich loaf
scotch fillet steak, partially frozen
fine olive oil
freshly ground black pepper

Garnish: (optional)
fine capers, drained
baby onion rings

Slice the beef on an electric slicer into paper thin slices. Cover each slice of bread with a slice of beef. Trim crusts off the bread cutting off overhanging beef at the same time and cut each slice into 4 equal squares. Paint over with a little oil and season. Garnish if desired.

Do ahead Up to 2 hours but keep covered
and refrigerate

HAM AND CHEESE RIBBONS
Make 1 day in advance

1 packet 250 g Philadelphia cream cheese, softened
2 teaspoons horseradish relish
1 teaspoon paprika

salt and pepper to taste
15 slices of ham from 3 × 125 g packets of square sliced ham

Beat cream cheese, add horseradish, paprika, salt and pepper to taste. Spread cheese mixture over the slices of ham, building them into sandwiches each taking five slices of ham with four layers of cheese, so you end up with three ham and cheese 'sandwiches'. Chill, covered with plastic wrap and keep them absolutely flat.

Next day, trim edges off the sandwiches keeping them square. Cut into four strips each way. Yield is 16 squares from each 'sandwich'. Serve standing on their sides so that you have a pink and white striped effect, rather similar to pink and white caramels.

Average times Preparation — 20 minutes
Standing — overnight

Do ahead Up to 3 days

SALAMI CHEESE CORNUCOPIAS

skinned salami, very finely sliced
cream cheese, softened

freshly snipped chives

Beat cheese until creamy and spoon into a piping bag fitted with a small star tube. Roll 1 slice of salami into a cornucopia, one at a time, and pipe enough cheese into it to fill. Secure ⅓ from the end with a toothpick. Repeat with remaining ingredients, scatter cheese with chives and refrigerate. Cover until ready to serve. Remove toothpicks and arrange on a plate.

Do ahead Up to ½ day

CELERY WITH BLUE CHEESE

blue vein cheese, softened
cream cheese, softened
sticks of celery, washed and stripped of strings

brown sandwich loaf
butter, softened
red pepper, cut into tiny uniform dice

Beat half-and-half blue and cream cheese together until creamy. Spread with a small spatula into 2 equal length celery sticks and face them towards each other so the cheese is in the centre. Secure with rubber bands, wrap in plastic film and refrigerate for at least 4 hours, preferably overnight.

Stamp out 3 mm ovals from the bread and butter them. Remove rubber bands from celery sticks and cut sticks into ½ cm slices and arrange 1 slice on each oval. Top with a piece of red pepper. Cover and refrigerate until ready to serve.

Do ahead Celery overnight. Finished savouries, up to ½ day

Wine notes Champagne is the perfect accompaniment to canapés —
A: Yellowglen Vintage Cremant
E: Bollinger Special Cuvée
U: Domaine Chandon Brut

SPRING

SPRING

MENU 1

———◆———

A delicious but deceptively rich luncheon or dinner menu, requiring only last minute attention to the main course.

PAW PAW AND AVOCADO SALAD

———◆———

500 g ripe paw paw, skinned, seeded and cut into 2.5 cm cubes
1 large ripe avocado, peeled, pitted and cut into 2.5 cm cubes
420 g can hearts of palm, drained and cut into 1 cm slices
2 large ripe tomatoes, skinned, seeded and cubed coarsely

¼ cup lemon juice
¼ teaspoon salt
⅛ teaspoon ground coriander
⅛ teaspoon ground allspice
¼ teaspoon ground white pepper
1 cup loosely-packed watercress leaves

———◆———

Place the first four ingredients in a large glass bowl, pour in juice, seasoning and spices and toss thoroughly but gently. Add watercress leaves and toss again. Cover and chill for 1 to 2 hours before serving.

Average times Preparation — 30 minutes
Standing — 1 to 2 hours

Wine notes Paw Paw and Avocado Salad calls for an aromatic white —
A: Lindemans Nursery Vineyard Rhine Riesling, from Coonawarra
E: Riesling (Trimbach) from Alsace
U: Krug (Napa) Johannisberg Riesling

Do ahead 1 to 2 hours

VEAL RIB CHOPS WITH LEEKS

6 veal middle loin rib chops, each weighing
   300 g approximately
80 g butter
salt and freshly ground black pepper to taste
½ cup dry vermouth
½ cup beef stock

3 medium leeks, washed thoroughly (both
   white and green parts) and sliced into ½ cm
   pieces
½ cup cream

Heat butter in a very large heavy-based pan until foaming and fry veal chops quickly on both sides until golden and season lightly. Pour in vermouth and stock, reduce heat and continue to cook until chops are tender, about 12 minutes. Lift out of pan, cover and keep warm. (If you don't have a pan large enough to take all 6 chops at once either cook half at a time or do in 2 separate pans.) Set pan juices aside until ready to make the sauce.

Steam leeks in a steamer or in a colander over a pan of boiling water (not touching) until *al dente*. Keep warm.

Return cooking pan to medium heat and whisk in cream. Taste and adjust seasoning if necessary. Continue to cook until sauce reaches a good consistency.

Spoon a little of the sauce onto each of 6 heated dinner plates and place one veal chop in the centre of each. Spoon leeks on top of chops and serve at once.

Accompany with steamed new potatoes.

Average times Preparation — 10 minutes
             Cooking — 20 minutes

Wine notes The veal cutlets with leeks re-
            quire a medium to full-bodied
            red —
            A: Rouge Homme (Coona-
               warra) Claret
            E: Château Talbot (St-Julien)
            U: Hacienda (Sonoma)
               Cabernet Sauvignon

BUTTERSCOTCH NONSENSE

4 tablespoons golden syrup
1½ teaspoons gelatine, dissolved in 1 tablespoon boiling water
5 egg whites

Sauce:
3 egg yolks
1 cup thickened cream
1½ tablespoons golden syrup

fresh or crystallized violets to decorate (see
   page 191)

Heat golden syrup in a heavy-based pan over medium heat and cook until it darkens a little. Stir in gelatine and cook for 2 minutes. Set aside.

Beat egg whites in an electric mixer to stiff and glossy peaks and gradually pour hot golden syrup mixture slowly onto egg whites and beat for 4 minutes. Spoon into 6 champagne saucers or goblets and leave to set in a peak-shape.

To make sauce: beat cream to soft peaks, whisk in yolks and golden syrup. Spoon a little sauce around base of each nonsense and refrigerate until cold. Serve remaining sauce in a custard jug. Garnish with violets and serve well chilled.

Average times Preparation — 15 minutes
             Cooking — 10 minutes
             Chilling — 1½ hours

Wine notes Butterscotch nonsense needs no
            wine

Do ahead Up to ½ day

7

SPRING

MENU 2

An outdoor picnic on a beautiful Spring day is always looked forward to, especially when the food can be prepared ahead. These recipes all pack and travel easily.

MEDITERRANEAN SANDWICH

6 fresh rolls
3 cloves garlic, peeled
12 black olives, stoned and halved
1 red and 1 green pepper, seeded and cut into
  rings

2 medium ripe tomatoes, sliced
45 g can anchovies, drained and chopped
3 gherkins, sliced lengthwise
6 lettuce leaves
¼ cup olive oil

Cut rolls in halves. Rub halves with garlic. Fill with all the ingredients. Drizzle a little olive oil over the filling, sandwich halves together and put under a heavy weight for 3 hours. Wrap each roll individually and take 1 for each person. Or make 1 large sandwich with a cottage loaf, and cut into wedges when you need it.

The Mediterranean sandwiches, Pan Bagnia as they are traditionally known, are available from many roadside stalls in the south of France. Made at home, they are ideal for any packed lunch or supper and are excellent for tennis parties.

Average times Preparation — 20 minutes   **Do ahead** Up to ½ day
Standing — 3 hours

TABBOULI IN LETTUCE CUPS

200 g fine burghel (cracked wheat) soaked in
  warm water for 30 minutes
1½ cups finely chopped parsley
3 tablespoons finely chopped mint
4 tablespoons olive oil
4 tablespoons lemon juice

3 tablespoons finely chopped spring onions
salt and freshly ground black pepper to taste
1 cup very finely chopped, skinned and seeded
  tomatoes
12–18 large lettuce leaves, washed, drained and
  crisped

Drain burghel, put in a clean tea towel and squeeze out all the water. Put burghel in a large bowl with all the remaining ingredients except tomatoes and lettuce and mix well. Gently fold in tomatoes, taste and adjust seasoning. Cover and refrigerate until ready to serve.
Present tabbouli in a salad bowl with a serving spoon with lettuce leaves in a basket beside it and allow guests to make their own parcels.

Average times Preparation — 25 minutes   **Do ahead** Prepare tabbouli and lettuce up to
Soaking — 30 minutes   1 day ahead

SAVOURY SALMON BREAD
Make 1 day ahead

2 × 220 g cans red or pink salmon
¼ cup softened butter
⅓ cup sweet fruit and vegetable pickle
3 tablespoons very finely chopped white onion
3 tablespoons mayonnaise

¼ cup coarsely chopped walnuts
¼ teaspoon white pepper
2 tablespoons gelatine
2 French sticks
100 g melted butter

Drain salmon and reserve stock. Remove black skin and bones. Break up salmon flesh with a fork. Mix butter, pickle, onion, mayonnaise, walnuts and pepper together. Fold in salmon. Dissolve gelatine in reserved stock (made up to ¼ cup with water if necessary) over heat and then cool a little before adding to salmon mixture.

To prepare the sticks: cut each in half across the middle and scrape out bread without breaking the crust, using a grapefruit knife, zucchini or apple corer. (Keep bread for breadcrumbs.) Paint the insides of sticks with melted butter.

When salmon mixture has cooled to blood temperature, spoon into sticks and shake down gently. Wrap each half in foil and refrigerate overnight. Next day, cut into 1 cm pieces.

Average times Preparation — 30 minutes
Cooking — 2 minutes
Cooling — 10 to 15 minutes
Setting — overnight

Do ahead 1 day

Wine notes With this picnic lunch, the wines need to be suitable for both the food and the outdoors. With the opening dishes, a fresh, fruity white with body —
A: Rosemount Fumé Blanc
E: Vouvray (Bredif)
U: Mondavi (Napa) Fume Blanc

HONEY-GLAZED CHICKEN WINGS

Marinade:
4 tablespoons honey
1 tablespoon French mustard
2 tablespoons sherry or lemon juice
4 tablespoons tomato sauce
freshly ground black pepper to taste

1.5 kg chicken wings
4 tablespoons butter

Whisk all marinade ingredients together in a large bowl. Marinate chicken pieces for 4 hours, covered and refrigerated.
Heat butter in a large heavy frying pan or baking dish. Drain marinade off chicken, reserving it. Sauté chicken pieces in butter, turning from time to time. After 10 minutes turn down heat, cover pan with a lid or foil and continue to cook until chicken wings are tender.
Pour in marinade and cook until it thickens and coats all the chicken pieces. Cool and serve cold.

Average times Preparation — 10 minutes
Standing — 4 hours
Cooking — 25 minutes
Cooling — 1 hour

Do ahead Up to 1 day

Wine notes With the chicken and tabbouli, a chilled, light red —
A: Montrose (Mudgee) Pinot Noir
E: Beaujolais Fleurie (Duboeuf)
U: Martini (Napa) Pinot Noir

ANZACS
Makes 30 to 36 approximately

1 cup flaked oats
1 cup raw sugar
1 cup desiccated coconut
1 cup plain flour
Pinch salt

½ cup chopped almonds
3 tablespoons water
1 tablespoon golden syrup
2 teaspoons soda bicarbonate
125 g butter

In a large bowl, mix the first 6 ingredients together thoroughly. In a small saucepan, bring water, syrup, carb. soda and butter to the boil and stir into dry ingredients, combining thoroughly. Drop the mixture in teaspoonfuls on a buttered oven tray leaving plenty of room for spreading. Bake in 160°C (325°F) oven for 20 to 25 minutes or until golden. Cool on wire racks and store in airtight containers.

Average times Preparation — 15 minutes
Cooking — 25 minutes

Do ahead Up to 1 week. Store in airtight containers

DATE AND GINGER SLICE

100 g unsalted butter
1 cup stoned dates, chopped
1 tablespoon mixed peel
90 g preserved ginger, drained and chopped
⅓ cup raw sugar
3 cups cornflakes

Icing:
250 g dark chocolate, broken into squares
80 g unsalted butter

Heat butter, fruits and sugar in a large pan over medium heat until sugar dissolves. Do not boil. Gently stir in cornflakes and remove from heat. Spread mixture into a 26 cm × 30 cm Swiss roll pan and level top with a spatula.
Melt chocolate and butter together over hot (not simmering) water until smooth. Pour over slice and spread quickly with a spatula. Leave until set. (In hot weather it may need refrigeration.) When cold cut into 5 × 7½ cm fingers and store in airtight containers.

Average times Preparation — 15 minutes
Cooking — 5 minutes
Setting — 30 minutes

Wine notes With the Date and Ginger Slice and Anzacs, a fresh, sweet white —
A: Allandale (Pokolbin) Fleur
E and U: Coteaux du Layon (Anjou)

Do ahead Up to 3 days

SPRING

MENU 3

◆

This menu was originally designed by me to demonstrate at the International Wine and Food Expo in Washington D.C. in 1982. Using two of Australia's best ingredients, Sydney rock oysters and lamb followed by pavlova filled with Spring fruits, it was such a success that it was featured in nine USA newspapers. It makes an ideal dinner for entertaining someone special.

OYSTERS BOTANY BAY

◆

6 dozen loose oysters, drained
2 tablespoons dry sherry
80 g butter
2 large cloves garlic, crushed
2 cups fresh breadcrumbs
2 tablespoons finely chopped parsley

2 teaspoons finely grated lemon rind
salt and coarsely ground black pepper to taste

6 lemon halves for garnish

◆

Sprinkle oysters with sherry and leave for 1 hour. Foam butter in a heavy-based frying pan and sweat garlic, but do not brown it. Stir in all remaining ingredients except oysters and cook until the breadcrumbs are golden. Butter 6 small shallow ovenproof dishes. Spoon oysters into them (without juices) and top with breadcrumb mixture. Bake in 200°C (400°F) oven approximately 12 to 15 minutes but do not overcook or let oysters become tough. Serve immediately, garnished with half a lemon.

Average times Preparation — 10 minutes
Cooking — 20 minutes
Standing — 1 hour

Wine notes Oysters spiced with these strong flavours call for a fairly neutral wine with high acidity, such as a sparkling white —
A: Seppelt Great Western Vintage Brut Champagne
E: Roederer Brut Premier Champagne
U: Mirassou (Santa Clara) au Naturel Champagne

MUSTARD SEED LAMB FILLETS

3 large fillets off whole racks of lamb, very well-trimmed (about 700 g)	45 g butter
	¾ cup dry white wine
3 tablespoons crushed mustard seeds (crushed in blender or in a pepper mill)	1 cup demi-glace (beef stock reduced to ½ original volume)
3 teaspoons salt	3 teaspoons red currant jelly
3 teaspoons milled black pepper	45 g softened butter

Roll fillets in crushed mustard seeds, salt and pepper and pat on well. In a heavy-based pan, heat butter and pan-fry fillets over high heat, cooking for 1 minute on each side. Reduce heat and cook a further 6 minutes or until done the way you like them, turning only twice. Lift fillets out of pan and rest in a warm oven for 10 minutes.

Discard all but 2 teaspoonfuls of butter remaining in the pan. Pour in wine and reduce over high heat, stirring to gather up the caramelized juices. When reduced to 2 tablespoons, add demi-glace and whisk till incorporated into sauce. Reduce by half. Whisk in jelly and when melted, reduce heat to low. Whisk in softened butter, 2 teaspoons at a time, only adding the next piece after the previous one is thoroughly incorporated into sauce. Do not let sauce boil or it will thin. As soon as the last of the butter is well amalgamated with sauce, taste and adjust seasoning if necessary. Remove from heat and keep warm.

Cut lamb into 2 cm slices and arrange on 6 preheated dinner plates. Spoon a little of the sauce over lamb and place remainder in a sauceboat.

Serve with steamed asparagus and orange stuffed potatoes (see next recipe).

Average times	Preparation — 10 minutes	**Do ahead**	Prepare lamb fillets to cooking stage, up to ½ day
	Cooking — 8 minutes		
	Resting — 10 minutes		
Wine notes	The lamb requires a full-bodied, astringent red —		
	A: Lindemans St George Vineyard (Coonawarra) Cabernet Sauvignon		
	E: Château La Mission-Haut-Brion (Graves) of a great year		
	U: Clos du Val (Napa) Cabernet Sauvignon		

ORANGE STUFFED POTATOES

6 medium pontiac (pink eye) potatoes, washed	grated zest of 2 oranges
4 tablespoons butter	salt to taste
3 tablespoons heavy cream	orange juice
2 egg yolks	25 g melted butter

Prick the potatoes and cook in their skins at 200°C (400°F) until just tender. Cut off the top third and scoop out pulp from lids and bases. Discard lids. Mash pulp with butter, cream, egg yolks, grated orange zest (reserve some for the tops) and salt to taste. Add enough orange juice to make a soft purée.

Using a 2 cm plain pastry tube and bag, pipe the purée into potato shells. Paint melted butter over the skins and cook until golden brown under a hot grill. Scatter remaining zest over the tops.

Average times	Preparation — 10 minutes	**Do ahead**	Prepare up to grilling stage up to ½ day ahead and heat through in 200°C (400°F) oven before browning tops.
	Cooking — 35 minutes		

PAVLOVA

6 egg whites
pinch salt
2 cups castor sugar
2 teaspoons vinegar
1 teaspoon vanilla essence

300 ml thick cream, beaten to soft peaks

fruits in season to garnish

Beat egg whites with salt until firm but not dry. Gradually beat in three-quarters of the castor sugar, and beat until very stiff. Fold in the remaining sugar, vinegar and vanilla.

Take a 25 cm cake pan and cut a circle of brown paper 5 cm bigger than the pan and wet it under the tap. Place the paper wet side up over base of *upturned* cake pan and use this as a base to mound pavlova. Pile pavlova mixture on top of paper and spread it to sides of the tin, *not* the paper. Smooth over the top and make as flat as possible.

Cook at 120°C (250°F) in centre of oven for 1¼ to 1½ hours. Turn upside down on to a serving platter and carefully remove paper while still hot. When cold, fill with cream and fruit.

Note: A pavlova should be filled at least 1 hour before serving to allow meringue, cream and fruit to mellow together

Average times Preparation — 20 minutes
Cooking — 1¼ to 1½ hours
Cooling — ½ hour

Wine notes The pavlova, to finish this grand meal, calls for a luscious dessert wine —
A: Peter Lehmann (Barossa) Semillon Sauternes
E: Château Rieussec (Sauternes) of a great year
U: Château St Jean (Sonoma) Late Harvest Johannisberg Riesling

Do ahead Pavlova up to 1 day and store in an airtight container

SPRING

MENU 4

◆

A very easy entrée which eliminates the pastry crust, followed by the most delicious light curry and ending with a superb ice-cream, this menu is ideal for lunch, dinner or supper.

CRUSTLESS HAM AND SPINACH QUICHE

◆

1 bunch spinach	salt and pepper, to taste
3 eggs	90 g Gruyère cheese, coarsely grated
1 cup thickened cream	90 g ham, chopped or cut into matchsticks

◆

Strip spinach leaves off stems and wash in several changes of cold water until there is absolutely no trace of sand or grit. Drain and place in a colander.

Bring a large pot of water to the boil, stand colander over the top (the boiling water must not touch colander), and place a lid over the top. Cook for 8 minutes to wilt spinach, lift out, drain and cool. Wring out excess moisture by hand.

Beat eggs, cream and seasoning until well combined, fold through remaining ingredients and pour into a buttered 23 cm ovenproof glass or ceramic quiche dish.

Cook in centre of 200°C (400°F) oven for about 30 minutes or until well risen, golden and set. Serve hot or cold, cut into wedges.

Average times Preparation — 20 minutes
Cooking — 40 minutes

Wine notes The quiche needs a fruity, full-bodied white —
A: The Rothbury Estate Cowra Chardonnay
E: Tocai di Lison ('La Fornarina') from the Veneto
U: Clos du Val (Napa) Chardonnay

Do ahead Wash and wilt spinach up to ½ day. If serving cold, make completely, 1 day ahead

VEAL KASHMIR

◆

Curry Sauce:

40 g butter
1 tablespoon Madras curry powder
1 medium apple, peeled, cored and roughly chopped
1 medium banana, skinned and roughly chopped
1 medium onion, roughly chopped
chilli sauce to taste
juice of 1 lemon
½ cup white wine
4 cups chicken stock
salt and pepper to taste
½ cup cream

1 kg veal fillets cut into 2 cm × 1 cm pieces
4 cups white, long grain rice
extra butter

Garnish:

1 mango
2 medium bananas
2 medium oranges
2 medium tamarillos
6–8 sprigs watercress

Accompaniments:

sambal oelek
plum sauce
fruit chutney

◆

Heat butter and cook curry powder in it over low heat, stirring for 5 minutes. Add all next 8 ingredients, and cook over medium heat for 40 minutes, stirring from time to time. Cool mixture and purée in a blender, stir in cream and adjust the seasoning.

While sauce is cooking, prepare and cook the rice. Bring a large pan of salted water to the boil over high heat, stir in the rice and continue to stir until water returns to the boil. Lower the heat and simmer for 9 minutes or until rice grains are just tender. Strain, rinse under running water (to prevent further cooking) and place in strainer over the same pan with a little water brought to the simmer. Steam for 5 minutes to dry rice, and take off the heat.

In a large frying pan, melt the extra butter and stir rice through it for a couple of minutes over medium heat. Divide mixture into 6 portions and pat down into a 16–18 cm ring mould (Savarin mould). Invert on a serving plate and tap out. Repeat this with remaining rice, making 1 ring for each person.

Slice all the fruits finely, and garnish top edge of each rice ring with 2 slices of each fruit and a sprig of cress. Serve with sambal oelek, plum sauce, and fruit chutney.

Reheat the sauce when ready to serve the curry and add the veal pieces. Cook them in the sauce over low heat until tender and serve in centre of individual moulded rice rings garnished with the fresh fruits and watercress.

Average times Preparation — 25 minutes
Cooking — 65 minutes
Cooling — 10 minutes
Wine notes Veal Kashmir, continue with the white from the first course

Do ahead Prepare sauce and cook veal in it up to 1 day ahead. Rice must be cooked only just before serving

PISTACHIO ICE-CREAM

◆

⅔ cup sugar
1 cup water
8 egg yolks

100 g shelled pistachios, blanched and chopped finely

◆

Dissolve sugar in water over medium heat. Beat egg yolks and pour in the warmed syrup. Cook the mixture in a double saucepan stirring all the time and remove from the heat as soon as it is thick. Do not let mixture boil.

Fold in the pistachio nuts and cream and cool the cream over ice. Churn or freeze quickly in ice-cream trays.

Average times Preparation — 10 minutes
Cooking — 10 minutes
Cooling — 10 minutes
Setting — 4 hours or overnight
Wine notes The ice-cream requires no wine

Do ahead At least ½ day and up to 3 days

SPRING

MENU 5

With the first and last courses made 1 to 2 days ahead, this is an excellent menu for busy people wanting to present a balanced menu within 1½ hours of arriving home.

TERRINE OF CHICKEN LIVERS WITH PORT

750 g chicken livers, cleaned
½ cup port
4 rashers of rindless bacon, chopped roughly
450 g finely minced pork
¾ cup dry white wine

salt and freshly ground black pepper to taste
very thin slices of pork fat (speck) unsalted and unsmoked to line terrine
2 bay leaves

Marinate chicken livers in port for 2 hours. Mince bacon and one-third of the livers. Mix with the minced pork, wine and seasoning.

Line terrine with speck and spread over this some of the minced liver mixture. Then run a layer of livers along the whole length of the terrine. Repeat these layers always finishing with a layer of the minced mixture and finish the terrine with speck. Put the bay leaves on top and then put on the lid.

Cook for 1½ hours in a water bath which comes half way up the sides of the terrine at 230°C (450°F) and then test with a metal skewer in the centre of the terrine. Insert skewer for exactly 30 seconds and immediately put it to the inside of your wrist. If it is very hot, the terrine is done. If it is only just hot then the terrine will take a further 10 minutes or so. Remove the lid and let cool. Refrigerate and serve sliced from the terrine.

Average times Preparation — 20 minutes
Marinading — 2 hours
Cooking — 1½ hours
Cooling — preferably overnight

Wine notes The terrine is complemented by a sparkling wine (or Sauternes, if you wish to try a different flavour combination) —
A: Yellowglen Brut Rosé Champagne
E: Bollinger Vintage Rosé Champagne
U: Schramsberg (Napa) Cuvée de Pinot

Do ahead At least 1 day and preferably 2 days

LAMB CUTLETS ANGELIQUE

1 medium egg-plant, cut into 2 cm cubes
1 large green cucumber, halved lengthwise, seeded, and cut into 1 cm slices
salt and pepper
1 tablespoon safflower oil
12 lamb cutlets, well trimmed
2 large zucchini, cut into 2 cm slices
1 large white onion, cut in 1 cm slices
1 green pepper, seeded and cut into 2 cm pieces
125 g white button mushrooms, halved or quartered, depending on size
1 × 425 g can tomatoes
½ cup veal stock
1 teaspoon cider vinegar
2 teaspoons dark brown sugar
1 bay leaf

Liberally salt egg-plant and cucumber and put a plate on top to weigh down. Leave to disgorge for 30 minutes.

Heat the oil in a heavy frying pan. Brown the cutlets well on both sides. Add all the vegetables to the cutlets together with all the other ingredients. Cover and simmer gently for 15 to 20 minutes. Remove lid for the final 5 minutes so that the sauce will reduce and thicken a little. Serve piping hot with Rice Pilaf (see next recipe).

Average times Preparation — 20 minutes
Standing — 30 minutes
Cooking — 25 minutes

Wine notes The cutlets are complemented by a solid red —
A: Mitchell Seven Hills Cabernet Sauvignon
E: Bandol (Domaine Tempier)
U: Rafanelli (Sonoma) Zinfandel

RICE PILAF

1 cup rice
2 cups veal or chicken stock
30 g butter
salt and pepper, to taste

Place all ingredients in a buttered ovenproof serving dish with a lid and cook for 25 to 35 minutes in 200°C (400°F) oven or until all the stock has evaporated.

Leave the rice to stand for 10 minutes before serving.

Average times Preparation — 5 minutes
Cooking — 30 minutes

PISTACHIO TARTLETS WITH LEMON ICING
Makes 15 to 18 tartlets

Short Pastry:

¾ cup plain flour
pinch salt
2 tablespoons castor sugar
60 g butter, chilled and cut into 6 pieces
2–3 tablespoons iced water

Filling:

⅔ cup pistachios, skinned
3½ tablespoons castor sugar
40 g butter, softened
1 egg
1½ tablespoons orange juice

Lemon Icing:

¾ cup icing sugar, sieved
1 tablespoon unsalted butter, softened
lemon juice to mix

To make the pastry: sift the flour and salt and add sugar. Rub in butter until mixture resembles oatmeal. Mix in just enough iced water to bring the mixture together. (Alternatively make in a food processor). Knead dough on a lightly floured board, flatten to 3 cm thickness, seal in plastic wrap and refrigerate for a minimum of 30 minutes.

Roll pastry on a lightly floured board until it is the thickness of a 5 cm coin. Butter 15–18 6 cm tartlet moulds. Stamp out 9 cm rounds with a scone cutter or a glass of the same diameter and press each into the buttered moulds pressing down well. Cover with plastic wrap and refrigerate for a minimum of 30 minutes.

Cook tartlet cases in 200°C (400°F) oven for 5 or 6 minutes. Remove from oven and press out any air bubbles which rise in the pastry. Return to oven and continue to cook until golden around the edges.

To make the filling: grind pistachios with castor sugar in a food processor until medium fine. Add softened butter and grind until fairly fine. Add the egg and orange juice and mix lightly.

Spoon the pistachio mixture into the pastry cases without over-filling and bake in centre of 190°C (375°F) oven for approximately 12 minutes or until the filling is well risen and a knife inserted in the centre comes out clean. Remove from the oven (tartlets will settle down a little as they cool). Leave to cool in the moulds for 10 minutes before removing and cooling on a wire rack.

To make the icing: mix icing sugar and butter together and add just enough lemon juice to make a soft mixture. When tartlets are quite cold spread a little of the icing over the top and leave to set.

Average times Preparation — 30 minutes
Standing — 2 × 30 minutes
Cooking — 25 minutes
Cooling — 30 minutes

Wine notes The pistachio tartlets are comp-
lemented by —
A: Henschke Auslese Rhine
Riesling
E: Château Climens (Barsac)
U: Château St Jean (Sonoma)
Late Harvest Johannisberg
Riesling

Do ahead Up to 2 days

SPRING

MENU 6

Two do-ahead dishes begin this menu and the pastry dough can be made up to the rolling stage, so only the rest of the dessert has to be made at the last minute.

BRAIN TERRINE

4 sets lamb brains
½ cup safflower or peanut oil
1 onion, chopped coarsely
½ cup chopped parsley, tarragon and thyme, mixed
½ cup dry white wine

4 eggs, beaten
½ cup coarsely chopped walnuts
½ cup finely chopped celery
salt and freshly ground black pepper to taste

Poach brains for 5 minutes in salted water. Drain, skin under running cold water and cut into large pieces. Heat oil in a frying pan and cook onion until softened. Add herbs, brains and wine. Simmer until liquids evaporate.

Cool and stir in eggs, walnuts and celery and season well. Spoon into an oiled 24 cm terrine and cook at 175°C (375°F) for 20 minutes. Cool in terrine, then refrigerate before turning out. Serve in 1½ thick slices with brown toast and unsalted butter.

Average times Preparation — 25 minutes
Cooking — 35 minutes
Cooling — 4 hours

Do ahead Up to 1 day

Wine notes Brain Terrine calls for a fruity white with fresh acidity to cut through the rich flavour —
A: Quelltaler (Watervale) Rhine Riesling
E and U: Sancerre Clos de la Poussie

BURGUNDIAN BEEF
Begin 1 day in advance

1¼ kg topside beef

Marinade:

2¼ cups dry red wine
2 carrots, coarsely diced
1 medium sized onion, quartered
1½ teaspoons fresh thyme
2 bay leaves

225 g fat streaky bacon, in 2 cm slices and diced coarsely
125 g pickling onions, skinned
125 g baby carrots, peeled, leaving 2 cm green tops on
2 tablespoons plain flour
1 bouquet garni
⅔ cup beef stock
1 cup water
2 cloves garlic, crushed
24 baby white button mushrooms
2 teaspoons grated orange zest
1 teaspoon tomato paste
salt and freshly ground black pepper, to taste
finely chopped parsley, to garnish

Cut the beef into 2½ cm cubes and place in a bowl with the marinade ingredients. Cover and leave overnight.

In a large heavy saucepan or casserole, sauté the diced bacon until it begins to crisp. Remove with a slotted spoon and reserve. Fry pickling onions and carrots in the bacon fat until lightly coloured. Drain and reserve together with the bacon.

Drain the beef well. Reserve marinade, discarding carrots and onions. Sauté the beef, a small amount at a time, in the remaining fat until brown. Sprinkle with flour and continue cooking until the flour browns, then add reserved marinade (including the bay leaves), bouquet garni, stock, water and garlic. Return the carrots, onions and bacon to the pan. Stir and bring to boil then reduce to a gentle simmer.

Simmer gently for 1 hour, uncovered. Stir in mushrooms and continue cooking for a further 30 minutes, or until meat is tender and sauce is reduced by half. Discard bouquet garni and bay leaves. Stir in orange zest and tomato paste. Season to taste with salt and freshly ground black pepper. Garnish with parsley and serve very hot.

Serve with a green salad with blanched snow peas and zucchini batons to accompany the beef burgundy.

Average times Preparation — 20 minutes
Standing — overnight
Cooking — 2 hours

Do ahead Up to 1 day but leave out mushrooms. Stir them into the dish before heating through

Wine notes Burgundian Beef calls for a hearty red —
A: Redbank (central Victoria) Sally's Paddock
E: Hermitage (Chave) of a good year
U: Sierra Vista (El Dorado) Zinfandel

SOUR APRICOT TART

Sweet Short Crust:
¾ cup plain flour
pinch salt
1½ tablespoons castor sugar
90 g butter, chilled and cut into 8 pieces
2-3 tablespoons iced water (depending on weather)

Filling:
200 g dried apricots
¼ cup lemon juice
2 tablespoons sherry
2 tablespoons icing sugar, sifted

To make short crust: sift flour and salt and stir in castor sugar. Rub butter into flour using finger tips until mixture resembles oatmeal. Stir in just enough iced water to bring the mixture together in a ball. Alternatively, make in a food processor.

Knead dough on a lightly floured board until it feels like chamois leather. Flatten to 3 cm. Wrap in greaseproof paper and put dough in refrigerator for 30 minutes.

Roll dough to fit a 26 cm × 30 cm Swiss roll tin, trim off overhanging pastry and prick all over with a fork. Cover and refrigerate for 30 minutes.

To make filling: soak apricots in lemon juice and sherry, turning them often so they are well coated.

Arrange the apricots very close together, stone side up on the chilled pastry and cook at 200°C (400°F) for 15 minutes on a preheated oven tray. Sift icing sugar over apricots and return to oven until pastry is golden and apricots glazed. Place under a hot griller if necessary. Serve warm with whipped cream.

Average times Preparation — 25 minutes
Resting — 2 × 30 minutes
Cooking — 20 minutes

Wine notes Sour Apricot Tart requires no wine

Do ahead Short crust dough, up to 1 day

SPRING

MENU 7

◆

A light menu which is suitable for lunch or dinner on a warm Spring day. If serving the gougère cold, there's very little last minute preparation.

GOUGÈRE

◆

150 ml water
60 g butter
75 g plain flour, sifted
pinch salt
2 eggs (55 g each)
60 g Gruyère cheese, coarsely chopped

Glaze:
1 egg yolk
pinch salt

◆

Put water and butter in a large saucepan and bring slowly to the boil over medium heat stirring so butter melts in the water before mixture boils. As soon as mixture boils pour in all the flour and salt and stir vigorously off the heat with a wooden spatula. Place pan back over low heat to dry the mixture, stirring constantly for 2 minutes. Cool for 2 minutes.

Whisk eggs and pour half at a time into the mixture, beating vigorously with a wooden spatula. (This step can be done in a food processor.) Fold in cheese and spoon mixture into a ring shape with a 6 cm centre on a well-buttered and floured baking sheet. Whisk glaze ingredients together and paint over the top. Cook in hottest part of 200°C (400°F) oven for 35 to 40 minutes without opening oven door. Gougère should be well risen with a crisp, golden crust. Serve at once cut into wedges. Alternatively serve at room temperature when the Gougère will deflate but is still excellent.

Average times Preparation — 10 minutes
Cooling — 5 minutes
Cooking — 50 minutes

Wine notes Gougère calls for a burgundy-style of red —
A: Robson (Pokolbin) Pinot Noir
E: Beaune Clos du Roi (Tollot-Beaut)
U: Firestone (Santa Barbara) Pinot Noir

Do ahead If serving cold, up to ½ day

SPRING LAMB SALAD

24 washed, dried and torn leaves of curly endive (frissée)
1 medium carrot peeled and cut into fine julienne 6 cm long and blanched
1 baby beetroot peeled with a vegetable peeler and cut into fine julienne
12 snowpeas stringed and cut into fine julienne and blanched
18 baby oyster mushrooms (optional)
12 walnut halves roasted until crisp (cool and rub off as much of the skins as possible)

Vinaigrette:
½ cup peanut oil
1 tablespoon red currant jelly mashed and melted
1 teaspoon French mustard
1 tablespoon red wine vinegar
salt and freshly ground black pepper to taste

3 medium lamb fillets
2 tablespoons peanut oil

6 tiny sprigs fresh thyme to garnish

Arrange salad leaves on 6 entrée plates. Scatter the julienne vegetables over the top with the mushrooms and walnut halves. Whisk vinaigrette ingredients together.

Heat the oil in a heavy-based frying pan and seal lamb fillets on all sides. Season and cook until tender, about 6–8 minutes (fillets must still be pink inside). Cut in 5 mm slices and arrange over salads. Dress immediately with vinaigrette. Garnish with thyme and serve at once.

Average times Preparation — 30 minutes
Cooking — 8 minutes

Wine notes Continue drinking the red with the lamb salad

Do ahead Prepare salad and vinaigrette up to ½ day ahead, but only cook lamb when needed

FLAMING BAKED BANANAS

12 ripe but firm bananas, peeled and halved lengthwise
1 tablespoon finely grated orange zest
3 tablespoons soft brown sugar
1½ teaspoons ground cinnamon

2 tablespoons butter, cut into 8 pieces
2 tablespoons orange juice
2 tablespoons Grand Marnier
¼ cup Grand Marnier, extra

Layer bananas in a casserole dish and scatter next 6 ingredients over the layers. Cover (use foil if you don't have a lid and tuck it around tightly) and leave to stand for 1 hour. Bake at 175°C (350°F) for 20 minutes.

Heat extra Grand Marnier, pour over bananas and ignite. Carry the flaming dish to table and serve with unwhipped cream.

Average times Preparation — 15 minutes
Standing — 1 hour
Cooking — 20 minutes

Wine notes Baked bananas need the aromatic sweetness of a muscat —
A: Brown Bros (northern Victoria) Spaetlese Lexia
E: Muscat de Beaumes de Venise (Domaine de Durban)
U: Fetzer (Mendocino) Muscat Canelli

Do ahead Up to oven stage, 1 hour

SPRING

MENU 8

A light and colourful first course begins this menu. Unmould the mousse while the chicken cooks, but remember, you do have to get up from the table to prepare the dessert.

SALMON MOUSSE WITH GREEN HORSERADISH SAUCE

¾ cup hot water
1 chicken stock cube
1½ tablespoons gelatine
220 g can red salmon
⅓ cup mayonnaise
1 tablespoon chopped parsley
3 teaspoons lemon juice
1½ tablespoons white onion, finely chopped
¾ cup thickened cream
salt and pepper to taste

Green Horseradish Sauce:
1 egg yolk plus 1 whole egg
1 teaspoon French mustard
¼ cup parsley sprigs, tightly packed
1 tablespoon white wine vinegar
salt and pepper to taste
1 cup salad oil
1 tablespoon horseradish relish

To make the mousse: place hot water, stock cube and gelatine in a blender or food processor and blend for 1 minute. Skin the salmon. Pour into blender/food processor, undrained, with all the remaining mousse ingredients and blend for 3 minutes. Pour into 6 × ½-cup wetted moulds. Place on a tray in refrigerator until set (approximately 2 to 4 hours).

To make the sauce: place egg yolk, egg, mustard, parsley, vinegar, salt and pepper in a blender or food processor and blend until parsley is finely chopped. With machine running on high, slowly pour in the oil, drop by drop, until half the oil is incorporated. Then pour in the rest of the oil in a thin, steady stream. If you add it too quickly you could curdle the sauce. Add horseradish relish and adjust seasoning if necessary.

To serve: pull away the set mousse from the top of each mould with your fingers. Dip moulds one at a time into warm water (it must not be hot). Invert onto a serving plate, shake out vigorously and spoon a little of the green sauce over the side of each mousse and pass the remaining sauce at the table.

The mousse may be garnished with tomatoes and lettuce leaves or dill cucumbers or simply topped with a sprig of fresh watercress or parsley.

Average times Preparation — 15 minutes
Setting — 2 to 4 hours

Wine notes Salmon mousse, with horseradish sauce, needs a crisp, aromatic white —
A: St Clare Watervale Rhine Riesling
E: Riesling (Kuentz-Bas) from Alsace of a good year
U: San Martin (Santa Clara) Johannisberg Riesling

Do ahead Up to 1 day

APPLE AND RAISIN STUFFED CHICKEN

Stuffing:

1 medium onion, chopped very finely
1½ green apples, peeled and chopped finely
1½ cups soft breadcrumbs
⅓ cup raisins, chopped
3 tablespoons sherry

1½ teaspoons mixed herbs
salt and fresh ground black pepper to taste
2 eggs

2 × 1.5 kg chickens
45 g butter

Mix chopped onion, apple, breadcrumbs, raisins, sherry, herbs, seasonings and eggs together. Stuff into chicken cavities. Roast in butter at 200°C (400°F) until golden and tender, approximately 40 minutes. Rest in warm oven for 10 minutes before serving.

Whole English spinach leaves, stewed lightly in olive or peanut oil to accompany the chicken.

Average times Preparation — 15 minutes
Cooking — 40 minutes
Standing — 10 minutes

Wine notes The chicken requires a big, fruity white —
A: Rosemount Wood Matured Show Chardonnay
E: Château Coutet Sec (Barsac)
U: Grgich Hills (Napa) Chardonnay

Do ahead Up to oven stage, ½ day

FLAMING RUM OMELETTE

For each omelette:

3 fresh eggs, separated
1½ tablespoons castor sugar

1 tablespoon cream
2 tablespoons rum
2 teaspoons butter

Beat egg whites until stiff, beat in yolks with 1 tablespoon of the castor sugar, cream and 1 tablespoon of rum.

Heat butter in an omelette pan over high heat until colour begins to change. Pour all the mixture into the hot butter and stir gently with a fork, moving mixture around in the pan and pulling back the setting mixture to allow the still liquid mixture to run underneath. Continue to do this until all the runny mixture is set and the top of the omelette is just set. Fold the omelette over on itself away from the handle and turn it out onto a warmed plate.

Warm remaining tablespoon of rum. Sprinkle remaining sugar over the omelette, pour over rum and ignite it. Serve immediately.

Average times for each omelette
Preparation — 5 minutes
Cooking — 3 minutes

Wine notes Rum omelette requires no wine

SPRING

MENU 9

This fruity and colourful menu is ideal for a special family celebration, especially for dinner. It is easily executed and mostly do-ahead. The main course is one on which my mother reared me.

BROCCOLI CRÊPES IN MALTAISE SAUCE

Batter:
½ cup plain flour
pinch salt
1 egg
1 teaspoon peanut oil
300 ml milk

extra peanut oil for cooking

Filling:
1 bunch broccoli

Maltaise Sauce:
1 teaspoon potato flour
1 tablespoon cold water
4 egg yolks
250 g butter, softened
white pepper, to taste
juice ½ blood orange
1 teaspoon finely grated zest blood orange
salt, to taste

To make batter: place flour and salt into a medium bowl. Add the egg and oil and slowly whisk in milk. Beat until batter is free of lumps. Alternatively, make in a food processor. Stand the batter for a minimum of 30 minutes.

To make filling: trim broccoli into 5 cm long florets and peel stems. Poach or steam until *al dente*.

To make crêpes: heat a 16 cm crêpe pan with a little peanut oil until hot. Pour off excess oil and ladle in enough batter to just cover base of pan. Cook over medium heat until bubbling on top. Turn over crêpe and cook until the second side is golden.
  Place on a buttered plate and keep warm. Make 12 more crêpes (the first is never the best) and stack one on top of the other. (They don't need interleaving unless they are to be put in freezer).

To make Maltaise Sauce: mix the potato flour, water and egg yolks in a pyrex jug or bowl over hot water (not boiling). Add softened butter in small pieces one piece at a time whisking constantly. Add pepper, juice and zest and salt if needed. Keep warm over warm water but do not reheat. *Note:* each piece of butter must be thoroughly incorporated into the sauce before adding the next.

To assemble: spread crêpes out on work surface — spotted sides (the second cooked side) face up. Place a broccoli floret in each with the head facing towards the edge of each crêpe and fold into quarters. Arrange 2 crêpes on each warmed entrée plate and spoon a ribbon of sauce over each crêpe. Pass any remaining sauce at the table.

Average times Preparation — 25 minutes
Cooking — 35 minutes
Standing — 30 minutes

Wine notes The predominant orange flavour in the Maltaise Sauce masks a wine

DRIED FRUIT AND NUT-STUFFED LOIN OF LAMB WITH HONEY GLAZE

Boned loin of lamb, 1 kg after boning

Stuffing:

½ cup sliced celery
1 cup chopped dried apricots
10 prunes, stoned and chopped
3 tablespoons chopped almonds
2 tablespoons chopped walnuts
½ cup freshly made breadcrumbs
2 tablespoons chopped white onion
2 teaspoons dried oregano or 1 tablespoon
    freshly chopped oregano
1 egg
1 teaspoon salt
¼ teaspoon pepper

1 tablespoon oil
salt and pepper

Honey Glaze:

2 tablespoons clear honey
2 tablespoons French mustard
1 tablespoon sherry
2 tablespoons tomato sauce
2 tablespoons soy sauce

Remove as much fat as possible from lamb. In a medium bowl, mix all stuffing ingredients together and press on to the inside of loin. Roll and then tie securely with butcher's twine.

In a heavy baking dish, heat 1 tablespoon of oil over high heat and seal loin on all sides for about 2 minutes. Salt and pepper loin and place in the hottest part of the oven. Bake at 200°C (400°F) for 35 minutes.

Mix together the honey and French mustard. Remove loin from oven and paint with honey glaze. Return loin to oven for a further 10 minutes. Cool, cover and refrigerate. Serve, sliced in 4 cm pieces, with Bean Sprout Salad (see next recipe).

Average times Preparation — 25 minutes
Cooking — 45 minutes
Cooling — 4 hours

Wine notes The honey-glazed lamb suggests
a full-bodied, fruity red —
A: The Rothbury Estate
   (Pokolbin) Carbonique
   Maceration Shiraz
E: Château Rayas Châteauneuf-
   du-Pape
U: Caymus (Napa) Zinfandel

Do ahead Up to 1 day

BEAN SPROUT SALAD

2 cups fresh bean sprouts, tailed
1 cup finely sliced baby white button mush-
    rooms
1 large red pepper, seeded and cut into 1 cm
    dice
6 spring onions, coarsely sliced, both green
    and white parts
2 tablespoons parsley, chopped finely

Dressing:

½ cup peanut oil
1 tablespoon white wine vinegar
salt and freshly ground black pepper to taste

Prepare all the salad ingredients and refrigerate, covered with plastic film, until ready to serve. Whisk together the dressing ingredients, pour over salad, toss well and serve.

Average times Preparation — 25 minutes

Do ahead Dressing up to 1 day

GUAVA CREAM

6–8 ripe, highly perfumed guavas, depending
    on size
¼ cup castor sugar
2 cups thickened cream
4 egg whites

Garnish:
1 extra guava
mint leaves

Skin the guavas and purée in a food processor or blender, and stir in castor sugar.

Beat cream until it forms soft peaks, and stir into the guava mixture. Beat egg whites until they form firm peaks and fold one-third into the mixture. Then fold in remaining whites and spoon into coupes or champagne saucers. Cover and refrigerate until firm (it will not set, but firms a little on chilling and standing). Decorate with fine slices of guava and a mint leaf.

Average times Preparation — 15 minutes
             Standing — 1½ hours

Do ahead Up to ½ day

Wine notes Guava Cream requires no wine

BURNT BUTTER BISCUITS
Makes 40 to 50 small biscuits

120 g butter
½ cup sugar
1 egg, 60 g
dash almond essence

⅔ cup self raising flour, sifted

almonds, halved, to garnish

Heat butter in a saucepan until it begins to brown. Stir in sugar and cook for 1 minute, stirring. Cool the mixture slightly. Beat the egg with almond essence. Mix the egg with the butter and sugar and fold in self raising flour. It should be a medium-stiff mixture.

Lightly butter a baking tray. Drop teaspoon-sized balls of biscuit mixture on to tray, leaving room for spreading. Top each biscuit with an almond and cook in 190°C (375°F) oven for approximately 15 minutes, or until golden. Cool on a rack and store in an airtight container.

Average times Preparation — 15 minutes
             Cooking — 20 minutes
             Cooling — 20 minutes

Do ahead Up to 1 week if stored in airtight
    containers

SPRING

MENU 10

This Italian-inspired menu is light and delightfully easy. The trick with the first course is to remember that the sauce is a delicate combination of four cheeses which need only to melt, not to cook, so use a water bath and be gentle with it.

PASTA WITH FOUR CHEESES

---

200 g fresh fettuccine or tagliatelle, see
    page 134
salt
oil

Sauce:

30 g butter
60 g Mascarpone cheese, chopped roughly
60 g Emmental cheese, chopped roughly
60 g Gorgonzola cheese, chopped roughly
60 g Parmesan cheese, finely grated

Bring a large pot of water to the boil with 1 tablespoon of salt and oil. While the water is coming to the boil prepare the sauce.

To make sauce: melt butter in a double boiler or small saucepan over hot water and stir in the four cheeses. Place pan over hot water and gently heat cheeses in butter until they are melted and well incorporated. Turn off heat and stand pan in the hot water bath.

To cook pasta: add pasta to the rapidly boiling water and stir once to prevent from sticking. Cook until *al dente.*

    Lift pasta out of water with a strainer into a warmed serving bowl. Do not pour pasta through strainer — you lose too much of the cooking water — it's better done the other way. Spoon in a quarter of the sauce and toss immediately. Spoon the remaining sauce over the top and serve at once.

Average times Preparation — 10 minutes
Cooking — 10 minutes

Wine notes The pasta could be accompanied by either a medium, astringent red, or a full-bodied white with crisp acidity; because a white is a more satisfactory partner for the veal with lemon and capers (the next course in this menu), a white is suggested —
A: Quelltaler Cachet Blanc
E and U: Vernaccia di San
    Gimignano ('Il
    Castelliere' —
    Poggibonsi) from
    Tuscany

(left) Passionfruit Tarts
(right) Butterscotch Nonsense

Wines (left to right):
Evans Family Coonawarra *Botrytis Cinerea* Rhine
    Riesling
Château St Jean (Sonoma)
Belle Terre Vineyards Johannisberg Riesling
    Individual Dried Bunch Selected Late Harvest
Château Coutet (Barsac)

Mustard Seed Lamb Fillets

Wine:
Clos du Val (Napa) Cabernet Sauvignon

VEAL WITH LEMON AND CAPERS

1 kg veal escalopes, beaten to 7 mm thick
3–4 tablespoons plain flour (approximately)
4 tablespoons butter
3 tablespoons olive oil

3 tablespoons lemon juice
salt and freshly ground black pepper to taste
3 tablespoons extra fine capers, drained

Dredge the veal escalopes in flour, shaking off the excess. Using a very sharp knife make tiny incisions into the edges of veal to prevent it from curling when it cooks.

Heat butter and oil in a very large heavy frying pan over high heat or alternatively use two pans at once. When butter and oil are sizzling sauté 2 to 3 escalopes at a time leaving plenty of space between them so that they will not stew. As soon as escalopes are golden on one side turn over and cook until golden on second side. Cook until just tender and set aside on a warmed plate.

When all escalopes are cooked, pour in the lemon juice and whisk over medium heat to gather up all the caramelized juices in base of pan. Season to taste and add a tablespoon or two of water if necessary. Cook until a good consistency and spoon over the veal. Scatter with capers and serve at once.

Follow the veal with a mixed salad in season.

Average times Preparation — 10 minutes
Cooking — 10 minutes

Wine notes Continue with the white from the first course

RASPBERRY ICE-CREAM

3 boxes raspberries, checked for condition
juice of 1 lemon

1 cup castor sugar
2 cups thickened cream, beaten to soft peaks

Push raspberries through a fine tamis or put through a mouli fitted with a fine grid to remove seeds. Stir in juice and castor sugar until sugar dissolves. Fold cream into raspberry mixture.

Either churn or set in ice-cream trays in refrigerator freezer, stirring as soon as ice-cream shows signs of setting around top edge. Cover with foil and freeze. Accompany with caraway seed meringues (see next recipe).

Average times Preparation — 10 minutes
Setting — 2 to 4 hours

Do ahead At least ½ day and up to 3 days
Wine notes The ice-cream requires no wine

CARAWAY SEED MERINGUES
Makes 12 dozen 2½ cm buttons approximately

3 egg whites
⅔ cups castor sugar

3 teaspoons caraway seeds

Beat egg whites in a copper or metal bowl until they form stiff peaks. Beat in 1 tablespoon of sugar at a time until two-thirds of the sugar is incorporated. Fold remaining sugar into the meringue mixture with the caraway seeds, using a rubber spatula and a very light hand.

Fit a large piping bag with a plain 1 cm piping tube and fill with the mixture. Pipe 2½ cm buttons on to a lightly buttered baking tray leaving a little room for spreading. Cook in centre of 120°C (250°F) oven for approximately 65 minutes or until the meringue buttons are set but not brown. Cool on a wire rack and store in an airtight container.

Average times Preparation — 20 minutes
Cooking — 65 minutes

Do ahead Up to 1 week if stored in airtight containers

SPRING

MENU 11

The seafood ragoût is an adaptation of one which was served 25 years ago in a famous Melbourne restaurant. I have simplified it, but it is still a bit of a fiddle, however it is very well worthwhile. The easiness of the lamb dish and the do-ahead dessert make the menu less demanding on last minute time.

SEAFOOD RAGOÛT

1 cup finely sliced baby egg-plant with skin
60 g butter
¼ teaspoon salt
2 tablespoons finely chopped shallots
½ cup finely sliced red and green peppers
1½ cups sliced white button mushrooms
1 cooked baby crayfish tail, 200 g approximately
60 g butter, extra

250 g fresh prawns, shelled and deveined
250 g scallops, cleaned
3 teaspoons plain flour
¼ cup dry white wine
1 cup fish stock
2 tablespoons thick cream
salt and pepper to taste
1 dozen loose oysters

Salt the egg-plant slices and leave to disgorge for 15 minutes. Heat 60 g butter in a medium-sized heavy pan and sauté the shallots and peppers for 3 minutes. Lift out with a slotted spoon and set aside. Sauté mushrooms for 1 minute, lift out with a slotted spoon and set aside. Wipe egg-plant with paper towel and sauté in same pan for 2 minutes. Set aside.

Remove flesh from crayfish tail, remove intestine and cut flesh into 1 cm medallions. Add the extra butter to pan and sauté prawns for 2 minutes. Lift out and reserve. Sauté scallops for 1 to 2 minutes (depending on size), lift out and reserve.

Whisk flour into pan juice and cook over medium heat, whisking for 2 minutes. Pour in wine and stock and cook, whisking, until sauce thickens to a thin coating consistency. Whisk in cream and seasonings to taste.

Heat crayfish in sauce for 30 seconds, then add all the other ingredients except oysters, plus their juices and stir gently with a wooden spatula until heated through. Add oysters, stir and serve at once.

Average times Preparation — 40 minutes
Cooking — 30 minutes

Do ahead Shell, clean and prepare seafood up to cooking stage, up to ½ day

Wine notes Seafood ragoût needs a strongly-flavoured white with crisp acidity —
A: Terrace Vale (Pokolbin) Semillon
E: Chablis Grand Cru Les Blanchots (Domaine Laroche)
U: Heitz (Napa) Chardonnay

LAMB IN PAPER

1 leg of lamb, trimmed of fat and weighing 1.5–2 kg
2 cloves garlic, bruised, peeled and slivered
2 tablespoons lemon juice
1 tablespoon olive oil

1 tablespoon salt
freshly ground black pepper

brown paper and string

Make several deep incisions in the meat with the point of a very sharp knife, and stuff each incision with a sliver of garlic. Rub the meat well with lemon juice, oil and seasonings. Wrap up meat in brown paper, making a neat parcel and tie well with string. Place parcel in a lightly-oiled roasting pan and cook in centre of 175°C (375°F) oven for approximately 1¼ to 1½ hours for pink lamb. (If you like lamb well done, then leave it for 2 hours.) Untie parcel, rest meat for 10 minutes, then carve. Serve with leek sauce (see next recipe).

Average times Preparation — 10 minutes
Cooking — 1¼ to 2 hours
Standing — 10 minutes

Wine notes Lamb in paper calls for a top quality, richly flavoured Cabernet —
A: Leeuwin Estate (Western Australia) Cabernet Sauvignon
E: Château Pichon-Lalande (Pauillac) of a great year
U: Beaulieu (Napa) Cabernet Sauvignon Georges de Latour

Do ahead Prepare up to oven stage, 1 hour ahead

LEEK SAUCE

1 bunch leeks very thoroughly washed, including green tops
60 g butter

1 cup thickened cream
1 teaspoon salt
freshly ground black pepper to taste

Slice leeks medium fine in a food processor fitted with the slicing disc.

Heat butter in a large heavy pan over medium heat and cook leeks, stirring for 10 minutes. Stir in cream and cook over high heat, stirring until sauce reaches a good consistency. Season to taste and serve.

Average times Preparation — 15 minutes
Cooking — 15 minutes

Do ahead Leeks may be prepared up to cooking stage ½ day

MACADAMIA NUT SOUR CREAM PIE

Filling:

1½ cups sour cream (full fat)
4 egg yolks
¾ cup castor sugar
2 tablespoons cornflour

vanilla essence to taste
juice ½ lemon
1 cup shelled and lightly roasted macadamia nuts
1 × 23 cm sweet pastry case baked

To make filling: pour sour cream into top of double boiler and heat over simmering water until moderately hot. (Cream will thin as it heats). In mixing bowl beat egg yolks slightly and whisk in castor sugar and cornflour. Slowly pour hot cream over yolk mixture, whisking vigorously. Return mixture to double boiler and cook, whisking constantly, over simmering water for 15 to 20 minutes or until thick. Do not boil. Remove from heat and stir in vanilla. Cool.

Pour lemon juice over nuts and stir into cooled cream mixture. Pour into prepared pastry case, cover and chill 4 hours.

Average times Preparation — 10 minutes
Cooking — 25 minutes
Chilling — 4 hours

Wine notes Macadamia nut pie calls for a muscat —
A: Baileys Late Harvest Lexia, from northern Victoria
E and U: Muscat de Beaumes de Venise (Jaboulet)

Do ahead Up to 1 day

SPRING

MENU 12

———◆———

This is a delightfully light menu which can be prepared almost entirely in advance. It is excellent for lunch or dinner on a warm Spring day and should be followed with a pyramid of fresh chèvre cheese and crusty bread, rather than dessert.

WHITEBAIT MOUSSE

———◆———

1½ teaspoons gelatine
2 tablespoons hot water
3 × 220 g cans whitebait
2 tablespoons lemon juice
300 ml thick cream, beaten to soft peaks

dash tabasco sauce
salt and fresh ground black pepper to taste

sprigs fresh watercress and lemon halves to garnish

———◆———

Dissolve gelatine in hot water and cool a little. Put whitebait and juices in a bowl with gelatine and remaining ingredients and fold together very carefully, keeping whitebait whole. Pour into a 5-cup wetted ring mould, cover with plastic wrap and set in the refrigerator.

To unmould, pull mousse away from top edges of mould with fingers. Dip in warm water, invert on a round serving plate and shake out. Fill centre with sprigs fresh watercress and serve with lemon halves, crusty brown French bread sticks and unsalted butter.

Average times Preparation — 15 minutes
Setting — 4 hours

Do ahead At least ½ day and up to 1 day

Wine notes Whitebait Mousse calls for a fresh, acid, dry white —
A: Allandale (Pokolbin) Semillon
E and U: Chablis Grand Cru les Clos (Regnard)

SMOKED CHICKEN SALAD

2 medium carrots, peeled and curled with a
  vegetable peeler
2 large green cucumbers, scrubbed and halved
  lengthwise and seeded
salt
1.5 kg smoked chicken, skinned and flesh cut
  into shreds (it doesn't need any cooking) or
  750 g smoked turkey roll, cut into shreds
1½ cups baby white mushrooms, finely sliced
6 spring onions, peeled and finely sliced

Dressing:
2 tablespoons ginger marmalade
⅓ cup peanut oil
2 tablespoons white wine vinegar
2 tablespoons soy sauce

Soak carrot strips in iced water until they curl. Cut 1 cucumber into quarters lengthwise, then into 6 cm strips. Slice other cucumber into very fine crescents keeping the two shapes separate. Salt them and weigh each down with a plate. Stand 30 minutes. Squeeze out juices and dry on paper towels. Drain the carrot curls. Arrange chicken or turkey, cucumber strips and carrot curls in little piles on a large plate, or on individual serving plates. Arrange cucumber crescents in the centre. Over the top, scatter the mushroom slices and sprinkle with spring onions.

To make dressing: whisk all the dressing ingredients together in a small bowl, and pour over salad 5 minutes before serving. Serve salad as it is without tossing.

Average times Preparation — 30 minutes
Standing — 30 minutes

Wine notes Smoked Chicken Salad requires
an aromatic white —
A: Barry (Clare) Jud's Hill Rhine
   Riesling
E: Riesling (Pierre Sparr) from
   Alsace of a good year
U: Mirassou (Santa Clara)
   Johannisberg Riesling

Do ahead Prepare vegetables and poultry
and refrigerate, covered and in
separate containers, up to ½ day

SPRING

MENU 13

◆

With the casserole made 1 to 2 days ahead and only needing to be heated through at the last moment, the salad and dessert are the only two dishes needing attention at the time of serving.

WARM SEAFOOD AND AVOCADO SALAD

◆

Fish Stock:

500 g fishheads and bones
½ onion
½ carrot
1 stick celery
1 bay leaf
3 black peppercorns, tied in muslin
3 cups cold water

12 green prawns
500 g scallops, cleaned

3 cups young English spinach leaves, stemmed, washed, dried and torn into bite-sized pieces
2 medium-firm ripe avocados
3 tablespoons lemon juice

Dressing:

2 teaspoons French mustard
¾ cup fine olive oil
salt and freshly ground black pepper to taste
2 tablespoons white wine vinegar

12 pecan halves

◆

To make fish stock: bring all fish stock ingredients to the boil over low heat, skimming just before it comes to the boil. Simmer for 25 minutes, strain through a colander into a medium sized pan.

To cook seafood: poach prawns in stock for 2 minutes and add scallops to poach for 1 minute. Turn off heat and when cool enough to handle, peel prawns, devein and cut in halves lengthwise. Slice scallops into thin rounds.

To make salad: halve and stone avocados and ball with a melon baller. Spoon lemon juice over them. Combine all the dressing ingredients together in a small pan and bring to a simmer. Divide spinach leaves between 6 heated entrée plates, arrange scallop slices and avocado balls on the leaves. Spoon over warm dressing and scatter with pecan halves.

Average times Preparation — 25 minutes
Cooking — 30 minutes (including fish stock)
Cooling — 10 minutes

Wine notes The salad needs a very crisp white to cut through the richness of the scallops and avocado —
A: Wyndham Estate Chablis Superior
E: Chablis (Bacheroy-Josselin)
U: Domaine Laurier (Sonoma) Chardonnay

Do ahead Prepare spinach leaves up to ½ day, keep airtight and refrigerate

SPRING VEAL CASSEROLE

◆

4 tablespoons oil
300 g streaky bacon in one piece, rind removed
  and cut into 18 pieces
1.5 kg shoulder veal, cut into 24 pieces
18 pickling onions, peeled
3 sticks celery, cut on the cross into 3 cm
  pieces
2 teaspoons sugar
2 leeks, split in halves, washed and cut into
  1.5 cm slices
2 cloves garlic, bruised, peeled and chopped
  finely
3 tablespoons plain flour
1 cup water
1 beef stock cube

½ cup dry white wine
1 teaspoon salt
¼ teaspoon pepper
pinch ground nutmeg
1 bouquet garni (2 pieces celery tied around 1
  bay leaf, 1 sprig thyme, 1 sprig parsley, 3
  strips orange zest)
500 g tomatoes, peeled and quartered
250 g white button mushrooms
250 g (drained weight) stuffed olives, sliced
250 g sour cream
2 tablespoons freshly chopped parsley

◆

Heat oil in a large heavy heatproof casserole and fry bacon in it over medium heat rendering as much fat as possible. Lift out with a slotted spoon and reserve. Seal the veal, 8 pieces at a time, until well browned on all sides, lift out and reserve with bacon. Turn heat down to low and fry onions for 3 minutes, shaking pan to brown onions lightly on all sides. Add celery, sugar and leeks and fry for 2 minutes. Stir in garlic, then flour mixing in thoroughly. Pour in water, stock cube and wine and stir well. Add seasonings and bouquet garni, making sure it is submerged in stock. Bring ingredients to a simmer, cover with lid, and cook in 170°C (350°F) oven for 45 to 60 minutes, or until meat is tender.

Stir in tomatoes, mushrooms and olives and return to oven for 10 minutes. Stir sour cream through ingredients, spoon into a heated serving dish and sprinkle over parsley.

Serve hot with boiled, buttered baby new potatoes or boiled raw rice.

Average times Preparation — 60 minutes
Cooking — 50 minutes

Do ahead 1 to 2 days but do not add sour
cream until heating through.

Wine notes The veal calls for a medium-
bodied red with light astrin-
gency —
A: Bowen Estate (Coonawarra)
   Cabernet Sauvignon
E: Château Carbonnieux
   (Graves) of a good year
U: Diamond Creek (Napa)
   Cabernet Sauvignon

CHINCHILLA

◆

6–8 egg whites
⅔ cup unsweetened cocoa powder, sifted
1½ tablespoons castor sugar

1 tablespoon ground cinnamon or powdered
  coffee, or very finely ground almonds

cream mixed with brandy to serve

◆

Beat egg whites until stiff. Gently fold in remaining ingredients, using a rubber spatula. Spoon into a buttered and sugared 4- or 5-cup soufflé dish and cook in 175°C (375°F) oven for 45 minutes or until well risen and golden on top. Serve at once with unwhipped cream to which you have added a little brandy to taste.

Note: this recipe is a good way to use left-over egg whites. Chinchilla is one of those marvellous desserts where you can change the flavour from cinnamon to coffee or almond, depending on your requirements at the time.

Average times Preparation — 10 minutes
Cooking — 45 minutes

Wine notes The dessert calls for a light,
chilled muscat —
A: Seppelt Rutherglen Muscat
E and U: Muscat de Mireval

SPRING

MENU 14

———◆———

A beautifully coloured menu which is full of palate surprises. Only the main course requires total last minute preparation.

BAKED AVOCADO

———◆———

Béchamel Sauce:

90 g butter
6 tablespoons plain flour
3 cups milk
⅓ cup finely grated Parmesan cheese
salt and pepper to taste

3 medium ripe avocados
6 slices ham, approximately 250 g, cut into matchsticks
3 cups béchamel sauce
3 tablespoons finely grated Parmesan cheese
3 tablespoons butter

———◆———

To make sauce: heat butter in a small pan and whisk in the flour. Cook over medium heat, whisking for 2 minutes. Pour in milk and whisk until the sauce thickens. Add cheese and season to taste.

To prepare avocados: cut the avocados in halves, lengthwise, remove stones and peel them. Slice into 1 cm thick slices, retaining the shape of the half avocado. Place each half in a buttered individual shallow gratinée dish, push over by hand to flatten slightly, scatter with ham, cover with béchamel sauce and scatter with Parmesan cheese. Dot with butter. (If not using immediately, cover with plastic wrap and refrigerate until ready to cook.) Place in the centre of 180°C (350°F) oven for 12 to 15 minutes, or until the cheese melts and the sauce is sizzling. To finish, place under a hot griller to brown evenly. Serve immediately.

Average times Preparation — 25 minutes
Cooking — 30 minutes

Do ahead Béchamel, up to 1 day. Up to oven stage, 30 minutes

Wine notes Baked Avocado needs a crisp, flavoursome white —
A: Château François (Pokolbin) Chardonnay
E: Pouilly-Fuissé (Château Fuissé) of a good year
U: Whitehall Lane (Napa) Chardonnay

VEAL WITH ORANGE

60 g butter
6 thin veal escalopes, flattened
1 tablespoon plain flour
3 large oranges
2 tablespoons brandy

1 cup beef stock
salt and pepper to taste

6 sprigs fresh thyme, with flowers if possible, to dress

Heat butter in a heavy-based pan until foaming, sauté 2 or 3 escalopes at a time until golden on each side. Lift out on to a plate. Whisk in flour and cook for 2 minutes. Finely grate the orange zest and stir in with the brandy and stock. Season and simmer for 5 minutes, whisking from time to time. Replace veal, cover and simmer gently for 10 minutes.

Peel both oranges (dip first in boiling water for 30 seconds) and remove all the white pith. Slice and warm on top of veal for 2 minutes. Serve dressed with fresh thyme.

Serve with a potato dish.

Average time Preparation — 25 minutes
Cooking — 27 minutes

Wine notes Veal with Orange needs a flavoursome red —
A: Penfolds St Henri Claret
E: Château Maucoil Châteauneuf-du-Pape
U: Ahlgren (Santa Cruz) Zinfandel

PARIS BREST WITH SPRING FRUITS

Pastry Ring:
½ cup milk
½ cup water
1 teaspoon castor sugar
110 g butter, cut into 8 pieces
1¼ cups (160 g) plain flour, sifted
4½–5 eggs, 55 g
3 teaspoons icing sugar, sifted

Filling:
1 pear, cored and sliced finely
1 apple, cored and sliced finely
1 banana, sliced finely
juice 1 orange
300 ml thickened cream beaten to soft peaks with eau-de-vie de poire to taste
1 mandarin, peeled and segmented
1 kiwi fruit, peeled and sliced

extra icing sugar to dust the top

To make pastry ring: place the first 4 ingredients in a large saucepan and bring slowly to the boil. The butter must melt in the liquids before the mixture boils. Immediately it boils pour in all the flour at once, stirring rapidly with a wooden spatula. Cook over low heat, stirring constantly for 2 minutes. (This is to evaporate some of the moisture in the mixture.)

Remove from heat and transfer mixture to a large heatproof bowl, spreading mixture up the sides of the bowl so as to cool it rapidly. Beat in the eggs one at a time with the wooden spatula. The mixture will improve by hard beating between the addition of each egg. Do not add the last egg (the 5th) until you are sure that you need all of it. Beat the 5th egg with a fork in a small bowl and add gradually to the mixture until you have a stiff dropping mixture (it should only leave the spatula after some coaxing and shaking).

Alternatively, cool the mixture and place in the bowl of a food processor. Beat in eggs one at a time, running the machine for 30 seconds between each addition. Beat the last egg and add only as much as you need to attain the correct consistency.

Lightly oil and flour a baking tray. Spoon mixture into a large pastry bag fitted with a large star tube. Pipe a circle on to the tray about 18 cm in diameter. It is important not to let it get too large because it will expand in the oven. Continue to pipe one circle on top of the other until you have used all the mixture. Sprinkle with icing sugar and cook in hottest part of oven at 220°C (425°F) for 15 minutes. Open oven door, carefully turn the tray around and close door, propping the handle of a wooden spoon in it, for a further 10 minutes. This is to allow steam to escape and keep pastry crisp.

Remove from the oven and cool away from draughts for 10 minutes. It will sink slightly. Split ring in halves with a bread knife and lift off the top to allow both top and bottom to cool. After 5 minutes, use a teaspoon and scrape away any uncooked pastry inside the two halves.

To make filling: dip the pear, apple and banana slices in orange juice. When pastry ring is completely cooled, fill the bottom half with cream and fruit, place top half over the filling and dust liberally with icing sugar. Serve cut into wedges.

Average times	Preparation — 30 minutes Cooking — 45 minutes Cooling — 40 minutes	**Do ahead** Pastry ring, up to 1 day. Completed recipe, up to 1 hour
Wine notes	Paris Brest needs a luscious, sweet wine — A: Lindemans Reserve Porphyry E: Château Rieussec (Sauternes) of a great year U: Bargetto (Santa Cruz) Late Harvest Johannisberg Riesling	

SPRING

MENU 15

This is a more demanding menu, in that all three courses require almost total last minute preparation, so it makes sense to make these dishes on a day when you're going to be at home.

SPRING VEGETABLE RISOTTO

---

1 white onion, finely chopped
50 g butter
250 g risotto rice
6 cups well seasoned beef stock, boiling
100 g asparagus or French beans, parboiled and cut into 2 cm pieces
100 g zucchini, parboiled and cut in 1 cm dice

50 g fresh podded peas
50 g white button mushrooms, halved or quartered
1 green pepper, skinned, seeded and diced finely
2 medium tomatoes, skinned, seeded and chopped
50 g butter, extra
40 g finely grated Parmesan cheese

In a large heavy-based pan, sauté onion in butter until tender. Add rice and stir for a few minutes. Pour in the boiling stock, 1 cup at a time, stirring constantly. As rice takes up the stock, add next cup and continue to cook, stirring. When rice is half cooked, add vegetables and continue to cook, adding more boiling stock as needed.

When the rice is *al dente* remove pan from heat and stir in extra butter and cheese. Mix well and serve immediately.

Average times Preparation — 25 minutes
Cooking — 40 minutes

Wine notes The risotto needs a full-flavoured white —
A: Morris (Rutherglen) Chardonnay
E: Chardonnay Atesino (Santa Margherita)
U: Chalone (Monterey) Chardonnay

SCALLOPED CRAYFISH

Fish Stock:

1 snapper head
1 onion, cut in halves
1 bay leaf
1 small piece carrot
2 peppercorns
4 cups water

3 × 1 kg green crayfish, split in halves and cleaned
90 g butter
3 tablespoons plain flour
¾ cup dry white wine
salt and pepper to taste
ground mace to taste
freshly ground nutmeg to taste
1 to 2 teaspoons anchovy sauce
1 tablespoon lemon juice
1 cup fresh white breadcrumbs
60 g butter, extra

To make stock: bring stock ingredients slowly to the boil and simmer uncovered for 25 minutes. Strain and measure 2¼ cups.

To prepare crayfish: remove flesh from crayfish halves and cut into 2 cm cubes. Heat butter in a large, heavy-based pan and cook flour for 2 minutes, whisking constantly. Set aside to cool. Bring fish stock to the boil in another large pan and cook crayfish shells in it until they turn bright red. Lift out and set shells aside.

Pour fish stock into the roux (butter and flour) and return to heat whisking constantly until sauce thickens. Add the wine, seasonings, anchovy sauce and lemon juice and cook until sauce no longer tastes of wine. Adjust seasoning and fold through the uncooked crayfish pieces. Cook for 3 to 4 minutes or until fish is just tender. Do not let it boil.

Place crayfish shells in a baking dish, spoon mixture into shells, dividing it equally among them. Scatter with breadcrumbs, dot with remaining butter and flash under a hot griller until golden on top. Serve at once.

Average times Preparation — 25 minutes
Cooking — 45 minutes

Wine notes Scalloped crayfish — continue with the white from the first course

Do ahead Fish stock, up to 1 day ahead

SABAYON OF SPRING FRUITS

2 firm ripe pears, peeled, cored and sliced in 1 cm slices
2 navel oranges, peeled and segmented with a sharp knife, omitting membranes
2 firm ripe bananas, sliced finely
2 kiwi fruits, peeled and sliced finely
4 very thin slices ripe pineapple, each cut into 6 wedges
1 box strawberries, hulled

Sabayon:
12 egg yolks
1 cup castor sugar
1 cup orange juice
½ cup Grand Marnier

zest of 2 limes, julienned, to garnish

Arrange fruits in 6 individual shallow, heatproof serving dishes. Place dishes on a baking tray and warm fruits in 175°C (350°F) oven for 10 minutes.

To make sabayon: bring some water to a simmer and turn off the heat. Place a large pyrex or metal bowl over the water (it must not touch the water) and whisk egg yolks and sugar in it. Pour in orange juice and Grand Marnier and whisk constantly until mixture thickens and doubles in volume.

To prepare fruits: remove fruits from oven and heat a griller. Boil julienned zest of lime for 30 seconds and drain thoroughly. Lavishly coat fruits with the sabayon and flash them under the griller to gratiné lightly. Garnish with lime zest and serve at once.

Average times Preparation — 25 minutes
Cooking — 25 minutes

Wine notes Sabayon of Spring Fruits requires no wine

SPRING

MENU 16

The spinach ricotta gnocchi were first cooked for me by a friend in Venice. I have perfected the recipe and today it is one of my Australian friends' favourites. A word of warning though, gnocchi need very careful handling. The next two courses are mostly do-ahead which makes the menu a little easier.

SPINACH RICOTTA GNOCCHI WITH BROWN BUTTER AND SAGE LEAVES

400–500 g fresh spinach (bunches vary in size so ask the greengrocer to weigh it)
250 g ricotta cheese
1 teaspoon salt
freshly ground black pepper
¼ teaspoon ground nutmeg
½ cup freshly grated Parmesan cheese
2 egg yolks
½ cup plain flour
½ cup freshly grated Parmesan cheese, extra, for serving

Brown Butter with sage leaves:
125 g butter
12 small fresh sage leaves

Strip spinach leaves off stems and wash them in several changes of cold water until there is no grit. Chop medium fine and steam over boiling water in a steamer or in a colander over a pan of boiling water with the lid on (the colander must not touch the water), but open lid a little to allow some steam to escape. This is to retain the colour in the spinach. Steam for 5 minutes, lift out and leave to cool.

Mix ricotta with salt, pepper, nutmeg, Parmesan and egg yolks. Squeeze spinach very dry in your hands and add to ricotta mixture, mixing in thoroughly with a fork. Taste and adjust seasoning. With floured hands, form into balls about 2½ cm in diameter. Place on a tray lined with foil. Refrigerate for minimum of 2 hours.

Bring a large pan of water just to simmering point — it must be deep enough for the gnocchi to float. Poach the balls in four batches, timing 4 minutes after they rise to the surface and float. If the water simmers too quickly the gnocchi will break up. Lift out with a slotted spoon and drain. Keep warm.

Heat butter and sage leaves in a small pan until butter begins to brown. Spoon over gnocchi and serve at once.

Note: Frozen spinach may be used. Buy enough to weigh 500 g after thawing and draining off juices. Commercially prepared frozen spinach can be very wet. The canned variety will be far too sloppy for this recipe.

Average times Preparation — 40 minutes
Cooking — 25 minutes
Standing — 2 hours

Wine notes The gnocchi call for a light red —
A: Château Le Amon (Bendigo) Beaujolais-style
E and U: Valpolicella (Masi)

Do ahead Can make gnocchi ½ day ahead

SPRING VEAL FILLETS

1.5 kg veal escalopes, flattened
2 tablespoons plain flour
salt and pepper to taste
3 tablespoons peanut oil
6 tablespoons butter
4 shallots, chopped finely
3 medium onions, chopped finely
2 cloves garlic, chopped finely

1 cup dry white wine
2 cups veal stock
1 tablespoon tomato paste
1 fresh bouquet garni
2 medium carrots, peeled and sliced on the
  cross into 1 cm slices
400 g shelled fresh green peas
1½ tablespoons chopped fresh parsley

Dredge escalopes in seasoned flour. Heat oil and butter in a large heavy pan and wait for the foaming to subside. Sauté several escalopes at a time (do not overcrowd the pan or they will stew) over medium/high heat. Turn each as soon as it is golden on the first side and repeat on the second side. Lift out and keep warm. Repeat with remaining escalopes.

Sauté shallots, onions and garlic over medium heat, stirring until softened — about 5 minutes. Add wine, stock, tomato paste and bouquet garni and reduce until sauce is a good consistency, stirring from time to time with a wooden spatula to prevent sticking. Remove bouquet garni and discard. Steam carrots and peas separately until they are *al dente*.

Warm escalopes in the sauce. Taste and adjust seasoning. Arrange on a warmed serving platter with parsley scattered over top.

Average times Preparation — 20 minutes
Cooking — 45 minutes

Wine notes Spring veal requires a medium
red —
A: Heemskerk Cabernet
   Sauvignon, from Tasmania
E: Château Chasse-Spleen
   (Moulis en Médoc)
U: Parducci (Mendocino)
   Cabernet Sauvignon

Do ahead Can prepare up to the reheating of
the escalopes and steaming of
vegetables, ½ day ahead

KIWI FRUIT SORBET

250 g ripe kiwi fruit (or 5 medium fruits), cut in halves, flesh scooped out and puréed, to measure 1 cup
1 cup water
½ cup sugar

juice of half a lemon, depending on ripeness of kiwi fruits

iced vodka, to accompany
fresh flowers to decorate

In a small saucepan (not aluminium) bring half the purée to the boil over a low heat and cook for 3 minutes. Cool. Heat water and sugar together and stir until sugar dissolves. Cool. In a bowl, stir all ingredients together, adding lemon juice to taste, and refrigerate for 4 hours. Churn or set by freezing in ice-cream trays until partly frozen. Beat and return to trays to freeze.

Serve spooned or scooped with iced vodka poured over at the moment of serving. Surround with fresh flowers and leaves from the garden.

Average times Preparation — 10 minutes
Cooking — 8 minutes
Cooling — 4 hours
Setting — 4 hours or overnight

Do ahead At least ½ day and up to 2 days

Wine notes Sorbet requires no wine; however, try a luscious dessert wine after the cleansing, fruit flavour of the sorbet has faded from your palate: a late picked, *botrytis*-affected Rhine Riesling —
A: Seville Estate Riesling Beerenauslese from the Yarra Valley
E: Niersteiner Orbel Riesling Trockenbeerenauslese (Rheinpfalz)
U: Château St Jean (Sonoma) Late Harvest Johannisberg Riesling

RICCIARELLI
Makes 36 approximately
Make at least 1 day in advance

2 cups blanched almonds, finely ground
1 cup castor sugar
¾ cup icing sugar
vanilla essence to taste

2 egg whites

extra icing sugar to dust

Pound almonds and castor sugar to a paste or blend in a food processor. Sift icing sugar and mix with vanilla into almond paste. Beat egg whites till frothy and fold into almond mixture. Add a little more icing sugar if necessary to make a stiff paste.

Pinch off small pieces approximately the size of almonds in shell and roll into egg shapes. Place on buttered trays, cover with greaseproof paper and leave at room temperature for 24 hours. Bake in very slow oven, 140°C (280°F) for 30 to 40 minutes, until dry and still white. Biscuits should not colour. Reduce to 120°C (250°F) and cover if necessary. Cool on wire rack and dust with icing sugar. Dust again before storing in airtight container.

The Ricciarelli are Venetian biscuits which will accompany any sorbet or ice-cream course in this book.

Average times Preparation — 30 minutes
Standing — 24 hours
Cooking — 30 to 40 minutes
Cooling — 45 minutes

Do ahead 4 days in advance. Store in an airtight container

SPRING

MENU 17

◆

This is a more demanding menu requiring good timing in the kitchen. It's a colourful menu with interesting textures and tastes and should be kept for special occasions.

WARM SQUID SALAD WITH PINK PEPPERCORNS

◆

350 g fresh baby squid (calamari) bodies, skinned and cut in 1 cm rings
Note: this is about 4 baby squid. If you can only buy larger ones cut them in halves lengthwise and then into strips 5 × 1 cm

Marinade:

1 cup olive oil
1 tablespoon lemon juice
1 teaspoon salt
freshly ground black pepper to taste

Salad:

1 small head red mignonette lettuce, washed, drained and crisped
8 cos lettuce leaves, washed, drained and crisped
8 curly endive leaves, washed, drained and crisped
½ cup very fine julienne of carrots
½ cup red peppers, skinned and cut into very fine julienne (see *note* in method)
2 teaspoons pink peppercorns, drained

◆

Wash, dry and tear salad leaves into bite-sized pieces.

To make marinade: mix marinade ingredients together and pour over squid leaving for 2 hours. Drain off marinade into saucepan and bring it to a simmer. Drop in squid and poach gently for ½ to 1 minute or until just tender.

To serve: arrange salad leaves on individual salad plates. Spoon hot squid over them and drizzle just enough of the marinade over squid and lettuce leaves to lightly dress. Scatter with carrot and pepper julienne and pink peppercorns and serve at once with crusty French bread.

Note: to prepare pepper, blister skin all over holding pepper over a gas flame with a fork or under a hot griller and rub off skin. Cut in halves and remove membranes and seeds.

Average times Preparation — 35 minutes
Standing — 2 hours
Cooking — 1 minute

Wine notes The squid salad is complemented by a fruity riesling —
A: Katnook (Coonawarra) Rhine Riesling
E: Bernkasteler Kurfustlay Spaetlese (Thanisch) from the Mosel
U: Chappellet (Napa) Johannisberg Riesling

Dried Fruit and Nut Stuffed Lamb with Honey Glaze

Wine:
The Rothbury Estate Carbonique Maceration Shiraz

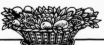

Seafood Ragoût

Wine:
Heitz (Napa) Chardonnay

SLICED BEEF WITH PORCINI

◆

12 dried porcini mushrooms
45 g butter
1 kg well hung rump steak, cut in one or two
    2.5 cm thick slices
salt and freshly ground black pepper to taste

½ cup dry red wine
1½ cups very well flavoured beef stock
45 g softened butter, extra

◆

Soak mushrooms in just enough warm water to cover for 30 minutes. Drain mushrooms and reserve the water. Cook mushrooms in 200°C (400°F) oven for 20 minutes.

In a large heavy frying pan, heat butter until it foams. Seal steak on both sides in butter over high heat and then season it. When steak is cooked the way you like it, set aside in a warm oven to rest 10 minutes before slicing.

Pour the wine into pan and whisk to catch up the caramelized juices in base of pan. When wine is reduced by half, add beef stock and soaking water from the mushrooms. Reduce over high heat until half its original volume. Reduce the heat to low and whisk in extra butter, about 2 teaspoons at a time, without allowing sauce to boil. (If sauce boils the butter will thin sauce instead of thickening it.)

Slice beef across the grain in 1 cm slices (they are in fact like long ribbons) and arrange on 6 heated dinner plates. Spoon sauce over the top and arrange mushrooms over steak.

Serve with Broccoli, Cauliflower Salad (see next recipe).

Average times Standing — 30 minutes
    Preparation — 5 minutes
    Cooking — 8 minutes

Wine notes The beef requires a full-bodied
    red with a firm tannin finish —
    A: Huntington Estate (Mudgee)
        Cabernet Sauvignon
    E: Château Grand-Puy-Lacoste
        (Pauillac) of a great year
    U: Robert Mondavi (Napa)
        Reserve Cabernet Sauvignon

BROCCOLI, CAULIFLOWER SALAD

◆

½ medium cauliflower, cut into florets
1 bunch broccoli, cut into florets
2 red peppers, cut into rings and seeded

Dressing:

juice of 1 lemon
3 tablespoons olive oil
½ cup thickened cream
salt and pepper to taste

◆

Blanch cauliflower in a large pan of boiling salted water for 2 minutes. Lift out with a perforated spoon and refresh in a large bowl of iced water. Repeat with broccoli using same water. The water must never leave the boil or broccoli will lose some of its colour. Refresh in same bowl with cauliflower. Drain very thoroughly and mix with red pepper in a salad bowl.

To make dressing: whisk all dressing ingredients together until creamy. Pour dressing over the top and serve.

Average times Preparation — 15 minutes
    Cooking — 4 minutes
    Cooling — 10 minutes

Do ahead Salad, up to ½ day. Dress only as
    serving

FLOATING ISLAND

◆

Island:

5 egg whites, at room temperature
pinch salt
½ cup castor sugar

Toffee:

¾ cup castor sugar
4 tablespoons cold water
pinch cream of tartar

Custard:

5 egg yolks
3 tablespoons sugar
2 cups milk
vanilla

◆

To make island: beat egg whites with salt until they form stiff peaks. Gradually beat in sugar, 1 tablespoon at a time, and beat until stiff. Butter the top rim and inside of an 18 cm round cake pan.

Spread egg white mixture into prepared pan and smooth over the top. Cover with a piece of buttered greaseproof paper. Stand in a baking dish of cold water and cook in 200°C (400°F) oven for 25 minutes or until well risen and set.

Remove from oven, keeping away from draughts. Remove paper and loosen edges with a knife. Invert over a flat-based serving dish with low sides (to hold the 'sea') and lift off cake pan.

To make toffee: while island is cooking, mix the sugar, water and cream of tartar together in a small pan and cook over a low heat, stirring until sugar dissolves. Cook over medium heat damping down sides of pan with a pastry brush dipped in cold water. This is to prevent sugar crystals from forming. Boil mixture until it is straw-coloured. Take off heat and stand until bubbling subsides. Spoon two-thirds of caramel over top of the island letting it run down the sides.

To make custard: whisk egg yolks and sugar together. Pour milk into remaining caramel and heat slowly. When nearly boiling, pour over whisked sugar and yolks mixture. Return to caramel pan and cook over a medium heat, whisking all the time until the custard thickens. Test with a wooden spoon — it should coat the back of it. Flavour with vanilla and sieve the custard. Leave to cool over iced water with a circle of greaseproof paper set directly on the top of it. This will prevent a skin forming.

Just before serving, carefully pour custard around the island, and stand at room temperature. If the dessert is left in a humid atmosphere like the refrigerator, the caramel will break down very quickly. Serve remaining custard in a jug.

Average times Preparation — 20 minutes
Cooking — 45 minutes
Cooling — 30 minutes

Wine notes Floating Island calls for a luscious dessert wine —
A: Peter Lehmann (Barossa) Semillon Sauternes
E: Château Rieussec (Sauternes) of a great year
U: Bargetto (Santa Cruz) Late Harvest Johannisberg Riesling

Do ahead No more than 2 hours before serving

SUMMER

---◆---

AUTHORS NOTE
Every recipe is designed to serve six unless stated otherwise.

---◆---

SUMMER

MENU 1

A light luncheon menu for a warm Summer day. The chicken liver pâté was devised in my catering kitchen in Melbourne and like all pâtés improves with aging for 1 to 2 days. I first tasted the salad at the Plaza Athenée in Paris and this is my adaptation of it. The cake should be served with coffee and can be accompanied with crème fraîche or whipped cream. It's mostly a do-ahead menu.

QUICK CHICKEN LIVER PÂTÉ

---

125 g butter
1 large white onion, coarsely chopped
2 cloves garlic, chopped
500 g chicken livers, cleaned
salt and freshly ground black pepper to taste
2 eggs, beaten

125 g butter, extra
3 tablespoons whisky
1½ tablespoons green peppercorns, drained

60 g clarified butter

Heat 125 g butter in a large, heavy-based frying pan, gently fry onion until soft and transparent. Add garlic and continue cooking for another minute.

Add livers to the pan and cook, turning them to brown on all sides, for about 8 minutes. They should be cooked, but still pink inside. Add salt and pepper. Reduce heat, stir in eggs and scramble them. Remove from heat while eggs are still soft.

Mince the mixture in a food processor or blender. Work in the rest of butter and the whisky. Fold in peppercorns and spoon into an earthenware pot. Cover with plastic wrap and refrigerate until firm. Melt 60 g clarified butter and spoon over top to seal the pâté. Refrigerate until set. Serve with toast.

Average times Preparation — 15 minutes
Cook — 15 minutes
Chilling — 2 hours

Wine notes The pâté calls for a dry, sparkling white —
A: Buring Vintage Brut Champagne
E: Château Moncontour (Vouvray)
U: Piper-Sonoma (Sonoma) Brut Champagne

Do ahead At least 1 day and up to 3 days

PARISIAN CHICKEN SALAD

I like to use roasted chickens for salads as I think the meat has a better flavour. You could buy a roasted chicken or rotisserie-cooked chicken if you are in a hurry.

---

1 cooked chicken, approximately 1.8 kg
2 hearts lettuce, washed, crisped and torn into bite-size pieces
½ cup stuffed olives, sliced
2 hard boiled eggs, quartered

2 × 45 g cans flat anchovies, drained
5 tablespoons mayonnaise, thinned with 5 tablespoons vinaigrette
50 g capers, drained

Skin chicken, joint it and shred flesh. Using a round serving platter, pile lettuce pieces into a pyramid in centre. Scatter over chicken and olives. Arrange eggs around base. Strew anchovies attractively around pyramid. Dress with thinned mayonnaise and scatter capers over top of salad.

Average times Preparation — 20 minutes

Wine notes With the salad, a light, chilled
red —
A: Wyndham Estate Pinot Noir
E and U: Beaujolais Village
Domaine de la
Chapelle de Vatre
(Sarrau)

MORELLO CHERRY CAKE
Serves 8 to 10

5 egg yolks
2 whole eggs
¾ cup castor sugar
140 g almond meal

50 g fresh white breadcrumbs
5 egg whites
700 g pitted morello cherries, drained very
thoroughly
icing sugar to dust

Cream egg yolks, whole eggs and castor sugar until pale and light. Fold in almond meal and breadcrumbs. Beat egg whites until firm, but not dry. Fold one-third into yolk mixture, then fold in remaining whites.

Place some of the drained cherries in the base of a well-buttered 26 cm cake pan or spring form. Fold the rest of the cherries into cake mixture and pour into pan. Bake in 175°C (350°F) oven for 45 to 55 minutes or until firm.

Cook on a rack. Sift icing sugar over top and serve with cream or crème fraîche (see next recipe).

Average times Preparation — 20 minutes
Cooking — 50 minutes
Cooling — 30 minutes
Wine notes Cherry cake needs a luscious,
sweet white —
A: Montrose (Mudgee)
Sauternes
E and U: Château Romer
(Sauternes) of a good
year

Do ahead Up to 2 days

CRÈME FRAÎCHE
Make at least 1 day in advance

1 cup thickened cream, at room temperature

1 tablespoon buttermilk or natural full fat
yoghurt, at room temperature

Mix the two ingredients together and leave to stand covered, preferably overnight and undisturbed until thickened. In the summer this will take approximately 24 hours and in cooler weather it can take up to 3 days. When thick cover and refrigerate until ready to use.

Average times Preparation — 5 minutes
Standing — 1 to 3 days

Do ahead At least 1 to 3 days. Store covered
and refrigerated for up to 4 days

SUMMER

MENU 2

Ideal for lunch or dinner on a warm Summer day, this is mostly a do-ahead menu with a strong Mediterranean influence.

POACHED TUNA WITH TARRAGON MAYONNAISE

Court Bouillon:

2 tablespoons sherry
slice of lemon
salt to taste
2 black peppercorns
1 white onion, halved and stuck with 2 cloves
a piece of carrot, chopped roughly
a piece of celery, chopped roughly
water

1 small fresh tuna weighing 3½–4 kg, or a piece about the same weight, scaled and cleaned (see *note* below)

salt and pepper
1 white onion, quartered
1 bay leaf
1 large sprig parsley

Mayonnaise:

2 egg yolks
½ teaspoon salt
½ cup peanut oil
½ cup olive oil
1 tablespoon lemon juice
1 tablespoon finely chopped fresh tarragon
pepper to taste

To make court bouillon: place court bouillon ingredients over rack of a fish kettle, and pour in only enough water to just cover the rack. Bring slowly to a simmer.

To cook fish: wash fish very thoroughly, removing any traces of blood. Season inside and place onion and herbs in the cavity. Wrap tail end in 2 layers of foil to slow down the cooking. Lie on rack. Cover kettle and poach gently until just cooked, approximately 25 minutes. Test with skewer or sharp knife at back of fish head. The flesh should be just cooked as this is the thickest part of fish. Lift out on rack and cool for 15 minutes before skinning carefully.

To make mayonnaise: blend egg yolks and salt together in a blender until pale and thick. (If making the mayonnaise in a food processor, double recipe to have enough volume to cover the blades.) With the machine running on high, slowly pour in the oil a few drops at a time until the mayonnaise is quite thick. Then pour in the remaining oil in a thin steady stream. Lastly add the lemon juice and pepper to taste. Add more salt if necessary. Spoon into serving bowl and fold through tarragon and set aside.

To serve: remove the onion and herbs from the cavity of the fish. Arrange on an oval platter and accompany with mayonnaise.

Note: small tuna are very hard to find but there are similar fish like doggy mackerel which are very good cooked this way. Alternatively, buy a piece of tuna and season it. Add bay leaf and parsley to the court bouillon.

Average times Preparation — 20 minutes
Cooking — 25 minutes
Cooling — 1½ hours

Do ahead Cook fish up to 20 minutes before serving. If serving cold, cook up to 1 day ahead. The mayonnaise up to 3 days ahead.

Wine Notes The tuna calls for a big-flavoured, acid white —
A: Quelltaler Wood Matured Semillon
E and U: Savennières (Domaine de la Bizolière), from Anjou

BEEF NIÇOISE

30 butter

750 g eye fillet or scotch fillet, very well trimmed and skinned

salt and freshly ground black pepper to taste

375 g snake beans, topped and tailed and cut into 7 cm lengths

4 medium ripe tomatoes skinned, seeded and chopped into 2 cm cubes

1 medium green pepper, seeded and cut into julienne

1 medium red pepper, seeded and cut into julienne

1 medium green cucumber, skinned, seeded and cut into 2 cm cubes

6 spring onions, peeled and cut into 4 cm lengths (both green and white parts)

6 small red radishes, sliced finely

3 sticks celery, stringed and cut on the cross into 3 cm pieces

Vinaigrette:

1 teaspoon French mustard

1 teaspoon salt

freshly ground black pepper to taste

1 clove garlic finely chopped

1 tablespoon white wine vinegar

5 tablespoons olive oil

¾ cup Niçoise olives (from Provence) or small black olives

2 × 45 g cans flat anchovy fillets

4 hard boiled eggs, shelled and quartered lengthwise

To cook beef: heat butter in a heavy-based baking dish over high heat until foaming. Add the beef and cook for 2 minutes or until sealed on the first side. Turn over and season cooked side liberally. Cook a further 2 minutes on second side, turn and season again. Place in the hottest part of 200°C (400°F) oven and cook for 16 to 18 minutes for medium-rare. Remove from baking dish and set aside to cool.

Cook beans in a pan of rapidly boiling, well salted water until *al dente*. Refresh under running cold water and drain.

Place the tomatoes, peppers, cucumber, spring onions, radishes and celery in a large salad bowl.

To make vinaigrette: whisk all vinaigrette ingredients together, taste and adjust seasoning if necessary.

To prepare for serving: cut beef into 2 cm cubes and add to salad. Pour over vinaigrette and toss gently. Scatter black olives over the top, drain anchovies and arrange over top of salad and surround with hard boiled egg quarters. Cover with plastic wrap and refrigerate for 30 minutes before serving.

Average times Preparation — 40 minutes
Cooking — 23 minutes
Cooling — 30 minutes
Chilling — 30 minutes

Do ahead Beef can be cooked up to 1 day ahead. Vegetables can be prepared up to ½ day ahead and packed into separate airtight containers in refrigerator until ready to mix. Vinaigrette can be made up to 1 day ahead

Wine notes Beef Niçoise calls for a sturdy red —
A: Henschke Hill of Grace
E: Cornas (Clape)
U: Ridge (Santa Clara) York Creek Zinfandel

51

STRABERRY ICE-CREAM

4 egg yolks
⅔ cup castor sugar
1 cup cream
3 tablespoons kirsch
400 g ripe strawberries, cleaned, hulled and
    puréed
300 ml thickened cream, whipped

Crystallized strawberries:

strawberries, preferably with stalks
1 egg white
castor sugar

Beat yolks and castor sugar until pale and light. Heat 1 cup cream in a medium-sized pan until almost boiling. Pour over egg yolks mixture, whisking constantly, and return to the pan. Cook, whisking constantly over low heat until mixture thickens enough to coat back of a wooden spoon. Cool over a bowl of iced water, whisking from time to time. Stir in kirsch and strawberries and fold in whipped cream.

Churn and spoon into a wetted 5-cup mould, cover and freeze until firm. Unmould by dipping in warm water, invert over a serving dish and shake out. Return to freezer to firm before garnishing and presenting. Garnish with whole strawberries dipped in lightly beaten egg white and castor sugar.

Average times Preparation — 25 minutes
Cooking — 10 minutes
Cooling — 30 minutes
Freezing — 2 hours

Wine notes The ice-cream requires no wine

Do ahead Up to 2 days, except for crystal-lized strawberries

SUMMER

MENU 3

The dessert is for those of you who are lucky enough to have your own fig tree. They must be bottled for at least 1 month before using, otherwise they will lack flavour. They are marvellous to have on hand at any time of the year. The first two courses contrast beautifully and make an ideal Summer lunch or dinner.

SEAFOOD SALAD WITH PAW PAW AND KIWI FRUIT

250 g cooked crayfish flesh, off the shell
250 g cooked prawns, shelled and deveined
125 g cooked crab meat off the shell
1 medium ripe paw paw, seeded and diced
3 kiwi fruit, peeled and quartered lengthwise

Mayonnaise:
2 egg yolks
pinch salt
1 cup safflower oil
lemon juice to taste
1 tablespoon tomato paste
salt and pepper to taste

watercress and alfalfa sprouts to garnish

Arrange seafood on 6 entrée plates, scatter over the paw paw cubes and kiwi fruit.

To make mayonnaise: in a blender, work egg yolks and salt until pale and thick. Slowly trickle oil in through the feed tube in a thin, steady stream with the blender running on high.

When mayonnaise is thick and all the oil is in, add lemon juice to taste, tomato paste and seasoning. If too thick, thin with equal quantities of water and lemon juice and readjust seasoning.

Spoon mayonnaise over seafood and garnish with watercress and alfalfa sprouts

Average times Preparation — 30 minutes
Wine notes The seafood salad with fruit requires a spicy white —
A: St Clare (Clare)
    Gewurztraminer
E: Gewurztraminer (Hugel)
    from Alsace
U: Souverain (Sonoma)
    Gewurztraminer

Do ahead Mayonnaise up to 3 days

MEDALLIONS OF PORK WITH SOUR CREAM GREEN PEPPERCORN SAUCE

750 g large pork fillets skinned
½ cup plain flour
3 eggs
2 tablespoons water
salt and freshly ground black pepper to taste
1¾ cups fine white fresh breadcrumbs
4 tablespoons clarified butter to cook

freshly snipped watercress to garnish

Sauce:

1 cup natural yoghurt
½ cup finely diced Granny Smith apple, with skin left on
¼ cup white onions, very finely chopped
½ cup fresh chives, finely snipped
2 tablespoons lemon juice
2 teaspoons *gros sel*
3 tablespoons drained green peppercorns

To prepare pork fillets: cut into 2.5 cm slices and flatten between two sheets of plastic wrap using a meal mallet. Dredge medallions in flour, shaking off excess. Beat eggs with water and seasoning. Dip pork medallions into beaten eggs and then into breadcrumbs, patting them on well. Cover and refrigerate in single layers or interleaved with plastic wrap until ready to cook.

To make sauce: fold all sauce ingredients together using a rubber spatula and spoon into a serving bowl.

To cook fillets: heat clarified butter in a large heavy-based frying pan or baking dish over medium heat until hot. Sauté medallions in butter until golden without overcrowding the pan. When sealed on one side, turn over and seal on the second side. Cook until just done and drain on crumpled paper. Serve at once garnished with watercress and accompanied with sauce.

Serve the pork with a potato salad dressed in vinaigrette.

Average times Preparation — 20 minutes
Standing — minimum ½ hour
Cooking — 15 minutes

Do ahead Medallions, up to cooking stage, up to ½ day ahead. Sauce up to 1 day ahead

Wine notes Medallions of pork require a medium-bodied, astringent red —
A: Moorilla Estate Cabernet Sauvignon, from Tasmania
E: St-Nicholas-de-Bourgueil (Touraine)
U: Burgess (Napa) Cabernet Sauvignon

WHISKY FIGS
Must be made one month ahead

½ kg sugar
1½ cups water

2 kg firm ripe figs, with skins left on
1 cup whisky

Bring sugar and water to the boil slowly stirring to dissolve sugar and cook for 5 minutes. Add figs and stir gently. Cover and simmer very slowly over low heat for ¾ hour. Remove lid and simmer very gently for a further hour without letting syrup burn. Set aside to cool.

When cold spoon figs into clean masons' jars. Mix syrup with whisky and pour over figs. Seal and refrigerate for 1 month.

Average times Preparation — 5 minutes
Cooking — 1¾ hours
Maturing — 1 month

Do ahead At least 1 month

Wine notes The figs require a luscious, sweet white —
A: The Rothbury Estate Gold Label Late Picked Semillon
E: Château Climens (Barsac) of a great year
U: Château St Jean Late Harvest Johannisberg Riesling

SUMMER

MENU 4

This is an easy do-ahead menu, especially if you are serving the ham cold. Ideal for pre-Christmas parties or buffets, it's an easily executed menu.

ICED BUTTERNUT PUMPKIN SOUP

---

1 kg butternut pumpkin, skinned, seeded and
    sliced finely
2 medium white onions, peeled and sliced
1 medium old potato, peeled and sliced
4 cups stock

salt, pepper and nutmeg to taste
1 cup thickened cream

toasted pumpkin seeds to garnish

Place all ingredients except cream and pumpkin seeds into a large soup pan and bring slowly to a simmer over medium heat. Cook steadily for 35 minutes without a lid, stirring from time to time. Cool the soup and purée. Cover and chill, preferably overnight. Stir in cream and adjust seasoning. Serve soup in chilled soup bowls and scatter with pumpkin seeds.

Average times Preparation — 10 minutes
    Cooking — 35 minutes
    Chilling — overnight

Do ahead 1 day

Wine notes Iced Butternut Pumpkin Soup could be accompanied by an aromatic white —
A: Capel Vale (Western Australia) Gewurtztraminer
E: Gewurtztraminer (Kuentz-Bas) from Alsace
U: Grand Cru (Sonoma) Gewurtztraminer

BAKED FRUIT-GLAZED HAM
Serves 20 to 30

◆

1 × 7 kg cooked leg of ham
whole cloves

Baste:
1 cup apple cider
1 cup pineapple juice
1½ cups soft brown sugar

Garnish (optional):

6 oranges
fresh basil

◆

Remove skin from ham and place ham fat side up in a heavy baking dish. Cook in centre of 220°C (425°F) oven for 30 minutes.

Cook basting ingredients together in a small pan until sugar dissolves.

Take ham from oven and using a very sharp knife score fat on the cross into 1½ cm diamonds. Stud each diamond with a clove. Pour hot basting mixture over top of ham and return to oven to cook for 20 to 30 minutes or until brown on top, basting every 10 minutes. Remove from baking dish and leave to cool. Keep refrigerated until ready to serve. Keeps about 2 weeks, wrapped in foil and refrigerated.

If serving hot: cut 6 oranges with good skins into ½ cm slices and caramelize in a heavy frying pan with 1 cup castor sugar. Melt sugar in bottom of the dry pan and as soon as it melts and turns brown, stir in orange slices, a few at a time. Arrange around the base of ham with sprigs of fresh basil.

Serve with Cabbage Salad (see next recipe)

Average times Preparation — 25 minutes
Cooking — 1 hour 10 minutes
Cooling — 4 hours

Wine notes Fruit-glazed ham could be accompanied by a rosé —
A: Houghton Moondah Brook Cabernet Rosé
E and U: Cabernet d'Anjou

Do ahead If serving cold, up to 3 days

CABBAGE SALAD

◆

½ white cabbage, sliced very finely omitting all core

Dressing:
1 teaspoon salt
1 teaspoon English mustard
2 tablespoons sugar

¼ cup white wine vinegar
1 tablespoon melted butter
2 hard boiled eggs, chopped finely

◆

Put cabbage in a large salad bowl, cover with plastic wrap and refrigerate until ready to serve. To make dressing, whisk all ingredients together and pour over salad, toss well and serve.

Average times Preparation — 10 minutes

Do ahead Prepare cabbage up to ½ day before needing, cover and store in refrigerator

ICE-CREAM PLUM PUDDINGS WITH FROZEN CHOCOLATE SAUCE

Ice-cream Plum Puddings:

⅓ cup red and green glacé cherries, halved
⅓ cup chopped mixed peel
⅓ cup raisins
⅓ cup sultanas
⅓ cup currants
⅓ cup slivered almonds, toasted
⅓ cup hazelnuts, toasted and skinned
⅓ cup skinned pistachios (optional)
¼ cup brandy
1 teaspoon mixed spice
½ teaspoon ground cinnamon

½ teaspoon ground nutmeg
2 tablespoons cocoa powder
2 eggs, separated
½ cup icing sugar, sieved
900 ml thickened cream, beaten to soft peaks

Frozen Chocolate Sauce:

80 g dark chocolate, chopped
3 tablespoons polyunsaturated vegetable oil

Mix fruits and nuts together in a large bowl and pour over brandy. Stir in spices and cocoa. In a medium bowl beat egg whites stiffly, add yolks and beat well. Beat in sugar then fold cream into egg mixture. Pour mixture over fruit and nuts and fold all together.

Pour into 6 individual cup moulds (can use tea cups) which have been rinsed out with cold water, but not dried. Cover with foil and freeze 1 to 1½ hours. Remove from freezer and stir each mixture thoroughly. Cover and freeze until solid, preferably overnight.

On the day of serving, dip moulds into warm water, run a warm knife around the top edge, invert over individual serving dishes, and shake out. If puddings melt even slightly, return immediatly to freezer to firm.

To make sauce: place chocolate and oil in a small saucepan. Stand saucepan in a large saucepan or baking dish of hot water over medium heat and stir from time to time. When chocolate has melted and is well blended with oil, spoon over the tops of puddings allowing it to drizzle down the sides and set. Dress with holly sprigs.

Note: the sauce can be spooned over puddings and returned to freezer, but only on the day of serving.

These puddings can be made up to 3 days before serving. If the weather is really hot, they should be taken from the freezer only 10 minutes or so before serving. Obviously they will be rock hard straight from the freezer, difficult to eat and rather tasteless. The puddings should be left to stand on the bottom shelf of the refrigerator 5 to 10 minutes before serving.

Average times *Ice-cream* —
Preparation — 25 minutes
Setting — 1½ hours
Chocolate Sauce —
Preparation — 5 minutes
Cooking — 10 minutes
Setting — 1 minute

Wine notes The ice-cream requires no wine

Do ahead Puddings, up to 3 days

SUMMER

MENU 5

A delightfully easy Summer luncheon, dinner, or supper menu which is mostly do-ahead. The dessert is from The Savoy in London.

MOZZARELLA WITH TOMATOES AND ANCHOVIES

5 boccancini, cut into 1 cm slices (fresh mozzarelle in their milk, sold in Italian delicatessens)
5 ripe, medium tomatoes, cut in 1 cm slices
2 × 45 g cans flat anchovies

3 tablespoons olive oil
2 tablespoons finely chopped fresh oregano
coarsely ground black pepper

Arrange slices of boccancini on a platter with tomato slices interleaved between each of the cheese slices. Place anchovy fillets in a criss-cross pattern over the top and drizzle the oil from the cans over them. Drizzle olive oil over the top and scatter over oregano. Grind plenty of black pepper over the platter, cover with plastic wrap and refrigerate for 30 minutes.

Average times Preparation — 15 minutes
Chilling — 30 minutes

Wine notes The entrée, with its strong anchovy flavour, calls for a fruity white with a touch of residual sugar —
A: Tisdall Fumé Blanc from Victoria
E: Vouvray (Bredif)
U: Congress Springs (Santa Clara) Sauvignon Blanc

Do ahead Up to ½ day but only open anchovies 30 minutes before serving

VEAL STROGANOFF WITH RICE PILAF

60 g butter
2½ tablespoons plain flour
3 cups veal stock
½ cup sour cream
½ cup tomato purée
60 g butter, extra
1.5 kg veal fillets, cut into 5 cm × 1 cm strips
½ cup finely chopped white onion
2 cloves garlic, finely chopped
salt and freshly ground black pepper to taste
150 g white button mushrooms, finely sliced

Rice Pilaf:
1 cup long grain rice
2 cups veal stock
30 g butter
salt and pepper to taste

To make stroganoff: in a large pan make a roux by melting butter and whisking in flour. Cook, whisking, for 2 minutes. Pour in stock and cook, whisking until thickened. Boil for 2 minutes, reduce heat and stir in sour cream and tomato purée. Stir until mixture returns to simmer but do not boil. Set aside.

In a large heavy frying pan heat the extra butter and sauté half the meat with half the onion and garlic. Cook until meat is golden. Lift out with a slotted spoon and add sauce. Repeat with remaining meat, onion and garlic. Taste mixture, season accordingly and simmer gently for 10 minutes. Add mushrooms and cook a further 10 minutes.

To make pilaf: put all pilaf ingredients into a buttered flameproof casserole and bring to boil. Cover and cook at 200°C (400°F) for 25 to 35 minutes or until all stock has evaporated. Leave rice undisturbed to stand for 10 minutes before serving.

Average times *Stroganoff* —
Preparation — 20 minutes
Cooking — 45 minutes
Pilaf —
Preparation — 5 minutes
Cooking — 30 minutes
Standing — 10 minutes

Do ahead Can be made 2 days in advance, providing sour cream is not stirred in until day dish is needed

Wine notes Veal Stroganoff requires a full-bodied red —
A: Rosemount Coonawarra Shiraz
E: Hermitage La Chapelle (Jaboulet) of a good year
U: San Martin (Santa Clara) Zinfandel

ICED GRAND MARNIER SOUFFLÉ

6 egg yolks
¾ cup castor sugar
5–6 tablespoons Grand Marnier
3 cups thickened cream, beaten to soft peaks

3 egg whites

3 glacé orange slices to garnish

Beat egg yolks and castor sugar together in a medium-sized bowl over simmering water until light and frothy. Cool, beating over iced water. Add Grand Marnier. Fold cream into the mixture. Beat the egg whites until firm. Fold into the mixture. Prepare a 3½-cup soufflé dish with a greaseproof collar, standing 5 cm above rim. Pour mixture into the prepared dish. (The mixture should be level with top of collar.) Place in freezer, until set like ice-cream.

To serve, remove collar and decorate top with glacé orange slices cut in halves.

Average times Preparation — 15 minutes
Cooking — 10 minutes
Cooling — 15 minutes
Setting — 4 hours or over-night

Do ahead Up to 3 days

Wine notes The dessert requires no wine

SUMMER

MENU 6

———◆———

A menu which requires only last minute attention to the cooking of the main course. It's colourful and easy to perfect for a hot Summer's day or night.

SMOKED TROUT MOUSSE WITH SMOKED SALMON

———◆———

1.25 kg smoked trout
½ cup thick cream
salt and freshly ground black pepper to taste
horseradish relish to taste

lemon juice to taste
6–8 thin slices smoked salmon

sprigs fresh dill to garnish

———◆———

Remove skin from fish and discard it. Carefully take the flesh from bones and mince or chop in a food processor. Whip cream until it makes 'ribbons' and fold into fish with salt, pepper, horseradish and lemon juice to taste.

Mix it with your hands and adjust seasonings. Mound on to a serving platter and smooth over with a spatula. Cover entire mound with thin slices of smoked salmon. Cover and refrigerate for at least 2 hours. Garnish with sprigs of fresh dill and surround with toasted brown bread triangles. No butter, it's rich enough as it is!

Average times Preparation — 25 minutes
Standing — 2 hours

Wine notes Smoked trout mousse needs a spicy Gewurtztraminer —
A: Brown Bros
Gewurtztraminer, from
northern Victoria
E: Gewurtztraminer (Kuentz-Bas) from Alsace
U: St Francis (Sonoma)
Gewurtztraminer

Do ahead Can be finished 1 day ahead,
except for toast

MEDITERRANEAN SALAD

———◆———

2 medium tomatoes, cored and cut into 1 cm cubes
1 medium cucumber, skinned and cut into 1 cm cubes
2 sticks celery, stringed and cut into ½ cm slices
½ red and ½ green pepper, seeded and cut into 1 cm slices
6 spring onions, sliced very finely, both green and white parts

Vinaigrette:
1 teaspoon Dijon mustard
1 large clove garlic, chopped very finely
½ cup olive oil
1 tablespoon white wine vinegar
salt and black pepper to taste

———◆———

Mix all the salad ingredients together, cover with plastic wrap and refrigerate until ready to serve.

Whisk all vinaigrette ingredients together, pour over salad and toss thoroughly 10 minutes before serving.

Average times Preparation — 15 minutes
Standing — 10 minutes

Do ahead Prepare salad and refrigerate
covered up to 2 hours: dressing
up to 1 day

BARBECUED POUSSINS WITH LEMON AND OREGANO

6 × no. 4 or 5 poussins (baby chickens)
½ cup olive oil
½ cup lemon juice

2 teaspoons freshly chopped oregano or 1 teaspoon dried oregano leaves
salt and freshly ground black pepper to taste

Using poultry shears or kitchen scissors split poussins open down one side of backbone, cut down other side of backbone and remove it. Spread out poussins, skin side up on a work surface, and using your fist, completely flatten poussin. Place poussins in a large flat dish and cover with remaining ingredients. Turn over poussins, cover with plastic film and refrigerate for 2 hours.

On a preheated barbecue grill, place poussins skin side down and seal. Turn them over, paint with residue oil and lemon mixture from the flat dish and leave to seal on the second side. Continue cooking and turning poussins until they are cooked through, about 15 minutes.

Serve whole and at once with Mediterranean Salad.

Average times Preparation — 15 minutes
Standing — 2 hours
Cooking — 15 minutes

Do ahead Prepare up to barbecue stage up to
½ day ahead

Wine notes The poussins require a medium-
bodied red with enough acidity
to balance the herb flavours —
A: Redman (Coonawarra)
  Claret
E and U: Chianti Classico

MANGO ICE-CREAM WITH PASSIONFRUIT CREAM ANGLAISE

Mango Ice-cream:

3 tablespoons Grand Marnier
1 cup fresh mango purée (2 small to medium
  mangoes)
8 egg yolks
1 teaspoon cold water
3½ tablespoons castor sugar
450 ml thickened cream

Passionfruit Cream Anglaise:

4 egg yolks
2 tablespoons castor sugar
450 ml thickened cream
pulp from 3 large ripe passionfruit

In a double boiler over simmering water whisk the first 5 ice-cream ingredients until thick. Do not allow water to boil. Remove from heat and continue to whisk until mixture is smooth and thick. Cool over a basin of cold water then fold in cream using a rubber spatula. Either crank in an ice-cream churn or set in ice-cream trays in the deep freeze. Serve in scoops in a sea of Passionfruit Cream Anglaise.

Note: Mangoes must be very ripe with a good perfume or the flavour will be bland. This recipe is also excellent made with the same quantity of fresh white peach purée.

To make Passionfruit Cream Anglaise: whisk egg yolks and castor sugar together in a medium bowl until pale and fluffy. Bring cream to boil in a medium heavy-based saucepan and pour slowly over yolk mixture whisking constantly. Return mixture to pan and cook over low heat, whisking all the time until mixture thickens and coats back of wooden spoon. Remove from heat and cool with a circle of greaseproof paper placed directly over custard. When cool, stir in passionfruit pulp. Makes 4 generous servings.

Note: Custard thickens considerably as it cools.

Average times Preparation — 20 minutes
Cooking — 15 minutes
Cooling — 10 minutes
Setting — 2 to 4 hours

Wine notes Mango ice-cream requires no
wine

Do ahead Make both ice-cream and Cream
Anglaise up to 1 day ahead

SUMMER

MENU 7

◆

This menu is for a cooler Summer's evening and requires a little last minute attention.

AVOCADO AND GINGER SALAD

◆

Dressing:

¼ cup white wine vinegar
1 tablespoon paprika powder
1 cup peanut oil
2 teaspoons salt
¼ teaspoon black pepper

1 large avocado, cut in halves, stone removed
  and peeled
2 tablespoons lemon juice
2 medium tomatoes, skin and core removed
1 cup julienne (matchsticks) of celery, carrot
  and cucumber (no seeds)
1 tablespoon julienne of fresh ginger
12 chives, whole
6 tiny sprigs fresh dill

◆

To make dressing: bring vinegar and paprika to boil in a small saucepan. Simmer gently for 5 minutes. Leave to cool. Strain through kitchen paper in a sieve into a glass jar. Add remaining dressing ingredients and shake to combine. Set aside.

To prepare salad: slice avocado into 1 cm slices and dip in lemon juice. Arrange on 6 entrée plates in a star pattern. Cut tomato in halves, from core through to base then slice into 1 cm pieces. Arrange between avocado slices. Pile julienne ingredients in centre of each plate and strew with whole chives. Shake dressing and sprinkle a little over each salad and garnish each plate with a sprig of dill.

Average times Preparation — 15 minutes
Cooking — 5 minutes

Wine notes The salad calls for a fruity riesling —
A: Enterprise (Clare) Rhine
   Riesling
E: Forster Jesuitengarten Riesling Kabinett (Rheinpfalz)
U: Zaca Mesa (Santa Barbara)
   Johannisberg Riesling

Do ahead Dressing up to 1 week, covered
and refrigerated

62

SPICY SWEET RABBIT

◆

3 young rabbits, saddles and hind legs only
2 tablespoons oil
2 rashers bacon, rind removed and chopped
2 cloves garlic, bruised and chopped finely
2 tablespoons Italian parsley, chopped finely
½ teaspoon dried red chilli peppers
1 tablespoon brown sugar

2 cups dry white wine
1 tablespoon tomato paste, mixed with 2 table-spoons water
¼ cup raisins
¼ cup blanched almonds
1 tablespoon red currant jelly
salt, to taste
2 teaspoons cornflour mixed with 2 table-spoons water (optional)

◆

Cut saddles through backbone, into 4 cm pieces and sever legs through thigh joints. Heat oil in a large casserole over a high heat. Brown bacon, stir in garlic and parsley and cook 1 minute. Lift out with a slotted spoon and reserve. Brown rabbit pieces on all sides, stirring with a wooden spatula. Return the first cooked ingredients, add chilli, sugar and wine. Cover and simmer, over low heat for 10 minutes. Stir in tomato paste, raisins and almonds. Cover and cook slowly over low heat until rabbits are tender, about 30 minutes. (Depends very much on the age of the rabbits.) Stir in jelly and taste. Add salt if needed. Over a high heat, reduce sauce until it is a syrup consistency or alternatively, thicken sauce with cornflour and water, over a low heat until sauce thickens and clears. Served with boiled green ribbon pasta (tagliatelle).

Note: 2 kg chicken pieces can be substituted for the rabbits.

Average times Preparation — 10 minutes
　　　　　　　　Cooking — 1 to 1¼ hours

Wine notes The spicy rabbit calls for a con-
　　　　　　tinuation of the Riesling served
　　　　　　with the first course

Do ahead Up to 1 day

MANGO MOUSSE

◆

4½ teaspoons gelatine
1½ tablespoons lemon juice
3 teaspoons orange juice
3 cups mango purée, canned or fresh

¾ cup whipped cream

1½ tablespoons skinned pistachios to garnish

◆

In a small saucepan, mix gelatine with fruit juices and heat gently until dissolved. Cool slightly. Stir purée and gelatine mixture together and fold cream through it. Pour into separate glasses or bowls and refrigerate until set. Serve with pistachios scattered over the top.

Average times Preparation — 10 minutes
　　　　　　　　Cooking — 5 minutes
　　　　　　　　Cooling — 5 minutes

Wine notes Mango Mousse calls for a rich,
　　　　　　long-finishing sweet white —
　　　　　　A: Rosemount
　　　　　　　　Trockenbeerenauslese Rhine
　　　　　　　　Riesling
　　　　　　E: Château Climens (Barsac) of
　　　　　　　　a great year
　　　　　　U: Freemark Abbey (Napa)
　　　　　　　　Edelwein

Do ahead Up to ½ day

SUMMER

MENU 8

The entrée must be made 3 days in advance so that it has time to gather flavour. It is traditionally served on the third Saturday in July, in Venice, at the Festival of Redentorre, when it is made with fresh sardines. This is a lovely dinner menu which requires quite a lot of forward planning.

VENETIAN FISH WITH SULTANAS AND PINE NUTS
Make 3 days in advance

⅓ cup plain flour
750 g fresh redfish, bream or whiting fillets, skinned
⅔ cup sunflower seed oil
750 g white onions, peeled and sliced medium fine

½ cup dry white wine
⅓ cup water
½ cup sultanas
¼ cup pine nuts
salt and freshly ground black pepper to taste
¼ cup white wine vinegar

Flour the fish lightly. In a large heavy frying pan heat oil and fry fish on both sides until just tender. Lift out with a fish slide and drain on crumpled paper. Using same oil, fry onions until soft but do not allow them to colour. Pour over the wine and water, turn down heat and cook slowly for 20 minutes.

Place fish in a criss-cross pattern in a shallow serving dish (not metal). Pour over onions with all the residual cooking oil and juices. Scatter over the sultanas and pine nuts, sprinkle with salt and pepper and pour vinegar over the top. Cover with plastic wrap and refrigerate for 3 days before serving.

Make sure there is plenty of juice during the maturing period in the refrigerator. If it seems a little dry, pour in equal quantities of water and vinegar. The juice should cover fish and come almost up to onions. Serve with crusty Italian bread.

Note: To make this recipe with sardines, break off heads and gut under running cold water, using fingers, and pull out backbones. There is no need to remove all small bones in small sardines. Proceed with recipe as for redfish but leave sardines whole.

Average times Preparation — 15 minutes
Cooking — 25 minutes
Standing — 3 days

Do ahead Must be prepared 3 days ahead

Wine notes Soused fish requires no wine; clear your palate of the vinegar with some mineral water and savour the red wine with the lamb

LAMB FILLETS WITH FRESH TOMATO FONDUE SPIKED WITH FRESH BASIL

12–18 lamb fillets, skinned
salt and freshly ground black pepper

Tomato Fondue with Fresh Basil:

1 kg tomatoes
1 tablespoon oil

salt and freshly ground black pepper
½ teaspoon sugar
10 basil leaves or ½ teaspoon dried basil leaves

To grill lamb: heat a heavy cast iron pan, preferably one with heavy ribbing (a French griller) until smoking. If you look after your pan and never wash it (simply wipe it out with paper towel after each use), it won't need oiling except the first couple of times you use it. Place fillets diagonally across ribbing and press down on them to achieve a scorch mark on the meat. Do not crowd pan or the meat will stew. When fillets are sealed, give them a half turn across the ribbing, still on the same side. This gives the meat a scorch mark in diamond shapes which is called a quadrillage. Turn them over, season first side and repeat the process on second side.

Depending on size of fillets and heat of pan, the lamb will take approximately 2½ to 3½ minutes on each side. You should aim for a good crusty seal on the meat with pink juices still running inside. Rest meat for 10 minutes, slice and serve immediately with Stuffed Zucchini (see next recipe).

To make tomato fondue: remove cores from tomatoes with a sharp paring knife. Dip them into boiling water for 15 seconds, then drain. Peel off skins, slice tomatoes in half crosswise and squeeze out all the seeds and juices into a strainer over a bowl. Discard seeds. Chop flesh into small cubes.

Heat oil in a shallow pan and cook tomato cubes, with the juice, seasoning and sugar. Stir from time to time so tomatoes do not burn. Continue to cook until most of the juices have evaporated and fondue is a thick but still moist texture, about 30 minutes. Stir in basil which should be pinched into fondue with fingernails. Serve hot or cold.

Note: Tomato Fondue is also excellent with some fish and veal dishes. A little finely chopped garlic can be added to tomato flesh as it first begins to cook, and of course, other herbs may be substituted instead of basil.

Average times	Preparation — 10 minutes	**Wine notes**	Lamb fillets call for a fresh
	Cooking — 37 minutes		Cabernet with crisp tannin —
	Standing — 10 minutes		A: Mt Mary Cabernet
			Sauvignon from the Yarra
			Valley in Victoria
			E: Château Calon-Ségur (St-Estèphe) of a good year
Do ahead	Can make tomato fondue ½ day ahead		U: Château Montelena (Napa) Cabernet Sauvignon

STUFFED ZUCCHINI

◆

Béchamel Sauce:

1 tablespoon butter
3 teaspoons plain flour
½ cup milk
salt and pepper to taste

12 × 10 cm zucchini
30 g butter

1 medium white onion, very finely chopped
¼ cup fine breadcrumbs
2 tablespoons finely grated Parmesan cheese
salt and pepper
2 tablespoons fine breadcrumbs, extra
2 tablespoons finely grated Parmesan cheese, extra
1 tablespoon butter, extra

◆

To make béchamel sauce: cook butter and flour together over medium heat in a saucepan for 2 minutes, whisking. Add milk and whisk until thickened. Season to taste and set aside.
To prepare zucchini: trim stems. Slice off top-third. Blanch both 'lids' and bottoms in boiling salted water for 3 minutes. Refresh under running cold water. Scoop out pulp from bottoms, being careful not to break them. Invert on a paper towel to dry. Mince the lids and pulp and squeeze out any excess juice.

Heat butter in medium pan and sauté onion until softened. Add minced zucchini and simmer for 5 minutes. Add béchamel sauce to zucchini mixture with breadcrumbs, Parmesan cheese and salt and pepper. Spoon mixture into zucchini. Sprinkle extra breadcrumbs and/or cheese on top. Dot with extra butter and put into buttered gratiné dish. Cook at 200°C (400°F) for 15 minutes, till tops are golden.

Average times	Preparation — 30 minutes	**Do ahead**	Up to oven stage, ½ day
	Cooking — 28 minutes		

INDIVIDUAL KIWI FRUIT TARTS

Short Crust Pastry:

1½ cups plain flour
pinch salt
120 g cold butter, cut into small pieces
2–4 tablespoons iced water

Filling:

3 eggs
¾ cup cream

3 teaspoons icing sugar
3 teaspoons kirsch
1 egg white, beaten
4 ripe kiwi fruits, peeled and sliced
3 teaspoons icing sugar, extra
extra cream, for serving

To make pastry: mix flour and salt in a medium bowl. Rub butter into dry ingredients, using fingertips, until mixture resembles oatmeal. With a knife, stir in 2 tablespoons water, adding the extra water, a little at a time, until mixture comes together to form a ball. Knead dough on a lightly floured board. Roll into a ball and flatten to about 3 cm. Wrap in plastic film or greaseproof paper and refrigerate for a minimum of 30 minutes. Alternatively, make in a food processor, stopping the machine as soon as mixture comes together in a ball.

On a lightly floured board, roll pastry dough to the thickness of a 10 cent coin. Roll up on rolling pin, and un-roll over 6 buttered individually prepared tart pans, approximately 11 cm in diameter. Gather dough into pans and tuck down with fingertips or a spare piece of dough rolled into a ball. Run rolling pin over the tops, cutting off excess pastry. Prick each thoroughly, place on a baking tray and line with 2 sheets of greaseproof paper. Fill with blind baking weights and refrigerate for 30 minutes. Bake in hottest part of oven at 200°C (400°F) for 10 minutes. Remove greaseproof paper and weights and return to oven for a further 5 to 10 minutes, or until golden and crisp.

To make filling: beat eggs, cream, icing sugar and kirsch together in a medium bowl. Paint egg white over base of each pastry case. Arrange kiwi fruit slices in the pastry cases, pour over egg mixture, sift over remaining icing sugar and bake in hottest part of oven at 180°C (375°F) for 15 minutes or until the mixture is set and golden on top. Remove tarts from pans and serve warm with running cream.

Average times Preparation — 30 minutes
Standing — 1 hour
Cooking — 35 minutes

Wine notes Kiwi Fruit Tarts, a rich sweet white —
A: Montrose (Mudgee) Sauternes
E and U: Château Suduiraut (Sauternes) of a good year

Do ahead Can make pastry and blind bake cases 1 day ahead

SUMMER

MENU 9

An Italian-inspired menu planned around some of Summer's best ingredients, it would be well received at lunch or dinner.

PASTA WITH UNCOOKED TOMATO SAUCE

---

750 g very ripe tomatoes
4 medium cloves garlic, peeled and chopped finely
⅔ cup fresh basil leaves, tightly packed, each torn into one-thirds
¼ cup coarsely chopped parsley
2 teaspoons fresh oregano leaves, chopped

¾ cup olive oil
salt, to taste
freshly ground black pepper, to taste
½ kg medium tubular pasta, such as penne (sometimes called mostachiolli or chiacciole)

Skin tomatoes, halve and squeeze out seeds. Cut into ½ cm dice. Place in a bowl with garlic and herbs. Add oil, salt to taste and a generous amount of pepper to bowl. Mix well. Cover bowl and place in refrigerator for at least 2 hours before serving time.

In a very large pot of boiling salted water, cook pasta until just underdone (*al dente*) (time depends on brand and specific shape, but should be about 10 to 12 minutes). Drain well.

While pasta is still extremely hot, pour refrigerated sauce over it. It is the reaction of very hot to very cold that releases the unique flavour of this dish. Mix very well and serve immediately. Do not add grated cheese.

Average times Preparation — 15 minutes
Cooking — 10 minutes
Chilling — 2 hours

Wine notes The pasta could be accompanied by a light red, slightly chilled —
A: Roseworthy Pinot Noir
E and U: Bardolino (Masi) from the Veneto

Do ahead Sauce up to 1 day

VENETIAN CALVES' LIVERS

1 kg calves' livers, skinned and very thinly sliced
salt
350 g butter

3 medium white onions, sliced
1 cup dry white wine
⅔ cup water, approximately
salt and freshly ground black pepper to taste

Remove any large gristly tubes from the liver. Salt the slices liberally and leave to disgorge for 30 minutes. Drain the liver slices and pat dry with paper towels.

Choose a frying pan large enough to accommodate all the liver in a single layer without crowding it, or use 2 pans. Melt butter in frying pan, and sauté onion, stirring for 5 minutes. Add a little wine and some water, adding more of these liquids as you need them. Continue to cook onions very slowly until limp and nicely browned, about 20 minutes.

Remove onions with a slotted spoon and keep warm. Make sure there is plenty of butter still in frying pan. Add more if necessary. Turn heat to high, and when butter is very, very hot put in liver slices.

As soon as liver loses its raw, reddish colour, turn it, add a large pinch of salt and some pepper, and return onions to frying pan. Turn everything once more, transfer to a warm platter and serve immediately.

Note: It takes almost longer to read this recipe than to cook the liver. If it is the correct thinness, the liver is done in less than 1 minute.

A lovely Summer salad would go well after the main course.

Average times Preparation — 15 minutes
Disgorging — 30 minutes
Cooking — 25 minutes

Wine notes Liver requires a medium-bodied red —
A: Botobolar (Mudgee) Shiraz
E and U: Barbaresco from Piedmont

STUFFED PEACHES

6 large freestone peaches, not overripe
2 tablespoons butter
125 g Amaretti biscuits, crushed finely

30 g butter, extra
⅓ cup sugar
⅓ cup brandy

Divide peaches in half and remove stones. To halve a peach without breaking it, find line that girdles peach and follow it cutting through with a sharp knife. Gently turn the two halves in opposite directions until they are free of the stone. With a teaspoon, enlarge the hole a little.

Butter baking dish with 2 tablespoons butter and arrange peach halves in it. Fill peach holes with Amaretti crumbs. Put a small piece of butter on top of crumbs, then sprinkle each peach with 1 teaspoon of sugar. Cook in 175°C (375°F) oven for 20 minutes.

Pour 1 teaspoon brandy over each peach half, and return to oven to cook 15–20 minutes longer. Arrange peaches on a serving dish. Let stand until cooled to room temperature. Do not refrigerate.

Average times Preparation — 10 minutes
Cooking — 35 minutes
Cooling — 40 minutes

Wine notes Stuffed Peaches call for a luscious, sweet white —
A: Peter Lehmann (Barossa) Semillon Sauternes
E and U: Moscato di Noto Liquoroso, from Sicily

Do ahead Up to ½ day

SUMMER

MENU 10

◆

This is a delightfully light and contrasting menu which is ideal for dinner. The first two courses require quite a lot of attention, so leave plenty of time to execute them. The red fruit salad is beautifully refreshing and the fruits can be changed to whatever is in season, as long as they are red or black. If it's very hot, you may need to chill the biscuits, which will soften if left out in the heat.

PRAWNS IN VERMOUTH

◆

4 tablespoons olive oil
36 green king prawns, shelled leaving tails intact, and deveined
45 g butter
2 small cloves garlic, crushed

salt and freshly ground black pepper to taste
⅓ cup dry vermouth
⅓ cup lemon juice

◆

Pour olive oil into a large heavy frying pan. When hot, add prawns and cook, stirring with a wooden spatula until golden all over, for approximately 2 to 3 minutes. Reduce heat and stir in butter, garlic, salt and pepper. Increase heat and pour in vermouth and lemon juice, stirring constantly with a wooden spatula and shaking the pan at the same time for 1 minute. Serve immediately with fluffy boiled rice.

Average times Preparation — 25 minutes
              Cooking — 5 minutes
Wine notes Prawns in Vermouth call for a
             mature, full, dry white —
             A: The Rothbury Estate Individual Paddock Semillon
             E and U: Hermitage Blanc
                (Chave or Jaboulet) of
                a good year

Do ahead Prepare prawns for cooking up to
           ½ day

SPLIT CHICKENS STUFFED WITH RICOTTA AND JULIENNE ZUCCHINI

Stuffing:

500 g small firm zucchini cut into fine julienne
   (use a food processor with julienne disc)
salt
45 g butter
1 large white onion, very finely chopped
freshly ground black pepper to taste
1 teaspoon finely chopped fresh marjoram
   leaves and flowers
1 egg
2 tablespoons finely grated Parmesan cheese
100 g fresh ricotta cheese

3 × 800 g chickens
3 tablespoons olive oil
1 teaspoon crumbled mixed dried herbs
   (thyme, oregano, savory)

To prepare stuffing: salt the julienne zucchini and leave to stand for 30 minutes.

In a medium heavy pan heat 1 tablespoon of butter and stew onion in it for 15 minutes over low heat stirring from time to time. Do not allow to colour. Set aside and cool.

Wrap the zucchini julienne in a clean tea-towel and squeeze out all the juices. Heat 2 tablespoons of butter in a large heavy pan and sauté the zucchini over high heat stirring constantly until *al dente* and all juices have reduced. Set aside and cool.

Combine cooked zucchini, onions, pepper, marjoram, egg, Parmesan cheese and ricotta cheese together and mix thoroughly.

To prepare chickens: remove tips from the wings and cut up one side of backbone with a pair of poultry shears or scissors. Lay chickens open skin side up on a work bench and beat flat using your fist. With poultry shears or scissors cut the broad piece of the backbone near the head end. Working from neck end, use fingers to release skin from flesh all the way through the carcasses and over to the drumsticks and the breasts, keeping it attached around the edges.

Stuff each of the chickens between flesh and skin with one-third of the stuffing mixture, spreading it evenly to cover the breasts and legs. Re-form chickens to make them look like 'toads', tucking neck flaps under and securing with a poultry pin.

Rub olive oil all over chickens and place side by side with skin sides up in a baking dish and sprinkle with herbs and seasoning. Cook in 200°C (400°F) oven for 50 to 60 minutes or until crisp skinned and brown. (If chickens brown too fast, cover with foil.) Lift out of baking dish and leave to rest for 10 minutes before carving.

To serve cut up one side of breastbone with poultry shears or scissors and serve one half per person.

Average times Preparation — 40 minutes
                 Standing — 30 minutes
                 Cooling — 20 minutes
                 Cooking — 75 minutes

Do ahead Chickens can be stuffed up to ½ day ahead, providing the stuffing is *thoroughly chilled* before putting into chickens. If serving chickens cold they can be cooked up to 1 day ahead

Wine notes The chicken is complemented by the style of white selected for the prawns, so you could continue with that wine, or change to a medium-bodied red —
A: Mt Pleasant Philip Hermitage
E and U: Chianti Classico

RED FRUIT SALAD

◆

1 box strawberries, wiped over and hulled
1 box raspberries or boysenberries
250 g cherries, stalked and stoned
125 g blueberries or red currants

6 blood plums, halved and stoned
200 g water-melon, seeded and balled
¼ cup kirsch

◆

Combine fruits in a large bowl, pour over kirsch, and chill for 1 hour.

Average times Preparation — 15 minutes
Chilling — 1 hour

Do ahead Up to ½ day

Wine notes Fruit salad requires no wine

COCONUT SWIRLS
Makes from 24 to 30

◆

3 tablespoons water
60 g unsalted butter cut into small pieces
1 teaspoon vanilla essence
2 cups pure icing sugar, sifted
8 tablespoons full-cream powdered milk (used
  dry)
2 cups desiccated coconut

Icing:
200 g dark cooking chocolate, chopped

◆

Bring water to boil in a medium saucepan with lid on. It is important that it does not evaporate. Remove from heat. Add butter cut into pieces and leave pan with lid on until butter has melted. Add vanilla. Mix together icing sugar and powdered milk. Pour into butter mixture ½ cup at a time and mix well after each addition. Work in coconut using wooden spatula. Place small teaspoon-size balls of mixture on to greaseproof paper on baking trays. Refrigerate until firm, about 30 minutes.

Melt chocolate in bowl over hot water until smooth. Using teaspoon, swirl melted chocolate on top of each coconut biscuit and set in refrigerator. Store in airtight containers.

Average times Preparation — 25 minutes
Cooking — 10 minutes
Setting — 40 minutes

Do ahead Up to 3 days. Stored in a cool
place in airtight containers

Wine notes Coconut Swirls with chocolate
call for a port —
A: Craigmoor (Mudgee) Rummy
  Port
E: Taylor's Late Bottled Vintage
  Port
U: Masson (Santa Clara) Rare
  Souzao Port

SUMMER

MENU 11

---◆---

This is a lovely family menu which is inexpensive and easily executed.

TOMATOES STUFFED WITH TUNA AND CAPERS

---◆---

6 ripe medium tomatoes
salt
¾ cup mayonnaise
2 teaspoons Dijon mustard

1½ tablespoons fine capers drained
2 × 220 g cans tuna (white preferably), drained

6 wisps Italian parsley to garnish

---◆---

Slice tops off tomatoes and remove all flesh using a melon baller, being careful not to break the skins. Salt insides lightly and invert over a plate to drain for 20 minutes.

Mix mayonnaise with mustard and capers. Break up tuna lightly using a fork and fold into mayonnaise. Taste and adjust seasoning.

Spoon mixture into prepared tomato skins and garnish each with a wisp of parsley. Cover and refrigerate for 30 minutes before serving.

Average times Preparation — 20 minutes
Standing — 20 minutes
Chilling — 30 minutes

Wine notes Stuffed tomatoes call for a fruity, crisp white —
A: Amberton (Mudgee)
Semillon
E and U: Vinho Verde
(Portugal)

Do ahead Up to ½ day

CHICKEN CURRIED WITH APPLES

◆

4 tablespoons peanut oil
60 g butter
2 × 1.3 kg chickens, each cut into 10 pieces (2
    wings, 2 thighs, 2 drumsticks and 4 breast
    pieces, discard the backs or keep for stock)
2 tablespoons curry powder

2 tablespoons plain flour
500 g white onions, minced
2 large Granny Smiths, peeled, cored and
    minced
2 cloves garlic, minced
salt and freshly ground black pepper to taste
1½ cups sour cream

◆

Heat half the oil and butter in a large heavy casserole and sauté a few chicken pieces at a time,
until golden all over. Lift out with a slotted spoon and set aside. Repeat with remaining chicken,
using remaining oil and butter when needed.

Return all chicken to casserole and sprinkle with curry powder and flour. Mix well so that all
the chicken is well coated. Stir in onions, apples and garlic, season to taste and simmer covered
over low heat for 30 minutes or until chicken is tender. Stir in sour cream and heat through.
Correct seasoning and serve.

Serve the curried chicken with boiled brown rice.

Average times Preparation — 20 minutes
Cooking — 50 minutes

Wine notes Curried chicken calls for aro-
matic white with some residual
sugar —
A: Hungerford Hill Coonawarra
    Spaetlese Rhine Riesling
E: Château de Belle-Rive Quarts
    de Chaume (Anjou)
U: Kenwood (Sonoma) Chenin
    Blanc

Do ahead Up to 1 day, stirring sour cream in
only on day served

PINEAPPLE FLUMMERY

◆

1 cup water
⅓ cup castor sugar
juice of 1 orange
juice of ½ lemon
2½ teaspoons gelatine

2½ teaspoons plain flour
1½ teaspoons extra lemon juice
440 g can unsweetened pineapple pieces,
    drained

◆

Bring water and sugar to boil stirring until sugar dissolves. Add citrus juices. Mix gelatine and
flour with extra lemon juice and whisk into syrup off the heat. Return to heat and cook a further
10 minutes stirring from time to time. Cool over a basin of iced water until it reaches blood
temperature (it should feel neither hot nor cold to the touch).

When the mixture is beginning to show signs of setting around the top edge, beat in an electric
mixer for 20 minutes. Fold in pineapple pieces. Pour into a wetted mould, cover and set in the
refrigerator.

When ready to serve, run a knife around the edge, invert over a serving platter and shake out.

Average times Preparation — 10 minutes
Cooking — 15 minutes
Cooling — 20 minutes
Beating — 20 minutes

Do ahead Preferably overnight and up to 1
day

Wine notes Pineapple Flummery calls for a
rich, sweet white —
A: Leasingham (Clare) Auslese
    Rhine Riesling
E: Moulin Touchais (Anjou)
U: San Martin (Santa Clara)
    Late Harvest Johannisberg
    Riesling

SUMMER

MENU 12

A delightfully light luncheon menu which is mostly do-ahead. Either the cheese course or the sorbet can be dropped if the menu is too long.

SUMMER SALAD

---

250 g snow peas or French beans, trimmed and
  stringed

Strawberry vinaigrette:

¼ cup strawberry vinegar
2 tablespoons fresh lime or lemon juice
salt and freshly ground white pepper to taste
⅓ cup light olive oil

1 small ripe rock melon or cantaloup halved,
  seeded and cut into julienne
2 cups small strawberries, hulled and cut into
  quarters
8 mignonette lettuce leaves
16 very thin slices prosciutto crudo

Blanch snow peas or beans in boiling salted water over high heat for 30 seconds for the peas and 1½ minutes for the beans. Drain immediately and refresh in a bowl of iced water for 5 minutes. Drain and pat dry on paper towel. Cut the snow peas or beans into fine julienne and place in a bowl.

Whisk all the vinaigrette ingredients together and pour over the peas or beans. Add melon and strawberries and toss lightly. Arrange the prosciutto slices draped and curled attractively between the lettuce cups. Pile the dressed salad into each of the cups and serve well chilled.

Average times Preparation — 30 minutes
　　　　　　　　Cooking — 1½ hours

Wine notes The Summer Salad calls for an
　　　　　　　aromatic white —
　　　　　　　A: Orlando Eden Valley
　　　　　　　　 Traminer Riesling
　　　　　　　E: Gewurztraminer (Pierre
　　　　　　　　 Sparr) from Alsace from a
　　　　　　　　 great year
　　　　　　　U: Souverain (Sonoma)
　　　　　　　　 Gewurztraminer

Do ahead Vinaigrette, up to 1 week

DEVILLED CHICKEN LEGS

Devilled Paste:

250 g butter, softened
3 tablespoons mango chutney
2 tablespoons lemon juice
1 tablespoon French mustard

1 teaspoon English mustard
2 teaspoons curry powder
freshly ground black pepper

12 chicken legs, scored with a sharp knife

Beat devilled paste ingredients together until smooth. Spred over chicken legs, cover and refrigerate for 4 hours.

Cook at 200°C (400°F) for 20 to 25 minutes or until tender. Finish under a hot griller painting the legs with the bubbling mixture until they are well coloured. Serve at once.

Serve the chicken legs with steamed baby summer vegetables.

Average times Preparation — 10 minutes
　　　　　　　　Cooking — 25 minutes
Do ahead Up to oven stage, up to 1 da
y

Wine notes With Devilled Chicken Legs,
　　　　　　　continue with the white from
　　　　　　　the first course

APRICOT ALMOND BREAD

1½ cups dried apricots
3 tablespoons butter
1½ cups castor sugar
2 cups plain flour
½ teaspoon salt

2 teaspoons baking powder
½ teaspoon bicarbonate of soda
⅓ cup milk
½ cup almonds in skin, coarsely chopped

Cover apricots with water, bring to the simmer and cook 5 minutes. Drain apricots, reserving juice. Chop apricots into small pieces.

Cream butter and castor sugar and stir in ½ cup of reserved apricot juice.

Sift flour with the salt, baking powder and soda. Stir into creamed butter and sugar, alternatively with the milk. Stir until batter is blended. Fold in apricots and almonds. Pour batter into a buttered loaf pan and cook in 175°C (350°F) oven for approximately 1 hour, or until risen, golden and tests done. Serve with unsalted butter and a tasty cheddar or Gruyère cheese.

Note: This bread slices more easily if allowed to stand overnight.

Average times Preparation — 25 minutes
Cooking — 1 hour 5 minutes
Standing — overnight

Wine notes Apricot and Almond Bread with cheese provides the opportunity to enjoy a red: light, fruity, perhaps chilled —
A: Peter Lehmann Pinot Noir
E: Chorey-les-Beaunes (Tollot-Beaut)
U: Acacia (Napa) Pinot Noir

Do ahead At least 1 day and up to 2 days and store airtight

PASSIONFRUIT SORBET

4 cups water
1¼ cups castor sugar
350 g passionfruit pulp

juice of 4 lemons
skins of 8 passionfruit

Mix all ingredients together, stirring until castor sugar dissolves. Refrigerate and leave to gather flavours for 4 hours. Lift the passionfruit skins out of mixture and discard. Churn mixture until it sets.

Average times Preparation — 10 minutes
Standing — 4 hours
Setting — 20 minutes

Wine notes Passionfruit Sorbet requires no wine

Do ahead Up to 3 days

75

SUMMER

MENU 13

◆

This is a delightfully colourful dinner menu with two completely do-ahead courses.

CARROT VICHYSSOISE

◆

60 g butter
1 medium white onion, peeled and sliced
4 medium carrots, peeled and sliced
4½ cups veal or chicken stock
1 stalk of celery, sliced finely

2 medium potatoes, sliced very thinly
salt and pepper, to taste
1 cup thickened cream
1½ tablespoons freshly snipped chives

◆

Heat butter over medium heat and cook carrots and onions with the lid on until tender. Add stock, celery, potatoes, and seasoning and simmer for 30 minutes. Cool soup over iced water then blend or sieve it.

Stir in cream and adjust seasoning. Chill soup and soup bowls, and serve garnished with chives.

Average times Preparation — 20 minutes
Cooking — 40 minutes
Cooling — 30 minutes
Chilling — 2 hours

Wine notes The carrot soup, with its sweet flavour from the vegetable, is complemented by a spicy white
A: Miramar Traminer, from Mudgee
E: Gewurtztraminer (Hugel) of a good year, from Alsace
U: De Loach (Sonoma) Gewurtztraminer

Do ahead At least 1 day and up to 2 days

BEEF FILLET WITH GREEN PEPPERCORN SAUCE

45 g butter
1.5 kg eye fillet, trimmed and skinned
salt and freshly ground pepper to taste
Sauce:
3 tablespoons cognac

1½ cups veal or beef stock
1 cup thick cream (optional)
2 tablespoons green peppercorns, drained
lemon juice to taste
salt to taste

◆

Heat butter in a large heavy baking dish and when foaming seal the beef on all sides over high heat. Season liberally and cook in hottest part of 200°C (400°F) oven for 27 minutes for medium-rare beef. Remove from pan and rest for 10 minutes in a warm oven before carving.
To make sauce: place pan over high heat and pour in cognac. Ignite it and shake pan until flame dies. Whisk in all the brown bits clinging to base and sides of pan. Add stock and cream (if using), and reduce sauce over medium heat to 2 cups, whisking from time to time. Stir in peppercorns, lemon juice and salt to taste. Serve beef sliced thickly and accompany with sauce.

Serve the beef with vegetables in season and Potatoes Savoyarde (see next recipe).

Average times Preparation — 10 minutes
Cooking — 35 minutes
Standing — 10 minutes
Wine notes Beef Fillet with Green Pepper-corn Sauce needs a full-bodied red —

A: Château Tahbilk Shiraz, from central Victoria
E: Hermitage (Chave) of a good year
U: Edmeades (Mendocino) Zinfandel

Spinach Ricotta Gnocchi with Brown Butter and Sage
Leaves

Wine:
Valpolicella (Masi)

Smoked Trout Mousse with Smoked Salmon

Wine:
Brown Bros (Milawa) Gewurztraminer

POTATOES SAVOYARDE

¾ kg old potatoes or pinkeyes
1 egg
salt and pepper, to taste

1½ cups veal stock
1 tablespoon butter

Peel and wash potatoes and slice them finely, so you can see through the slices if you hold them up to the light. A food processor fitted with a fine slicing disc is the quickest way to do this.

Beat the egg with seasoning and stock. Butter a 20 cm square × 7 cm deep ovenproof dish. Layer potatoe slices into prepared dish, seasoning every third layer. Pour stock over potatoes to prevent raw potatoes browning.

Cut butter into small pieces over the top and cook in 200°C (400°F) oven for 45 minutes or until tender. Serve hot, cut into squares.

Average times Preparation — 15 minutes
Cooking — 45 minutes

PASSIONFRUIT TARTS
Makes ten 8 cm tarts

Pastry:
1½ cups plain flour
2 teaspoons castor sugar
125 g butter, chilled and cut into 6 pieces
1½–2 tablespoons iced water

Filling:
180 g unsalted butter
1 cup castor sugar
7 egg yolks
½ cup passionfruit pulp

To make pastry: mix flour and castor sugar together and rub in butter until mixture resembles oatmeal. Mix in enough water until the mixture comes together in a ball. Do not knead. Flatten to 3 cm and wrap in plastic film and refrigerate for a minimum of 30 minutes. (In very hot weather rest in the deep freeze.)

Roll out on a lightly floured board until the pastry is the thickness of a 10 cent coin. Butter 10 cm × 8 cm base (10 cm top) tart pans. Cut the pastry into 10 and line each tart pan with the pastry pressing down well with fingers or a small ball of left-over dough. Trim off the overhanging pastry, prick the tarts' bases and sides thoroughly with a fork and place on a baking tray. Cover and refrigerate for a minimum of 30 minutes.

Place a double layer of greaseproof paper on each of the cases and weigh down with blind baking weights. Cook tarts in 200°C (400°F) oven for 12 to 15 minutes or until golden around the top edge. Remove the greaseproof paper and the blind baking weights. Return tarts to oven until dry and crisp. Cool on a wire rack.

To make filling: cook butter and sugar together in a heavy-based medium pan. Stir in yolks, and whisk mixture until it thickens over medium heat. It must not boil or it will curdle. (If the mixture curdles put in a blender and blend until smooth.) Remove from heat and stir in passionfruit pulp. Cool in a bowl of iced water, stirring from time to time. Spoon into prepared tart cases and leave to set in the refrigerator overnight. Serve with ice-cream or cream.

Average times Preparation — 25 minutes
Standing — 2 × 30 minutes
Cooking — 35 minutes
Cooling — 30 minutes
Setting — overnight

Do ahead At least 1 day and up to 2 days

Wine notes Passionfruit Tarts require a long-finishing sweet white —
A: Mitchelton Coonawarra *Botrytis* Rhine Riesling
E: Moulin Touchais (Anjou)
U: Freemark Abbey (Napa) Edelwein

SUMMER

MENU 14

A lovely Summer luncheon or dinner menu, requiring quite a lot of time and attention.

SCALLOP MOUSSE WITH FRESH TOMATO SAUCE

375 g scallops, cleaned with roe removed and
   set aside, chilled
1 egg white, chilled
1 cup thickened cream, chilled
1 teaspoon lemon juice
salt and freshly ground white pepper to taste
freshly grated nutmeg to taste

Fresh Tomato Sauce:
500 g ripe tomatoes, skinned, cored and seeded
1 teaspoon tomato paste
salt and freshly ground black pepper to taste
1 tablespoon freshly chopped basil
⅓ cup olive oil

To make mousse: purée scallops in a food processor until smooth. With the machine on high, add egg white, cream, lemon juice and seasonings. Turn off machine the moment the ingredients are well mixed. Cover and chill for 30 minutes.

Lightly oil a 4-cup mould and spoon half the mousse into it. Cover mousse with the roes and spoon remaining mousse on top. Gently tap mould on work bench to settle the contents. Cover with buttered greaseproof paper and place in a baking dish of hot water which comes half-way up sides of mould.

Cook at 175°C (350°F) for 25 to 30 minutes or until set. Cool thoroughly and then refrigerate.
To make tomato sauce: purée tomatoes in a food processor. Stir in the tomato paste, seasonings and herbs and whisk in olive oil a little at a time.
To serve: unmould the mousse, dip into warm water, invert over a serving dish and shake out. Serve cut into thin slices and accompany with fresh tomato sauce.

Average times Preparation — 20 minutes
                  Chilling — 30 minutes
                  Cooking — 25 minutes

Do ahead Mousse up to 1 day. Sauce up to
             2 days

Wine notes The Scallop Mousse with Fresh
             Tomato Sauce needs a fruity,
             crisp white —
             A: Horderns (Wybong) Semillon
             E and U: Pinot Grigio dell'Alto
                 Adige (Santa
                 Margherita)

POACHED LEG OF LAMB WITH SPICY MUSTARD SEED SAUCE

2 kg leg of lamb
250 g leeks, washed and chopped
200 g carrots, peeled and chopped
200 g turnips, peeled and chopped
green leaves from 1 bunch celery
Bouquet garni: sprig parsley, sprig thyme, 1
   bay leaf
1 tablespoon salt
½ teaspoon white pepper

Mustard Seed Sauce:
500 ml thickened cream
2 sprigs fresh tarragon, or 1 teaspoon dried tarragon leaves
3 tablespoons wholegrain mustard
1 teaspoon dried crushed red pepper
½ teaspoon ground cumin
freshly ground black pepper

Place lamb in a large stock pot, with vegetables, celery leaves, bouquet garni and salt and white pepper. Cover and bring slowly to boil. Turn down and simmer for approximately 50 minutes until lamb is pink. Remove all fat and skin from lamb, cover with foil and keep warm until ready to carve.

To make sauce: reduce cooking stock over high heat with lid off. Simmer cream in a frying pan (it will reduce more quickly in a low-sided pan) until it is reduced by one-third. Stir in tarragon, mustard, red pepper, cumin and black pepper and 1 cup of reduced cooking stock. Continue to simmer until sauce is a good consistency. Taste and add salt only if necessary.

Carve lamb into thin slices and serve with creamy sauce. Accompany with a steamed green vegetable, like broccoli, french beans or snow peas.

Average times Preparation — 30 minutes
Cooking — 1½ hours

Wine notes Poached lamb needs a big, tannic red —
A: Château Tahbilk Cabernet Sauvignon, from central Victoria
E: Château Meyney (St-Estèphe)
U: Duckhorn (Napa) Cabernet Sauvignon

RASPBERRY TART WITH RASPBERRY CREAM

◆

Pastry:

1 cup plain flour
1 tablespoon castor sugar
125 g unsalted butter, cut into 8 pieces
1 egg yolk
2–4 teaspoons iced water

Raspberry Cream:

⅓ cup plain flour
4 egg yolks
2 cups milk
1 tablespoon eau de vie de framboise

1 box raspberries, picked over
1 tablespoon pure icing sugar, sieved

◆

To make pastry: mix flour and sugar together and rub butter into it using fingers until the mixture resembles oatmeal. Mix in egg yolk and just enough water to bring the dough together into a single mass and knead lightly on a lightly floured board. Flatten to 3 cm, wrap in greaseproof paper and refrigerate for 30 minutes.

Roll pastry on a lightly floured board to fit a 23 cm tart pan. Butter tart pan and line with pastry. Trim off overhanging pastry. Prick pastry thoroughly, cover with plastic and refrigerate for a minimum of 30 minutes.

Place 2 layers of greaseproof paper in pastry case and fill with blind baking weights. Bake for 15 minutes in 175°C (350°F) oven. Remove paper and weights and set aside pastry case.

To make raspberry cream: whisk flour and yolks together with a little of the milk until smooth. Heat remaining milk and gradually pour onto yolk mixture whisking constantly. Return to pan and cook until cream is smooth and thick, whisking constantly. Place a circle of greaseproof paper directly on top of cream while it is cooling, to prevent a skin forming. When cool, stir in eau de vie de framboise.

Strain cooled cream into partly cooked pastry case and bake for 20 minutes at 175°C (350°F). Remove from oven and cover with raspberries. Sieve over icing sugar and serve either at once or at room temperature.

Average times Preparation — 25 minutes
Resting — 2 × 30 minutes
Cooking — 45 minutes
Cooling — 30 minutes

Do ahead Pastry case up to filling stage, up to 1 day. Raspberry cream up to ½ day

Wine notes Raspberry tart calls for a rich, sweet white —
A: St Leonards (Rutherglen) Late Harvest Semillon
E: Château Lafaurie-Peyraguey (Sauternes) of a good year
U: Phelps (Napa) Late Harvest Johannisberg Riesling

SUMMER

MENU 15

A beautifully colourful and contrasting menu with excellent flavours and textures, it is perfect for lunch or dinner. It does, however, require last-minute attention for the first and second courses.

PRAWNS CARLINA

100 ml peanut oil
3 eggs
pinch salt
3 tablespoons water
1 kg green king prawns, shelled and deveined
½ cup plain flour

2 tablespoons capers, drained
4 dill gherkins, finely sliced
2 medium ripe tomatoes, peeled, seeded and
  chopped finely
80 g butter, melted

Heat the oil in a large frying pan or wok. Beat eggs with salt and water. Flour prawns lightly shaking off any excess flour. Dip them in egg mixture.

Sauté the prawns in two batches in the oil until golden and crisp and drain on crumpled paper towels. Place them in a warm serving dish. Sprinkle over capers and dill gherkins. Spoon tomatoes over the top and pour over melted butter. Warm through in 150°C (300°F) oven and serve at once accompanied with a rice pilaf cooked in fish or chicken stock, see page 17.

Average times Preparation — 35 minutes
Cooking — 8 minutes

Wine notes Prawns Carlina need a crisp,
  fruity white —
  A: Bowen Estate (Coonawarra)
    Rhine Riesling
  E: Maximin Grünhäuser-
    Herrenberg from the Ruwer
  U: Martini (Napa) Johannisberg
    Riesling

RATATOUILLE NIÇOISE

3 tablespoons olive oil
2 medium white onions, cut in 1 cm slices
2 cloves garlic, chopped finely
1 large green pepper, cored, seeded and sliced
  in 1 cm slices
1 medium egg-plant, halved and cut in 1 cm
  slices
3 medium zucchini, peeled in 1 cm strips (to
  give them a striped effect), cut in 2 cm slices

3 medium tomatoes, cored, skinned and each
  cut into eighths
salt and freshly ground black pepper to taste
1 sprig of fresh thyme
1 fresh bay leaf

Heat oil in a large heavy frying pan and stir fry onions with garlic until golden. Add peppers and egg-plant and stir fry until golden. Add zucchini and stir fry until golden. Add tomatoes and stir. Season to taste.

Spoon mixture into a buttered gratiné dish, top with thyme and bay leaf and cook covered with foil for 30 minutes in 200°C (400°F) oven. Serve hot or cold.

Average times Preparation — 25 minutes
Cooking — 45 minutes

Do ahead If serving cold, up to 1 day

LAMB STEAKS WITH GARLIC AND THYME
Begin 1 day in advance

◆

6 lamb steaks, cut from the top of the leg,
1.5 cm thick

Marinade:

3 cloves garlic, bruised

3 teaspoons fresh thyme leaves
½ cup olive oil
salt and freshly ground black pepper to taste

◆

Remove the small, round bone from the centre of each lamb steak. Crush the garlic with the flat, heavy end of a big knife and peel off the skin. Cut into small pieces and put into a large flat china or glass dish. Lay steaks over the garlic, sprinkle over thyme and pour over olive oil. Cover and leave for 24 hours in a cool place, turning once.

Heat a griller or barbecue until very hot. Lift lamb steaks from marinade and seal them quickly on both sides. Then salt them and grind some black pepper over each steak and leave to cook to individual taste. If they are not to dry out, it is best to cook them so they are still a little pink inside, about 5 minutes on the first side and 3 on the second side, and paint with marinade, during cooking.

Serve steaks with Ratatouille Niçoise (see previous recipe).

Average times Preparation — 5 minutes
Standing — 24 hours
Cooking — 8 minutes

Do ahead Marinade at least 24 hours in advance

Wine notes Lamb steaks need a Cabernet —
A: Sandalford Cabernet
Sauvignon, from Western
Australia
E: Sassicaia (Antinori) from
Tuscany
U: Château Montelena (Napa)
Cabernet Sauvignon

PEACH BRÛLÉE

◆

6 large yellow peaches, peeled, stoned and
sliced into 1 cm thick slices
30 g preserved ginger, drained (reserve syrup
and make up to 2 tablespoons), chopped
finely
¼ teaspoon ground cinnamon

⅛ teaspoon ground allspice
½ cup flaked almonds
900 ml thickened cream beaten to soft peaks
1½ tablespoons castor sugar
1½ tablespoons brown sugar

◆

Layer peach slices in bottom of a large gratiné dish and sprinkle with ginger, ginger syrup, cinnamon, allspice and almonds. Cover completely with beaten cream and level the top using a spatula. Cover with plastic film and refrigerate for at least 3 hours.

Heat the griller. Mix the two sugars and sieve an even layer over the top keeping it as even as possible. Place under griller to caramelize, watching it carefully so that it doesn't burn. Turn the dish to ensure even cooking. As soon as the top has caramelized to an even golden brown remove and cool. Return to refrigerator for 30 minutes before serving.

Average times Preparation — 20 minutes
Standing — 3 hours
Cooking — 3 minutes
Cooling — 30 minutes

Do ahead At least ½ day

Wine notes With the peaches, a luscious,
sweet white —
A: Lindemans Reserve Porphyry
E: Château Rieussec (Sauternes)
U: Jekel (Monterey) Late Har-
vest Johannisberg Riesling

MENU 16

———◆———

Perfect for lunch, dinner or supper, this is a menu which requires quite a lot of last minute preparation.

GREEN TAGLIATELLE WITH PROSCIUTTO

———◆———

Mornay Sauce:

20 g butter
1 tablespoon plain flour
½ cup milk
½ cup cream
salt and white pepper to taste
1 tablespoon finely grated Parmesan cheese

Prosciutto Sauce:

50 g butter
150 g prosciutto cut into julienne
150 g leg ham cut in julienne
1 cup thin cream
1 cup mornay sauce
½ cup thickened sour cream, full fat

Pasta:

500 g spinach tagliatelle, see page 134
1 tablespoon salt
1 tablespoon cooking oil
½ cup finely grated Parmesan cheese, extra

———◆———

To make mornay sauce: in small pan melt butter and cook flour in it over medium heat, whisking constantly for 2 minutes. Pour in milk, cream and seasonings, and whisk until sauce thickens. Turn down heat and cook very slowly for 10 minutes, whisking from time to time. Whisk in Parmesan cheese, taste and adjust seasonings if necessary and set aside.

To make prosciutto sauce: heat butter in small frying pan and cook prosciutto and ham for 1 minute, stirring over medium heat. Add cream and mornay sauce and whisk until boiling. Whisk in sour cream and leave to simmer gently over low heat for 5 minutes.

To cook pasta: bring 2 litres of water to the boil, add salt and cooking oil. When it returns to a rapid rolling boil drop in all the pasta. Stir gently to ensure all strands are submerged and leave to boil until pasta is *al dente*. Strain with a pasta catcher or sieve and pour the pasta into a warm serving bowl. Spoon one-quarter of sauce over pasta and toss very thoroughly. Spoon remaining sauce over the top and scatter with extra Parmesan cheese. Serve at once.

Average times Preparation — 15 minutes
Cooking — 35 minutes

Wine notes Tagliatelle needs a crisp,
flavoursome white —
A: Mitchelton Marsanne from
central Victoria
E and U: Orvieto ('Il Castelliere'
— Poggibonsi)

Do ahead Mornay sauce up to 1 day

WHITING DUGLÈRE

6 ripe medium tomatoes, skinned, seeded and
    chopped roughly
3 shallots, finely chopped
6 fat whiting each weighing approximately
    250 g, filleted and skinned
⅔ cup dry white wine
1½ cups fish stock

salt and pepper to taste
60 g butter, softened
2 tablespoons plain flour

1 tablespoon freshly chopped tarragon to
    garnish
6 lemon halves to accompany

Butter a ceramic gratiné dish large enough to hold the fish fillets, folded in two, in a single layer.
Put tomatoes and shallots in the dish and arrange the fillets folded in two on top. Pour over wine,
fish stock and season. Cover and cook in 180°C (350°F) oven until fish is tender. Do not overcook
them. (The last part of the fillets to cook will be the fold. Insert a fine skewer into the folds and
if tender then remove the fish from the oven.)

Lift fish carefully off vegetables and set aside on a warm serving platter. Scrape vegetables and
juices into a medium pan and reduce over medium heat until half original volume. Mix together
softened butter and flour to make a beurre manie and whisk into reduced sauce until it thickens.
Continue to whisk for approximately 5 minutes. Taste and adjust seasoning and sieve sauce. Pour
sauce around fish and garnish with tarragon.

Serve with lemon halves and boiled new potatoes.

Average times Preparation — 20 minutes
    Cooking — 30 minutes

Wine notes With the whiting, continue with
    the white from the first course

FRESH PEACHES WITH PEACH SAUCE

Peach Sauce (Make 24 hours in advance):
6 yellow peaches, stoned, skinned and
    chopped coarsely
castor sugar to taste

cream sherry to taste
red food colouring

6 white peaches, skinned and sliced

To make sauce: purée peaches in food processor or blender with sugar and sherry to taste until
smooth. Add approximately 2 drops of red food colouring to give the sauce a 'blush'. Pour into
an airtight container and refrigerate.

At the last minute, arrange white peach slices onto 6 dessert plates and spoon over sauce. Pass
any remaining sauce in a sauceboat at the table.

Average times Preparation — 25 minutes

Wine notes Fresh Peaches with Peach Sauce
    need a rich, long-finishing sweet
    white —
    A: The Rothbury Estate Len
      Evans Dessert Blend
    E: Château Climens (Barsac) of
      a great year
    U: Jekel (Monterey) Late Har-
      vest Johannisberg Riesling

Do ahead Sauce, 1 day

SUMMER

MENU 17

———◆———

A delightful Summer luncheon menu for serving outdoors. If serving the main course cold, then it's all do-ahead.

CUCUMBER AND CREAM CHEESE MOUSSE

———◆———

400 g green cucumber
250 g cream cheese, softened or cottage cheese
½ cup mayonnaise
1¼ teaspoons gelatine
½ cup cold water

½ teaspoon salt
2 teaspoons castor sugar
½ cup thickened cream, lightly whipped

watercress to garnish

———◆———

Peel cucumber, cut in halves lengthwise and remove the seeds with a teaspoon. Chop it finely. Blend cheese until smooth or sieve it. Add mayonnaise and mix well.

Dissolve gelatine in cold water over low heat and stir in salt and sugar. Cool mixture until it reaches blood temperature. Immediately stir gelatine into cheese, fold in cucumber and cream. Mix thoroughly. Pour into individual glass bowls, cover and refrigerate until set. Garnish with baby sprigs of watercress.

Average times Preparation — 15 minutes
Cooking — 10 minutes
Setting — 2 hours

Wine notes The mousse needs a chilled fino sherry to cut through the cream cheese —
A: Burings Flor Fino Sherry Reserve Bin S114
E and U: Ynocente Sherry (Valdespino)

Do ahead Up to ½ day

COULIBIAC OF SMOKED SALMON

Pastry:

4 cups plain flour
2 teaspoons salt
300 g chilled butter, cut into 10 pieces
6 egg yolks
4 tablespoons olive oil
about ½ cup iced water, approximately

Filling:

400 g smoked salmon in one piece and skinned
1 cup finely chopped white onion
1 large clove garlic, finely chopped
¼ cup finely chopped fresh dill or fresh parsley
2 hard-boiled eggs, coarsely chopped
1 cup sour cream, full fat
¼ cup butter, melted
salt and freshly ground black pepper to taste

Glaze:

1 egg yolk
1 tablespoon cream

Sauce:

1 cup butter, melted
lemon juice to taste

8 sprigs fresh dill or parsley to garnish

To make pastry: place flour and salt in the bowl of food processor with butter. Process with quick on-off turns until mixture resembles oatmeal. In a small bowl, beat egg yolks and oil together with a fork. Turn on the machine, pour in all the yolk mixture at once and as much water as is necessary to bring dough to a single mass. Do not overwork dough. Place on a lightly-floured board and knead with lightly-floured hands until dough is chamois-like. Cover and refrigerate for a minimum of 30 minutes.

Cut two-thirds of pastry and roll it into a large oval or circle. Lift it on rolling pin and place on a lightly buttered baking sheet. Rest in refrigerator for 30 minutes. Meanwhile, roll remaining third to form a lid and rest in refrigerator on a tray or large plate.

To make filling: chop salmon coarsely and place in a large bowl with all the other filling ingredients using cream and butter to bind. Taste and adjust seasoning if necessary. Spoon into centre of the prepared pastry base.

To cook coulibiac: beat the glaze ingredients together with a fork. Tuck the pastry edges over the filling. Glaze top of pastry and stick down, gently pinching the pastry together with fingertips. Paint all over with glaze and slash 3–4 good slits in the lid to let out steam. Flowers and leaves can be cut from any remaining rolled pastry and stuck on with glaze. Glaze pastry flowers and leaves.

Cook in 190°C (375°F) oven for approximately 45 minutes or until hot right through and golden on top. Heat the butter and lemon juice together. Serve with the coulibiac.

Follow the coulibiac with a mixed green salad.

Average times Preparation — 35 minutes
Cooking — 45 minutes
Resting — 2 × 30 minutes

Wine notes Smoked salmon coulibiac is a grand dish calling for something out of the ordinary —
A: Yellowglen Brut Rosé Champagne
E: Bollinger Vintage Rosé Champagne
U: Schramsberg (Napa) Cuvée de Pinot

Do ahead Pastry before rolling, up to 1 day.
Up to cooking stage, 2 hours. If serving cold, up to 1 day

FIG AND ALMOND TORTE

4 egg whites
1 cup soft brown sugar
1 cup dried figs (not dessert figs), chopped
1 cup almonds in skins

vanilla essence to taste

Garnish:

1 cup cream, whipped to soft peaks
3 glacé figs, cut in halves

Beat egg whites to stiff peaks. Gradually beat in brown sugar, 2 tablespoons at a time, and beat to a stiff but glossy meringue mixture. Fold in figs, almonds and vanilla. Spoon into a well buttered 23 cm spring form pan and bake in centre of 170°C (350°F) oven for 35 to 40 minutes. Cool in pan for 20 minutes before turning out onto a wire rack.

When cool, thickly spread the whipped cream over the top and arrange the fig halves around outside edge.

Average times Preparation — 25 minutes
Cooking — 35 minutes
Cooling — 1 hour

Wine notes Fig and Almond Torte calls for
a luscious sweet white —
A: St Leonards (Rutherglen)
Late Harvest Semillon
E: Château Suduiraut
(Sauternes) of a good year
U: Château St Jean (Sonoma)
Late Harvest Johannisberg
Riesling

Do ahead Up to garnishing, 1 day

SUMMER

MENU 18

A light dinner menu which requires quite a lot of last-minute attention for the first and second courses.

CHICKEN QUENELLES WITH FRESH TOMATO SAUCE

Fresh Tomato Sauce:

60 g butter
1 onion, finely chopped
1 clove garlic, peeled and chopped
1 kg ripe tomatoes, skinned, seeded and chopped roughly
½ cup water
1 teaspoon finely chopped fresh marjoram
1 teaspoon finely chopped fresh oregano
salt and pepper to taste

Quenelles:

500 g boneless chicken breasts, skinned and chilled
½ very small onion, roughly chopped
2 egg whites, chilled
salt and white pepper to taste
300 ml thick cream, chilled
1 litre chicken stock

6 sprigs fresh oregano to garnish

To make tomato sauce: heat butter in saucepan, stir in onion and garlic and sauté 2 to 3 minutes. Add remaining ingredients and simmer uncovered for 15 minutes. Purée tomato sauce through mouli into another pan.

To make quenelles: cut chicken breasts in large pieces. Put chicken, onion, egg whites, salt and pepper into food processor or blender. Blend until smooth. With machine still running, gradually pour in cream. Cover and refrigerate for 30 minutes.

Bring stock to a simmer. Dip 2 dessertspoons into cold water and form oval shaped quenelles from chicken mixture; using the second spoon to help with the shaping. Drop chicken quenelles into large saucepan of simmering chicken stock. Simmer gently, uncovered 10 minutes. Drain with a slotted spoon. (Use the stock for soup.)

To serve: reheat sauce and spoon onto 6 heated entrée plates. Arrange 2 quenelles in the sauce on each plate and serve at once, garnished with sprigs of fresh oregano.

Average times *Quenelles —*
Preparation — 20 minutes
Chilling — 30 minutes
Cooking — 10 minutes
Sauce —
Preparation — 10 minutes
Cooking — 15 minutes

Wine notes Chicken quenelles need a full-flavoured, dry white —
A: Rosemount Wood Matured Show Semillon
E: Puligny-Montrachet les Combettes of a good year
U: Stag's Leap (Napa) Chardonnay

Do ahead Quenelle mixture up to chilling stage, ½ day. Sauce, 1 day

JOHN DORY AND MANGO

◆

¾ cup sugar
2 tablespoons white wine vinegar
6 cups beef stock, made up of 4 cups of canned
  beef consommé and 2 cups water
2 cups mandarin or tangerine juice, strained
½ cup cointreau
salt and pepper to taste

juice of 4 limes
6 medium John Dory, filleted and skinned
1 cup plain flour
¼ cup peanut oil

Garnish:

6 cooked prawns, shelled and deveined
2 large ripe mangoes, sliced

◆

Heat sugar in a large, heavy-based pan over medium heat, until it caramelizes (watching that it does not burn). Pour in vinegar (keeping your hands away, for it hisses furiously), and stir with a whisk until it is well incorporated. Add beef stock, mandarin or tangerine juice, cointreau and seasonings, and cook uncovered over medium heat for approximately 20 minutes. The quantity should reduce by half and be of a light coating consistency. Add lime juice and adjust the seasoning.

Dip fish fillets in flour and shake off excess. Heat oil in a large frying pan and cook a few fish fillets at a time, lightly, until just done. Drain on crumpled kitchen paper. Keep warm on a serving platter until all the fish are cooked. Spoon over prepared sauce, garnish with prawns and mango slices and serve.

Serve fish with a green vegetable in season.

Average times Preparation — 15 minutes
Cooking — 35 minutes

Do ahead Sauce, up to ½ day

Wine notes John Dory needs a rich, yet crisp
white —
A: Lake's Folly (Pokolbin)
  Chardonnay
E: Continue with the Puligny-
  Montrachet
U: Continue with the Stag's
  Leap Chardonnay

ICED STRAWBERRY SOUFFLÉ

◆

4 boxes strawberries, cleaned, hulled and
  picked over
1¼ cups castor sugar

1½ cups cream, whipped

½ cup extra whipped cream to garnish

◆

Reserve the 6 best strawberries and lightly purée the rest in a blender or food processor. Stir in sugar until it dissolves. Fold in whipped cream.

Make a double collar of foil standing 3 cm above the tops of 6 × ¾ cup soufflé dishes, and tie securely with string. Pour in strawberry mixture. Freeze until firm, unmould and remove foil. Decorate with extra whipped cream and remaining strawberries. Serve with Ricciarelli, see page 43.

Average times Preparation — 15 minutes
Freezing — 4 hours or over-
  night

Do ahead Up to 2 days

Wine notes Iced Strawberry Soufflé calls for
a sweet white —
A: Kaiser Stuhl Purple Ribbon
  Auslese Rhine Riesling
E: Monbazillac of a good year
U: Phelps Late Harvest
  Johannisberg Riesling

SUMMER

MENU 19

A colourful and light menu which evokes all the right moods of Summer. It's perfect for lunch, dinner or supper, with only the fish needing to be cooked at the last minute. At the end of Summer, when the salmon trout are running, substitute salmon trout for rainbow trout, if you are lucky enough to find them.

ICED CUCUMBER AND SPINACH SOUP

60 g shallots, finely chopped
2 tablespoons butter
2 large green cucumbers, peeled, seeded and chopped coarsely
3 cups chicken or veal stock
200 g spinach leaves, washed very thoroughly and chopped roughly

1 medium potato, peeled and sliced
salt and pepper to taste
lemon juice to taste
¾ cup cream

thin slices of red radishes and spring onions to garnish

In a large pan, sauté shallots in butter until softened. Add cucumbers, stock, spinach, potato, salt, pepper and lemon juice to taste. Simmer mixture for 25 minutes. Cool over iced water.

Purée soup in batches. Stir in cream, taste and adjust seasoning. Chill until ready to serve. Serve in chilled bowls and garnish with radish and spring onions.

Average times Preparation — 25 minutes
Cooking — 30 minutes
Chilling — ½ day

Wine notes The soup needs a chilled, medium sherry —
A: Lindemans Reserve Bin Z898A Amontillado
E and U: Dry Sack Sherry

Do ahead At least 1 day and up to 2 days

RAINBOW TROUT WITH WHIPPED CREAM SORREL SAUCE

◆

Sorrel Sauce:
3 egg yolks
180 g butter
3 tablespoons lemon juice
white pepper to taste
⅓ cup cream beaten to soft peaks

½ cup finely sliced fresh sorrel, tightly packed

6 fresh rainbow trout
salt and pepper to taste
60 g butter

◆

To make Sorrel Sauce: place egg yolks in a blender and run at high speed for 2 minutes. Meanwhile, heat butter in a small pan until boiling. Quickly spoon off foam and discard. While butter is still very hot spoon quickly into egg yolks with the machine running at top speed. (The hot butter will cook yolks and thicken sauce at the same time.) With the machine still running add lemon juice and pepper to taste. Set aside to cool. When sauce is cold, fold in beaten cream and sorrel. *To cook fish:* season the insides liberally. Butter a large heavy-based baking dish liberally and lie the fish on it. Cook in the centre of 200°C (400°F) oven for 8 to 12 minutes, depending on size of fish, or until they are tender. Serve fish at once on warmed dinner plates and spoon a thick ribbon of sauce across each. Pass remaining sauce in a bowl with a ladle at the table.

Serve with boiled and peeled potatoes.

Average times	Preparation — 15 minutes	**Wine notes**	Rainbow trout calls for a fruity
	Cooking — 12 minutes		white with sufficient acidity to
	Cooling — 30 minutes		match the acidity of the sorrel in
			the sauce —
			A: Tyrrell's (Pokolbin)
			Chardonnay Vat 47
			E: Chablis Grand Cru les Clos
			(Regnard)
			U: Carneros Creek (Napa)
Do ahead	Sauce, up to ½ day		Chardonnay

FRUITS IN WINE AND HONEY

◆

Syrup:
rind of ½ orange
rind of ½ lemon
rind of ½ grapefruit
2 cups white wine
2 tablespoons clear honey

Fruits:
1 box strawberries, hulled
1 cup cherries, pitted, or blueberries
½ ripe rock melon or cantaloup, seeded and
    balled
6 apricots, halved and pitted
2 bananas, cut in 2 cm pieces on cross
2 kiwi fruit, peeled and quartered lengthwise

◆

Pare rind from orange, grapefruit and lemon using vegetable peeler, taking care to remove only rind and no white pith. Place a few strips of rind together and using a sharp cook's knife cut rinds into thin matchsticks. In a small saucepan combine the wine and honey, add rind and cook for 20 minutes or until rinds are translucent. Taste and add more honey if needed. Leave to cool.

Put fruits in a large glass bowl, cover and chill. Pour chilled syrup over fruits 1 hour before serving and stir.

Average times	Preparation — 35 minutes	**Wine notes**	Fruits require an aromatic,
	Cooking — 20 minutes		sweet white —
	Cooling — 30 minutes		A: Orlando Spaetlese
	Chilling — 2 hours		Frontignac
Do ahead	Up to ½ day. Syrup up to 3 weeks		E: Muscat de Beaumes de
	if stored in airtight containers and		Venise (Jaboulet)
	refrigerated		U: Fetzer (Mendocino) Muscat Canelli

90

SUMMER

MENU 20

A grand dinner-party menu with a main course which is equally good hot or cold. The first course should be finished at the table, but is mostly do-ahead. The last course, however, requires a certain amount of dexterity and should be finished as close to serving time as possible. In very humid days the toffee will break down very quickly.

SHRIMP SALAD WITH TARRAGON AND CHIVES

2 teaspoons freshly chopped tarragon
1 teaspoon salt
1 teaspoon dry mustard
2 tablespoons freshly chopped parsley
2 tablespoons freshly snipped chives
1 egg
juice of 1 lemon
½ cup salad oil
¾ cup light sour cream

1 cup fresh or canned shrimps, drained
12 spinach leaves, washed, drained and torn into bite size pieces
12 red mignonette lettuce leaves, washed, drained and torn into bite size pieces
12 lettuce leaves, washed, drained and torn into bite size pieces
freshly ground black pepper

Place the first 7 ingredients in a large glass salad bowl. Whisk in salad oil until well blended, then whisk in sour cream. Fold in shrimps.

Toss in all the salad greens and toss well at table. Finish with a few twists of the pepper mill.

Average times Preparation — 10 minutes

Do ahead Prepare all salad ingredients up to tossing stage 2 hours ahead. Cover and refrigerate until needed.

Wine notes The salad needs a full-flavoured white —
A: Allandale Chardonnay from Pokolbin
E: Chassagne-Montrachet les Caillerets (Delagrange-Bachelet)
U: Mount Eden (Santa Clara) Chardonnay

TURKEY BREAST STUFFED WITH HERB BUTTER WITH A FRESH CHERRY SAUCE

◆

Herb Butter:

125 g butter
salt and pepper to taste
1 teaspoon chopped fresh rosemary leaves
1 teaspoon chopped fresh thyme
1 teaspoon chopped fresh sage
1 tablespoon chopped fresh parsley

½ boned turkey breast with skin attached
salt and freshly ground black pepper to taste

Fresh Cherry Sauce:

3 tablespoons black sugar
2 tablespoon malt vinegar
2 cups poultry stock
2 tablespoons coarsely grated orange rind
2 tablespoons coarsely grated lemon rind
2 tablespoons orange juice
2 tablespoons brandy
375 g fresh cherries, whole or pitted
2 tablespoons potato flour
3 tablespoons orange juice, extra

◆

To make herb butter: mix all ingredients together in a food processor. On a piece of plastic wrap form mixture into a roll, cover with plastic wrap and place in freezer until firm.

To prepare turkey: remove skin carefully from turkey breast and set aside. Using a very sharp knife, cut turkey breast from one end almost through to the other end and open into a butterfly. When herb butter is quite cold, cut into thin slices and place two-thirds of it over turkey breast. Leave the remaining butter out to soften. Roll turkey breast firmly and secure with large and small skewers to hold roll in place. Cover roll with turkey skin taking special care to cover broken pieces of turkey. Tie roll at 4 cm intervals using butcher's twine. Then tie twice around length of ro'l tucking in ends. Remove skewers and spread remaining herb butter over the outside.

Wrap firmly in foil and cook at 200°C (400°F) for 50 minutes. If serving hot, rest in foil for 10 minutes before carving. If serving cold, cool in foil then remove it and wrap turkey breast in plastic wrap and refrigerate, preferably overnight.

To make Cherry Sauce: put the first 7 ingredients in a medium saucepan and bring to boil, stirring. Add cherries and cook 1 minute. Stir potato flour into remaining orange juice and stir into sauce. Cook over low heat stirring constantly with a wooden spatula for 2 to 3 minutes or until sauce is thick. This sauce can be served hot or cold.

Average times *Turkey Breast —*
Preparation — 15 minutes
Freezing — 30 minutes
Cooking — 50 minutes
Standing — 10 minutes
Cherry Sauce —
Preparation — 10 minutes
Cooking — 10 minutes

Wine notes Turkey breast requires a medium-bodied, fruity red, still or sparkling —
A: Seppelt Great Western Sparkling Burgundy
E: Volnay-Santenots of a good year
U: Acacia (Napa) Pinot Noir

Do ahead *Turkey —*
Up to oven stage, 1 day ahead. If serving cold, cook up to 2 days ahead
Cherry Sauce —
If serving cold, up to 2 days ahead. Thin with extra orange juice if necessary

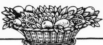

Rainbow Trout with Whipped Cream Sorrel Sauce

Wine:
Tyrrell's (Pokolbin) Chardonnay Vat 47

Turkey Breast Stuffed with Herb Butter

Wine:
Seppelt Great Western Sparkling Burgundy

SNOW EGGS

◆

Snow Eggs:
6 egg whites
pinch salt
⅓ cup castor sugar

Crème Anglaise:
13 sugar lumps
2 oranges with good skins
1½ cups milk
6 egg yolks

Toffee:
½ cup castor sugar
3 tablespoon water
pinch cream of tartar

Garnish:
¼ cup chopped, mixed glacé fruits
¼ cup sultanas
¼ cup rum
¼ cup toasted slivered almonds

◆

Fill a large baking dish about 10 cm deep three-quarters with water and add 1 tablespoon of salt. Bring to just below simmering point so that there are air bubbles on the bottom of the pan.

To make Snow Eggs: beat egg whites with salt until they hold soft peaks. Beat in sugar, 2 tablespoons at a time. Beat until very stiff. Form egg shapes by dipping a slotted spoon into mixture and rounding over the top surface with a ladle. Release eggs from the ladle into hot water bath. (The water coming up through the perforations in the spoon will ensure that the Snow Eggs slip off easily.) Poach eggs for 25 minutes then flip over on the backs of 2 spoons and poach for a further 25 minutes on the other side. Lift eggs out one at a time with a skimmer and drain on a tray lined with a clean tea-towel.

To make Crème Anglaise: rub sugar lumps over orange skins, gathering as much flavour as possible. Bring milk and sugar lumps slowly to the boil. Whisk egg yolks and pour the boiling milk slowly into egg yolks, whisking constantly. Return mixture to pan and cook over low heat whisking until mixture thickens enough to coat back of wooden spoon. Place a circle of greaseproof paper directly on top of cream and leave to cool.

To prepare garnish: place fruits in a small bowl and pour over rum. Mix and leave until ready to use.

To assemble Snow Eggs: pour cooled custard into a deep comport, and arrange Snow Eggs over it in a pyramid. Scatter over slivered almonds and spoon macerated fruits over Eggs.

To cook toffee: combine ingredients together in a small pan and cook over medium heat whisking constantly until sugar dissolves. Leave to cook until the toffee reaches a light caramel colour. Immediately remove from heat and stand until bubbling subsides. Drizzle toffee over Snow Eggs and leave to set a couple of minutes.

Average times Preparation — 30 minutes
Cooking — 1 hour 10 minutes
Cooling — 30 minutes

Wine notes Snow Eggs need a rich, sweet white —
A: Lindemans Reserve Porphyry
E: Château de Malle (Sauternes) of a great year
U: Bargetto (Santa Cruz) Late Harvest Johannisberg Riesling

Do ahead Cook Snow Eggs up to 2 hours before assembling
Crème Anglaise, up to 1 day.
Macerate fruits for up to 12 hours

SUMMER

MENU 21

◆

A perfect light Summer luncheon menu, which requires last-minute cooking for the first and second courses.

EGGS FLORENTINE

◆

1 bunch English spinach, leaves stripped off
    stems
45 g butter
salt and freshly ground black pepper
freshly grated nutmeg

6 eggs
6 tablespoons thick cream
90 g Kraft Swiss cheese, grated finely

◆

Wash spinach in several changes of water until grit free. Drain thoroughly squeezing out excess water.

Heat butter in a heavy-based frying pan and sauté spinach over high heat, stirring constantly for 2 minutes. Season with salt, pepper and nutmeg to taste. Drain off any remaining juices.

Spoon mixture into 6 well buttered egg cocottes (or custard cups or individual soufflé dishes). Break eggs on top, spoon over cream and scatter over cheese. Cook in 200°C (400°F) oven for 5 to 6 minutes or until the whites are set. Brown tops under a hot griller and serve at once.

Note: If using individual soufflé dishes, you will need 2 eggs for each dish and a little extra cooking time.

Average times Preparation — 15 minutes
                Cooking — 6 minutes

Wine notes Eggs Florentine call for a chilled
              fino sherry —
              A: Buring Flor Fino Sherry Re-
                serve Bin S114
              E and U: La Ina Sherry
                (Domecq)

Do ahead Wash spinach, drain thoroughly and keep airtight and refrigerate until ready to cook

STUFFED TROUT WITH JULIENNE VEGETABLES AND LIME BEURRE BLANC

◆

6 fresh trout, each weighing about 225 g,
    cleaned through the gills
45 g butter
2 small onions, cut into fine julienne
1 carrot, cut into fine julienne
1 parsnip or turnip, cut into fine julienne
1 large stick celery, cut into fine julienne
⅓ cup finely chopped parsley

salt and pepper to taste
1½ tablespoons lemon juice

Lime Beurre Blanc (to make 1 cup):

3 tablespoons lime juice
3 tablespoons dry white wine
2 shallots, very finely diced
250 g unsalted butter, creamed in food
    processor
salt and white pepper

◆

To prepare trout: sit them up on a work bench on their stomachs and with a very sharp knife cut from the back of the head down to the last little fin on the back, just before the tail. Using short, sharp strokes, gently cut away the flesh from backbone. (Fingers can be used to pry the flesh away and work just as well after making the initial cut.) When backbone is exposed, use a pair of scissors to snip backbone through right behind the head and again at the base of the tail. Carefully ease backbone out of fish, taking all the rib cage bones as well, and discard.

In a heavy-based frying pan, heat butter and sauté onion for 1 minute. Add carrot and parsnip or turnip and sauté a further minute. Add celery and cook, stirring, over medium heat until vegetables are *al dente* and still a little crunchy. Stir in parsley and season to taste. Remove from heat.

Generously butter a baking dish which will hold the fish sitting upright and comfortably together without crowding them. Spoon vegetable mixture into pockets in each fish and stand in prepared baking dish. Pour lemon juice over fish and bake at 200°C (400°F) for 10 to 15 minutes, depending on size of fish. Serve at once with Lime Beurre Blanc.

To make Lime Beurre Blanc: boil juice or vinegar, wine and shallots in a small pan (not aluminium) till reduced to 1 tablespoon. Cool till base of pan is just hot to touch. Set over pan of hot (not simmering) water and whisk in butter, a little at a time. Season to taste and serve as soon as possible.

Average times *Fish* —
    Preparation — 40 minutes
    Cooking — 10 to 15 minutes
    Beurre Blanc —
    Preparation — 3 minutes
    Cooking — 12 minutes

Wine notes The trout calls for a
    flavoursome, aromatic white —
    A: Rouge Homme
        (Coonawarra) Rhine Riesling
    E: Piesporter Goldtropfchen
        Kabinett (Mosel) of a good
        year
    U: Beringer (Napa)
        Johannisberg Riesling

Do ahead Prepare fish up to oven stage up to
    ½ day ahead

COLD LEMON SOUFFLÉ

2 boxes strawberries, hulled
2 tablespoons castor sugar
¼ cup sherry
4 eggs, separated

1 cup castor sugar, extra
1 cup lemon juice
1 tablespoon gelatine, dissolved in ½ cup water

Halve strawberries lengthwise, sprinkle with castor sugar and pour over sherry. Cover and leave to macerate until ready to serve.

Beat egg yolks and extra sugar until pale and fluffy. Gradually beat in lemon juice and dissolved and cooled gelatine. Beat egg whites till they form soft peaks. Fold one-third of the whites into the yolk mixture using a rubber spatula. Fold the remaining whites into mixture and spoon into 6 individual ¾ cup soufflé dishes or a 4½ cup dish. Fill to 2 cm below the rims. Cover and refrigerate until set. Spoon strawberries on top and serve.

Average times Preparation — 15 minutes
Setting — 1½ to 2 hours

Wine notes Cold Lemon Soufflé requires no wine

Do ahead Up to ½ day, but only dress with strawberries at the time of serving

SUMMER

MENU 22

A light, two-course luncheon menu which is mostly do-ahead but requires a certain amount of dexterity for the first course.

GALANTINE OF DUCK WITH ORANGE AND PISTACHIO NUTS

---

large duck weighing 1.7 kg
350 g veal shoulder, cut into cubes
350 g chicken livers, cleaned
1 small white onion, peeled
2 cloves garlic, peeled
coarsely grated rind of 1 orange

½ cup pistachios
1 egg white
salt and freshly ground black pepper to taste

watercress or fresh herbs to garnish

Bone duck beginning at neck end. Sew up tail end after removing fat at back. Mince veal, livers, onion and garlic and mix with all the remaining ingredients. Taste and adjust seasoning if necessary.

Cook in a well buttered baking dish at 150°C (300°F) for 1½ hours. Allow to cool, cover and refrigerate. When cold, cut into 1 cm slices, garnish with watercress or fresh herbs, and serve with Four Seasons Salad.

Average times Preparation — 35 minutes
Cooking — 1½ hours
Cooling — preferably overnight

Do ahead At least 1 day and up to 2 days ahead

Wine notes The duck calls for a lightly chilled, fresh, young Pinot —
A: Prince Albert Pinot Noir from Victoria
E: Santenay Gravières (Prosper Maufoux)
U: Martini (Napa) Pinot Noir

FOUR SEASONS SALAD

---

1 witloof (Belgian endive), bitter core removed, washed and drained
12 baby cos lettuce leaves, washed and drained
12 rocket leaves (or baby curly endive leaves), washed and drained
1 medium carrot, cut into fine julienne

6 sprigs watercress, washed and drained
2 tablespoons pomegranate seeds
cracked black pepper to taste
2 tablespoons virgin olive oil
2 tablespoons hazelnut oil
1 tablespoon lemon vinegar (or lemon juice)

Arrange the three salads attractively on large entrée plates, scatter with carrot, watercress, pomegranate seeds and a little pepper. Dress with the oils and vinegar and serve with galantine of duck, and follow with chèvre or goats' cheese.

Average times Preparation — 15 minutes

Do ahead Wash and drain salads and keep refrigerated and airtight up to ½ day

STRAWBERRIES GRAND MARNIER

2 boxes strawberries	2 oranges with good skins
4 sugar cubes	Grand Marnier to taste

Pick over the strawberries, hulling them as you go and cutting out any green or white pieces which would make the result tart. Get rid of grit as far as possible, but do not wash them. Cover and chill.

Rub sugar cubes over orange skins, collecting the beautiful aromatic flavours of the oranges. Drop the zested sugar lumps into a glass bowl and squeeze the juice of the oranges over the sugar. Leave until sugar has dissolved. Add Grand Marnier to taste and 10 minutes before serving, pour over the chilled strawberries. Serve with Sweetheart Biscuits (see next recipe).

Average times Preparation — 15 minutes
Standing — 30 minutes

Do ahead Prepare strawberries up to 2 hours in advance, but only dress 10 minutes before serving

Wine notes The strawberries require no wine

SWEETHEART BISCUITS
Makes 18 to 24 approximately

1½ cups plain flour	pinch salt
½ cup custard powder	180 g unsalted butter, at room temperature
½ cup icing sugar, sifted	vanilla essence to taste

Sift the first 4 ingredients together. Rub butter in like shortbread and add essence. Roll to 5 mm thickness on a lightly floured, chilled board. Stamp out heart-shaped biscuits and bake on a lightly buttered tray at 175°C (350°F) for approximately 20 minutes, or until lightly coloured. Cool on a wire rack and store in airtight containers until needed.

Average times Preparation — 15 minutes
Cooking — 20 minutes

Do ahead 3 days

AUTUMN

AUTUMN

MENU 1

A quick, easy and delicious family menu, suitable for lunch or dinner; it's also inexpensive.

VEGETABLE SOUP

---

2 tablespoons butter
4 tablespoons olive oil
1 medium white onion, chopped
1 cup lightly packed fresh basil leaves, finely chopped or 1 tablespoon dried
810 g can peeled tomatoes, drained and chopped
3 medium carrots, peeled and diced

3 medium zucchini, diced
3 medium potatoes, peeled and diced
4 cups beef stock
salt to taste
10 green beans, strung and cut into 2 cm pieces
12 spinach leaves, steamed

Heat butter and oil in a large heavy pan and cook onion over low heat for 15 minutes, stirring from time to time. Retain 1 tablespoon of basil and 2 tablespoons of tomatoes for garnish. Stir in the remaining basil, tomatoes and the rest of the ingredients except beans and spinach. Bring slowly to the simmer and cook, covered over medium heat for 20 minutes or until vegetables are tender. Stir in beans and cook for 5 minutes.

In a blender, purée half the soup with the spinach. Leave remaining soup unpuréed. Combine all the soup and heat through. Taste and add seasoning if necessary.

Serve piping hot, and garnish each soup bowl with reserved basil and tomato.

Average times Preparation — 25 minutes
Cooking — 45 minutes

Wine notes The soup needs a nutty sherry —
A: Seppelt Show Amontillado Sherry
E and U: Tio Diego Sherry (Valdespino)

Do ahead At least 1 day except for basil leaves for garnish

MEAT LOAF

1 kg minced topside
1 large white onion, chopped finely
1½ cups fresh breadcrumbs
3 tablespoons finely chopped fresh parsley
3 tablespoons tomato ketchup
1½ tablespoons Worcestershire sauce
1½ tablespoons French mustard
220 ml evaporated milk
2 eggs
salt and freshly ground black pepper to taste

Glaze:
1 teaspoon dry mustard
2 tablespoons brown sugar
½ cup tomato ketchup

Mix all the meat loaf ingredients together in a large bowl. Spoon into a buttered loaf pan or terrine. Cook in 180°C (350°F) oven for 25 minutes.

Whisk the glaze ingredients together and pour over the loaf. Return to oven for a further 50 to 60 minutes or until cooked through. Rest 10 minutes before serving if serving hot, and slice in pan. Alternatively if serving cold cool in pan before turning out. Cover and chill until ready to serve.

Serve with any vegetable in season.

Average times Preparation — 10 minutes
Cooking — 1¼ hours
Resting — 10 minutes

Wine Notes With the Meat Loaf —
A: Hardy's Nottage Hill Claret
E: Beaujolais Villages Domaine
de Riberolles (Jaffelin)
U: Sebastiani (Sonoma) Mountain Burgundy

Do ahead If serving cold, up to 3 days

DELICIOUS BANANA SUNDAE

6 medium bananas, just ripe
1½ tablespoons blackberry, strawberry, raspberry or boysenberry jam
vanilla ice-cream

6 tablespoons cherry brandy
150 ml cream, whipped
4 tablespoons toasted ground almonds or toasted coconut

Peel the bananas and cut into 1 cm slices on the cross. Divide equally between 6 goblets and top each with a teaspoon of jam, then a spoonful of ice-cream, then the liqueur. Top with cream and dress with almonds or coconut.

Average times Preparation — 10 minutes

Wine notes The sundae needs no wine

AUTUMN

MENU 2

━━━◆━━━

This cold menu is suitable for lunch or dinner and is all do-ahead except for the salad. The salad is a combination of superb flavours which makes it extremely popular.

ICED ORANGE TOMATO SOUP

━━━◆━━━

1 kg ripe tomatoes, skinned, seeded and chopped roughly
1 medium onion, sliced
1 medium carrot, peeled and sliced
5 cups chicken stock
1 bay leaf
2 pieces of lemon zest

6 peppercorns, tied in muslin
salt to taste
juice of 2 oranges
3 tablespoons potato flour

Julienne zest of 2 oranges to garnish

━━━◆━━━

Place the first 8 ingredients in a medium-sized pan and bring slowly to the boil. Simmer for 30 minutes with lid on. Cool slightly. Mouli or blend the soup until it is smooth and return to pan.

Mix ¼ orange juice with potato flour in a small bowl. Pour into soup and thicken over medium heat stirring with a wooden spoon. Simmer gently for 10 minutes. Cool over a sink of cold water changing water from time to time as necessary. Refrigerate until ready to serve.

Add remaining orange juice, taste and adjust the seasoning. Serve into chilled soup bowl and float orange zest on top.

Average times Preparation — 20 minutes
Cooking — 40 minutes
Cooling — 2 hours or preferably overnight

Wine notes The soup requires no wine

Do ahead Like all soups and casseroles this recipes is best made at least 24 hours in advance, except for garnish

ROMAN LOIN OF VEAL

━━━◆━━━

1.5 kg loin of veal
3 cloves garlic, skinned and cut into slivers
2 tablespoons olive oil
100 g smoked bacon, cut into 1 cm dice

salt and freshly ground black pepper to taste
1 tablespoon butter
1 tablespoon tomato paste
¾ cup dry white wine

━━━◆━━━

Pierce the loin in 8 places near the bone and insert the garlic pieces in it. In a heavy roasting pan heat olive oil and bacon and stir until bacon is browned and well rendered. Add loin and brown on all sides over high heat. Salt and pepper all over and add butter and tomato paste, blended with the dry white wine. Cover the baking pan (if you don't have a lid make a lid with foil). Roast meat at 150°C (300°F) for 1½ to 2 hours or until just cooked. Baste meat from time to time. If veal appears too dry pour in some stock or a little water.

Allow veal to cool in the cooking juices, cover and refrigerate overnight. Serve carved in 2 cm slices and accompany with Pasta, Fig and Basil Salad (see next recipe).

Average times Preparation — 10 minutes
Cooking — 2 hours
Standing — 4 hours or preferably overnight

Do ahead Prepare at least ½ day ahead or preferably overnight

Wine notes See note after accompanying salad

PASTA, FIG AND BASIL SALAD

◆

Honey Vinaigrette:

1 tablespoon pure honey (clear)
¼ teaspoon salt
freshly ground black pepper to taste
1 tablespoon red wine vinegar
4 tablespoons olive oil

2 cups cooked small pasta shells
1 cup finely chopped fresh basil leaves
12 ripe fresh figs, skin left on and quartered

◆

Whisk together the vinaigrette ingredients in a small bowl. Pour over the pasta shells in a large bowl and toss thoroughly with the basil leaves. Pile into a salad bowl and dress with the quartered figs.

Average times Preparation — 10 minutes

Wine notes Veal, with the elegant salad, needs a fruity, medium-bodied red —
A: Yalumba Signature Series Claret
E: Château Cissac (Cissac, Haut-Médoc) of a good year
U: Souverain (Sonoma) Cabernet Sauvignon

Do ahead Up to 1 hour

DOLCE TORINESE
Serves 10 to 12

◆

250 g dark chocolate, broken into squares
½ cup Amaretto di Saronno
125 g unsalted butter, softened
2 tablespoons castor sugar
2 eggs, separated
¾ cup finely chopped blanched almonds

pinch salt
8 Savoiadi or lady's finger biscuits cut into 1 cm × ½ cm pieces

icing sugar to dust

◆

Lightly oil a 5-cup loaf pan and place a triple layer of foil folded the length of the pan plus the ends to enable you to lift it out. Oil the foil.

In a heavy-based large saucepan, melt chocolate stirring constantly over low heat. When chocolate is dissolved, stir in Amaretto and remove from heat. Cool to room temperature.

Cream butter until light and fluffly. Beat in castor sugar, then egg yolks one at a time. Stir in almonds and cooled chocolate. Beat egg whites and salt in a clean bowl until mixture forms stiff peaks. Fold one-third of the whites into chocolate mixture using a rubber spatula. Fold in remaining egg whites in the same manner. When thoroughly incorporated, fold in cut-up biscuits discarding crumbs. Spoon mixture into prepared loaf pan and smooth top with a spatula. Cover tightly with plastic wrap and refrigerate for at least 4 hours or overnight.

Unmould loaf 1 hour or so before serving, by inverting on to a chilled serving platter and pull out. Smooth top and sides with a spatula and return to refrigerator. Just before serving, dust with sifted icing sugar. Cut into thin slices.

Average times Preparation — 25 minutes
Cooking — 5 minutes
Cooling — 20 minutes
Setting — 4 hours

Wine notes With Dolce Torinese, a rich muscat —
A: Morris (Rutherglen) Liqueur Muscat
E: Moscato Passito di Pantelleria Extra (Tanit) from Sicily
U: Novitiate (Santa Clara) Black Muscat

Do ahead At least ½ a day and up to 5 days

AUTUMN

MENU 3

◆

Beginning with a warm and very rich tart which has to be prepared at the last minute, this is a menu for lunch or dinner on a cooler Autumn day. For a warm Autumn day at lunch, I would omit the tart and simply serve the salad and the frozen pudding, which, of course, must be done in advance.

MUSHROOM TART

◆

Short crust:
1 cup plain flour
pinch salt
60 g butter, chilled and cut into 6 pieces
2 tablespoons iced water (approximately)

Filling:
60 g butter
500 g white button mushrooms, quartered
1 cup thickened cream
¼ cup port
salt and fresh ground black pepper to taste
¾ cup grated Gruyère cheese
1 egg white, beaten lightly

To make pastry: mix flour and salt and rub in butter so the mixture resembles oatmeal. Mix in water and knead dough on a lightly floured board. Roll into a ball, flatten to 3 cm, wrap in plastic film and refrigerate for 30 minutes or overnight. Alternatively make in a food processor.

Roll pastry on a lightly floured board to the thickness of a 10 cent coin. Roll the pastry up on the rolling pin and unroll over a buttered 20 cm shallow pie pan. Run the rolling pin over the top to trim off excess pastry. Prick gently all over (sides too), cover and refrigerate for 30 minutes.

Line pastry with 2 layers of greaseproof paper, fill with blind baking weights and bake on pre-heated oven tray in hottest part of 200°C (400°F) oven for 15 minutes. Remove paper and weights. Return to oven until top edge is just golden.

To make filling: heat butter in a large heavy pan and sauté mushrooms over high heat reducing as much juice as possible. Stir in cream and port and cook until smooth and creamy. Season to taste.

Paint a little egg white over pastry base and pour hot filling into the shell. Sprinkle with grated cheese and cook in 200°C (400°F) oven for 10 minutes. Gratiné the top under a hot grill and serve at once.

Average times Preparation — 20 minutes
Resting — 2 × 30 minutes
Cooking — 25 minutes

Do ahead Pastry up to rolling stage 1–2 days

Wine notes Mushroom Tart is complemented by a lightly chilled, fruity red —
A: Hardy's Keppoch Pinot Noir
E: Beaujolais: Brouilly Château de la Chaize
U: Lohr (Monterey) Gamay

CHICKEN SALAD

Mayonnaise:

2 egg yolks, at room temperature
1 teaspoon salt
½ cup olive oil
½ cup peanut oil
2 tablespoons lemon juice or to taste
finely ground white pepper to taste

1.7 kg cooked chicken
300 ml mayonnaise
4–6 sticks celery, stringed and diced
1 small onion, chopped finely

125 g sultana grapes
2 red apples, cored and sliced finely
juice 1 lemon
60 g shelled walnuts
60 g shelled hazelnuts, skinned
½ cup whipped cream or sour cream
1 teaspoon freshly chopped tarragon leaves
salt and pepper to taste
cos or mignonette leaves, washed and drained

6 watercress sprigs to garnish

To make mayonnaise: using a food processor or blender, work egg yolks and salt until mixture is pale and thick. With the machine running, slowly pour in the oils, drop by drop, until a quarter of the oils are added. Add lemon juice and pour in remaining oils in a thin steady stream, ceasing if the mayonnaise looks as though it's going to curdle. As mayonnaise thickens, the oils can be added a little more quickly. Season with white pepper to taste and turn off the machine. If the mayonnaise curdles, set the curdled mixture aside, wash the blender or food processor and begin again with 2 fresh egg yolks and another teaspoon of salt. When they are thick and pale, slowly ladle curdled mixture into new base with the machine running on high.

Note: it is important that all the mayonnaise ingredients be at the same temperature, preferably room temperature.

To prepare chicken salad: skin chicken and carve in long slices and cut into strips. Mix chicken and mayonnaise with the next 6 ingredients in a large bowl. Fold in cream and tarragon and season to taste.

Arrange a bed of lettuce leaves on a serving platter and pile salad on top. Garnish with watercress.

Serve with a basket of Melba toast made from bagels and a dish of unsalted butter.

Note: If the apples are a variety which discolour quickly, slice them into a bowl of water with a little lemon juice in it. Dry the slices before adding them to the salad.

Average times Preparation — 35 minutes

Wine notes Continue with the red for the Chicken Salad

Do ahead Make the mayonnaise up to 1 week in advance and keep covered in refrigerator. If it separates slightly, whisk before using

FROZEN YOGHURT PUDDING

1½ cups plain yoghurt
⅓ cup sultanas, macerated in 2 tablespoons brandy
⅓ cup red and green glacé cherries, sliced

⅓ cup slivered almonds, toasted
⅓ cup crushed pineapple, drained
⅓ cup icing sugar, sifted
3 egg whites

Place yoghurt in a medium-size bowl and fold in the next 5 ingredients. Beat egg whites until they form soft peaks and fold into yoghurt mixture. Spoon into a 3½-cup mould, which has been rinsed with cold water. Cover and freeze until firm, preferably overnight.

To serve, dip mould into warm water and invert over a serving plate. Shake out pudding and return to freezer if the outside has begun to melt. If too hard, leave on bottom shelf of the refrigerator for ½ hour before serving.

Average times Preparation — 10 minutes
Setting — 6 hours or preferably overnight

Do ahead Preferably 1 day in advance
Wine notes Yoghurt pudding requires no wine

AUTUMN

MENU 4

This is an ideal family menu, preferably for the evening. It has contrasting colours and flavours. The fruit salad can be changed to include any green fruits in season.

RED SALMON QUICHE

Short Crust Pastry:

½ cup plain flour
pinch salt
40 g chilled butter, cut into small pieces
1¼–2 tablespoons iced water

Filling:

4 spring onions both green and white parts, cut into 1 cm slices
220 g can red sockeye salmon, drained thoroughly
2 tablespoons green pepper, finely chopped
2 tablespoons red pepper, finely chopped
150 ml thickened cream
2 eggs
salt and freshly ground black pepper to taste
2 teaspoons freshly snipped dill or 1 teaspoon dried dill leaves

---

To make pastry: mix flour and salt together and rub in butter until mixture resembles oatmeal. Mix in just enough iced water until the mixture comes together to form a ball. (This can be done either in a food processor or by hand.) Knead on a lightly floured board, flatten to 3 cm, wrap in greaseproof paper and refrigerate for a minimum of 30 minutes.

Roll dough on a lightly floured board until it is large enough to fit a 23 cm shallow quiche pan. Lightly butter quiche pan and line with dough, tucking it into the corners of pan. Trim off overhanging dough by rolling pastry pin across the top. Prick the dough all over with a fork. Return to refrigerator in a plastic bag for a minimum of 30 minutes.

To prepare filling: scatter onions in prepared pastry case. Break up salmon into large 2.5 cm pieces including skins and bones. Spoon over onions with the peppers.

Beat cream, eggs and seasonings together and pour into prepared case. Scatter over with dill and cook in hottest part of 200°C (400°F) oven for 25 minutes or until risen and golden. If serving hot, then serve at once. If serving cold leave to cool in the quiche pan before removing from pan.

Average times Preparation — 25 minutes
Standing — 2 × 30 minutes
Cooking — 25 minutes

Wine notes Salmon quiche needs an aromatic white —
A: Leeuwin Estate Rhine Riesling from Western Australia
E: Eltviller Sonnenberg Spaetlese (Rheingau) of a good year
U: Ventana (Monterey) Johannisberg Riesling

Do ahead Pastry dough, up to 2 days. Pastry up to cooking stage, ½ day

MEDITERRANEAN LAMB SHANKS

◆

45 g butter	salt and freshly ground black pepper to taste
6 lamb shanks, cut in two	90 ml cream
3 medium carrots, cut into 5 mm slices	3 egg yolks
3 medium white onions, sliced medium fine	1½ tablespoons lemon juice
¾ cup veal or chicken stock	coarsely grated rind of 1 lemon

◆

Heat butter in a large heavy pan until changing colour. Sauté shank pieces on both sides, scatter vegetables over meat and pour in stock. Season, and cook covered on low heat until tender, about 45 minutes to 1 hour depending on size of shanks.

Whisk the cream and yolks together and stir into the hot sauce with lemon juice and rind. Return to low heat to warm through but do not boil or sauce will curdle. Taste and adjust seasoning and serve accompanied by fluffly boiled rice or hot buttered noodles and a green vegetable.

Average times Preparation — 15 minutes
Cooking — 60 minutes

Wine notes Lamb shanks require a big, astringent red —
A: Taltarni Cabernet Sauvignon from central Victoria
E: Château Lanessan (Haut-Médoc)
U: Ridge (Santa Clara) Cabernet Sauvignon — Monte Bello

Do ahead Up to thickening sauce with egg yolks and cream, 1–2 days ahead

GREEN FRUIT SALAD

◆

Syrup:	2 kg mixed green fruits: Granny Smith apples, green skinned pears, honeydew melon, greengage plums, kiwi fruit, sultana grapes or seeded muscatels
2 cups water	
⅔ cup castor sugar	
½ lemon	

◆

To make the sugar syrup: whisk water and sugar together over medium heat until sugar dissolves. Squeeze lemon juice into syrup and add lemon skin. Boil until reduced slightly until a light syrup. Leave to cool.

To prepare salad: core and quarter the apples leaving the skins on and slice them finely. Drop into cooled syrup to prevent browning. Do the same with the pears but cut into fine wedges. Ball melon, or cut into chunky cubes. Cut flesh off plums and peel and slice the kiwi fruit. Pull grapes from stalks and mix all the fruits through the syrup. Cover and chill until ready to serve. Remove lemon skin from syrup before serving.

Average times Preparation — 20 minutes
Cooking — 10 minutes
Cooling — 1 hour

Wine notes The fruit salad requires no wine

Do ahead Sugar syrup up to 3 weeks. Fruit salad up to ½ day

COCONUT ICE

180 g copha
450 g pure icing sugar, sieved
225 g desiccated coconut

2 egg whites
vanilla essence, to taste
food colouring, red or green

Melt the copha but don't let it get too hot. Remove from the heat. Stir in the icing sugar and coconut. Break up the egg whites with a fork but don't beat them. Fold into the coconut mixture and work very thoroughly using your hands if necessary. Add vanilla essence and work very well tasting the mixture to ensure it has enough vanilla.

Divide the mixture in half. Press one half into a flat pan measuring approximately 13 × 15 cm and level the top. Colour the remaining mixture a pale pink or pale green, kneading the colouring in very thoroughly. Press onto the white layer of coconut ice and smooth over the top. Cover and refrigerate until firm, preferably overnight. When set, turn out and cut into 2½ cm squares. Store in an airtight container and refrigerate.

Average times Preparation — 20 minutes
Heating — 5 minutes
Setting — 4 hours or over-
night

Do ahead At least ½ day and up to 1 week

AUTUMN

MENU 5

A short menu of only two courses, with an Indonesian main course which was taught to me in the early 1960s when I was living in The Hague. It requires a lot of last minute preparation but is always very welcome. Traditionally, and sensibly, it should always be followed by a fruit salad, and tropical fruits at this time of the year are at their best.

BAMI GORENG

300 g butter
1 tablespoon peanut oil
500 g shoulder or leg pork cut in 1 or 2 thick slices
salt and pepper to taste
½ cup water
250 g bami egg noodles
250 g speck, diced (unsmoked, unsalted pork)
4 cloves garlic, chopped finely
500 g white onions, sliced medium fine
500 g leeks (white part only), washed thoroughly and sliced medium fine
½ white cabbage, cored and sliced medium fine
1 cup (loosely packed) Italian parsley leaves chopped roughly
2–4 teaspoons sambal oelek (chilli paste)
1 tablespoon sweet soy sauce
1 teaspoon sugar

Garnish:

6 eggs
salt and pepper to taste
2 tablespoons water
30 g butter
200 g ham, sliced and cut into long strips

Accompaniments: tomatoes, cucumbers, Dutch cocktail onions, dill cucumbers, extra sambal oelek, 30 prawn crackers

Heat butter and oil over high heat in a heavy-based pan and seal the pork well on both sides. Season and pour in ½ cup water, cover and cook until tender. Set aside.

Heat speck in another very large heavy frying pan or wok and render it well. Lift out speck with a slotted spoon and discard. Stir fry garlic and onions in pork fat over high heat for 3 minutes. Add the leeks and stir fry a further 3 minutes. Add the cabbage and parsley and stir fry 4 minutes. Cut meat into 1.5 cm dice and add to mixture. Stir in the sambal oelek to taste (it's very hot so only add a little at first), soy sauce, seasonings, and sugar.

To cook noodles: put noodles in a large pan of boiling water for 5 minutes or according to directions on pack. Drain and refresh in cold water. Drain and set aside.

Fold the well drained noodles through the meat mixture, reduce heat and warm through. Taste and adjust seasonings and sambal.

Beat eggs and seasonings and water. Heat butter in a frying pan, when foaming, pour in eggs and scramble over low heat, using a wooden spatula.

Spoon bami mixture into a large warmed bowl. Spoon scrambled eggs around the edge. Strew ham strips on top, and serve at once. Accompany with a cooling salad of tomatoes and cucumbers, pickles, extra sambal oelek and prawn crackers.

To cook prawn crackers: heat oil until very hot and fry 1 cracker at a time over medium heat holding it below oil with tongs, until puffed up and tripled in size. (If they brown, oil is too hot.) Drain on crumpled paper and keep airtight until needed.

Average times Preparation — 45 minutes
Cooking — 1 hour 10 minutes

Wine notes Bami Goreng, with its range of spicy flavours, does not need a wine

Do ahead All forward preparation (but no cooking) up to ½ day. Prawn crackers, up to 1 day

TROPICAL FRUIT SALAD

1 medium paw paw, seeded and skinned and cut into big chunks
1½ cups fresh lychees, peeled and stoned
2 ripe firm bananas, peeled and sliced on the cross in 2 cm pieces

1 small pineapple, skinned, cored and cut into bite-sized wedges
1 cup freshly squeezed orange juice

Put the fruits into a large glass bowl, pour over juice and toss well. Cover and chill for 2 hours.

Average times Preparation — 15 minutes
Standing — 2 hours

Wine notes Tropical Fruit Salad requires no wine

Do ahead 2 hours

AUTUMN

MENU 6

This menu is ideal for the evening but needs last minute attention for all three courses. You will need to buy the best oranges available to make the dessert worthwhile and remember that if the humidity is high the toffee will not last more than 1 hour.

MUSSELS STEAMED WITH TOMATO AND FENNEL

1.5 kg fresh mussels in the shell
6 large ripe tomatoes, peeled, seeded and diced
½ cup chopped spring onions
3 tablespoons dry white wine

3 teaspoons fennel seed
salt and freshly ground black pepper
dash tabasco sauce

fresh fennel leaves, chopped, to garnish

To clean mussels, put them in a sink of cold running water. With a coarse brush, scrub shells to remove any particles clinging to them and remove the shaggy beards.

Put tomatoes in a steaming pot with spring onions, wine, fennel seeds, salt and pepper. Cover pot and simmer over medium heat, shaking pan occasionally to prevent tomatoes from sticking. Cook for 15 minutes, or until tomatoes have given off their liquid. Add mussels and tabasco, cover and steam over high heat until the mussels open — about 5 to 6 minutes. Discard any mussels which fail to open. Serve at once in large soup plates and garnish with fennel leaves.

Average times Preparation — 25 minutes
Cooking — 20 minutes

Wine notes Mussels with their fennel flavour
need an aromatic white —
A: Yalumba Pewsey Vale Rhine
Riesling
E: Oppenheimer
Krötenbrunnen (Guntrum)
from Rheinhessen
U: Jekel (Monterey)
Johannisberg Riesling

Do ahead Preparation up to ½ day — but no
cooking

SAFFRON RABBIT WITH CUCUMBERS

3 young rabbits with livers or 3 chicken livers
4 tablespoons olive oil
2 medium white onions, chopped roughly
1 head garlic, broken up but not peeled
pinch sugar
2 tablespoons plain flour
pinch cayenne pepper
salt to taste
¾ cup saffron threads, soaked in 1 tablespoon
   warm water

½ cup white wine
2 cups veal stock
3 medium green cucumbers, 500 g approximately, skinned, seeded and sliced thickly
125 g butter
8 medium ripe tomatoes, cored, skinned, seeded and chopped coarsely

Remove forelegs from rabbits and discard. Cut through rabbit carcasses in 5 cm pieces until you reach the hind quarters. Split them between the legs down the sides of the backbones.

Heat oil in a large heavy-based casserole and sauté rabbit pieces a few at a time until brown. Stir in onions, garlic and sugar and cook until onions are softened. Stir in flour and cook for 2 minutes. Add cayenne pepper, salt, saffron and its water, the wine and stock. Cover and cook gently until rabbits are tender.

Cook cucumbers in a pan of boiling salted water until *al dente*. Drain and refresh in cold water. Drain thoroughly and pat dry on paper towels.

Heat half the butter and sauté tomatoes for 10 minutes, stirring occasionally. Heat remaining butter and sauté cucumbers until warmed through.

Lift rabbits out of casserole and arrange on a warmed serving dish. Keep warm. Strain sauce and return to casserole. Stir in tomatoes, taste and adjust seasonings. Spoon over rabbit and arrange cucumbers around the outside.

Serve with a potato dish.

Average times Preparation — 40 minutes
Cooking — 60 minutes

Wine notes Saffron rabbit calls for a medium-bodied, spicy red —
A: Miramar Shiraz, from Mudgee
E: Château de Fonsalette (Côtes du Rhône)
U: McDowell (Mendocino) Zinfandel

Do ahead Up to 2 days, except for cucumbers

TOFFEE ORANGES

6 beautiful navel oranges
6 tablespoons Grand Marnier

Toffee:

1 cup castor sugar
¾ cup water

Garnish:

Orange rind
12 Angelica leaves

Using a marmalade shredder, remove rind from 4 oranges and blanch it for 20 seconds. Drain and dry on paper towel. Skin oranges with a very sharp knife, removing all pith. Slice oranges and put back together again. Spoon 1 tablespoon of liqueur over each.

To make toffee: boil sugar and water stirring until sugar dissolves. When toffee is straw coloured, spoon over each orange forming a complete case. Quickly decorate with angelica leaves. When set hard, sprinkle over with rind. Serve as soon as possible with or without cream.

Average times Preparation — 20 minutes
Cooking — 10 minutes

Wine notes Toffee Oranges require no wine

AUTUMN

MENU 7

This menu begins with one of my family's favourite soups, made simply with the tops of celery which gives the soup a wonderful flavour and colour. It improves with age like most soups. With the soup and the pudding out of the way the only last minute attention required is cooking the trout.

CELERY TOP SOUP

45 g butter	5 cups water
2 medium onions, coarsely chopped	2 beef stock cubes
tops of 1 large bunch celery, chopped roughly	salt and pepper to taste

In a large saucepan, heat butter and sauté onion until softened. Stir in all the remaining ingredients and simmer, covered, for 45 minutes. Cool over iced water and blend until smooth or put through mouli. Reheat before serving and adjust seasoning.

Average times Preparation — 10 minutes
Cooking — 55 minutes
Cooling — 20 minutes

Wine notes Celery Top Soup needs a medium sherry —
A: Seppelt Show Reserve Amontillado
E and U: Sandeman Dry Don Amontillado

Do ahead At least 2 days and up to 4 days

TROUT IN FOIL WITH LEMON AND FENNEL

6 trout, each weighing 225 g approximately	3 tablespoons dry vermouth
salt and pepper	3 tablespoons olive oil
6 stalks fresh fennel	6 lemon slices
3 shallots, chopped finely	

Wash and dry the fish carefully. Season inside with salt and pepper and put a stalk of fennel in each. Cut a large circle of foil which will comfortably hold each fish. Lie fish on foil and sprinkle with shallots, vermouth, olive oil and a slice of lemon.

Pinch the edges of foil to completely encase fish, so you have a pasty-shaped packet. Lie foil packages in a large baking pan and bake at 230°C (460°F) for 10 to 15 minutes.

Open a package to check the fish is properly cooked. Serve in package on a plate, snipping foil slightly to make opening easier.

Serve with boiled potatoes, skinned.

Average times Preparation — 15 minutes
Cooking — 15 minutes

Wine notes The trout needs a fruity Chablis-style white —
A: Amberton Semillon from Mudgee
E: Chablis (Domaine de l'Eglantière — Jean Durup)
U: Parducci (Mendocino) Chardonnay

Do ahead Up to oven stage, ½ day

APRICOT SOUFFLÉ WITH CHOCOLATE SAUCE

6 eggs, separated
1¼ cups castor sugar
2 tablespoons gelatine
juice 1 lemon
2 cups apricot purée (stew dried apricots in just
   enough water to cover)
3 tablespoons maraschino
2 cups thickened cream, beaten to soft peaks
pinch salt
safflower or almond oil
3 glacé apricots, split in halves

Hot Chocolate Sauce:
100 g dark chocolate broken into small pieces
1½ tablespoons unsalted butter
1½ tablespoons pure icing sugar, sifted
¾ cup cream

Beat egg yolks and sugar in a medium pan over just simmering water until pale and doubled in volume. Mix gelatine with lemon juice and heat over hot water until granules dissolve. Set aside to cool. Stir the apricot purée and maraschino together and fold into yolk mixture.

Stir cooled gelatine mixture into mixture and fold in the cream.

Beat egg whites with a pinch of salt until mixture forms firm peaks. Fold one-third of egg whites into apricot mixture using a rubber spatula. Fold remaining whites into mixture using a very light hand.

Prepare a 4-cup soufflé dish with a double collar of foil which comes 5 cm above top of dish. Tie down tightly with string. Lightly oil dish and collar with safflower or almond oil. Spoon prepared mixture into dish and set in refrigerator for 4 hours or overnight.

To serve, carefully remove foil collar and garnish top of soufflé with glacé apricots. Serve with hot chocolate sauce.

To make sauce: melt chocolate with butter and icing sugar over a pan of warm water, stirring with a wooden spoon until smooth. Remove from heat and set aside. Bring water back to a simmer and remove from heat. Place chocolate mixture back over water and stir in cream until thoroughly mixed. Cool and serve with the apricot soufflé.

Average times *Soufflé —*
            Preparation — 30 minutes
            Cooking — 10 minutes
            Setting — 4 hours
            Chocolate Sauce —
            Preparation — 5 minutes
            Cooking — 10 minutes
            Cooling — 40 minutes

Wine notes Apricot Soufflé with Chocolate
            Sauce, needs a chilled muscat —
            A: d'Arenberg (McLaren Vale)
                White Muscat of Alexandria
            E: Muscat de Beaumes de
                Venise (Domaine de Durban)
            U: Concannon (Alameda)
                Muscat Blanc

Do ahead *Soufflé —*
            Up to 1 day
            Chocolate Sauce —
            Up to 3 days

AUTUMN

MENU 8

───────◆───────

This is a lovely dinner-party menu requiring no great expertise, however, the galette does take some time to prepare and cook.

OYSTER MUSHROOM SALAD

───────◆───────

100 g snow peas, topped and tailed
200 g snake beans, topped and tailed and cut into 6 cm lengths
200 g small oyster mushrooms
1 punnet small cherry tomatoes, wiped over (halved if too large)

Dressing:
2 teaspoons coarse grain mustard
½ cup fine olive oil
white wine vinegar to taste
salt and freshly ground black pepper to taste

───────◆───────

Steam snow peas and snake beans separately until *al dente*. Refresh in iced water and drain well on paper towels. Place in a large bowl with the mushrooms and tomatoes.

Whisk dressing ingredients together. Taste and pour over salad. Toss well and serve.

Average times Preparation — 15 minutes
Cooking — 10 minutes

Wine notes The Oyster Mushroom Salad is complemented by an aromatic white with fresh acidity —
A: Mitchell (Watervale) Rhine Riesling
E: Dom Avelsbacher Altenberg Kabinett (Ruwer)
U: Trefethen (Napa) Johannisberg Riesling

Do ahead Up to tossing, ½ day

NUTTY NUTTY ENTRECÔTE

◆

Hazelnut Pâté:

60 g butter, softened
½ cup skinned hazelnuts, finely ground
1 tablespoon cognac
salt and freshly ground black pepper to taste

1.5 kg piece entrecôte (porterhouse)
3 tablespoons peanut oil
salt and freshly ground black pepper to taste

6 sprigs watercress to garnish

◆

To make hazelnut pâté: beat butter until creamy and fold through the remaining ingredients. Spread into a flat dish so that the pâté is 1 cm thick. Cover with plastic film and refrigerate until hard, preferably overnight.

To cook entrecôte: heat oil in a heavy baking pan and seal entrecôte, fat side down, over medium heat. Turn over entrecôte and season sealed side liberally. Place in hottest part of 200°C (400°F) oven to cook for 20 minutes. Turn over meat and season the second side. Return to oven for a further 20 minutes. Turn again and prick with a roasting fork. Press down on the hole to see if juices still run red. If so, return to oven for a further 10 minutes for medium-rare beef.

When beef is cooked to the way you like it remove from baking dish and rest in a warm oven for 10 minutes before carving.

To serve: slice meat into 6 thick slices and arrange on 6 heated dinner plates. Cut the hazelnut pâté into small squares and place one piece on the top of each serving. Garnish with watercress and serve at once with Galette of Two Pommes (see next recipe).

Average times Preparation — 10 minutes
Chilling — overnight
Cooking — 50 minutes
Resting — 10 minutes

Wine notes The nutty entrecôte should be
accompanied by a full-flavoured,
tannic red —
A: Redman (Coonawarra)
    Cabernet Sauvignon
E: Château Léoville-Las-Cases
    (St-Julien)
U: Sterling (Napa) Cabernet
    Reserve

Do ahead Hazelnut pâté overnight or up to
2 days

GALETTE OF TWO POMMES

◆

2 large Granny Smith apples, peeled and cored
3 medium potatoes, peeled and halved
salt and pepper, to taste

¾ cup cream
30 g butter, cut into 8 pieces

◆

Cut apples in halves and slice as finely as possible. (A food processor, fitted with the finest slicing disc, is the easiest way to do this.) Slice potatoes the same thickness. Butter 6 × 8 cm diameter tart pans. Arrange a layer of potatoes, with the slices just overlapping in the base of each. Season lightly. Do the same with a layer of apple slices and season. Continue in this manner until all apples and potatoes are used. Pour cream over the tops and dot with butter pieces. Place on a baking tray and cook in hottest part of 220°C (425°F) oven for 50 to 60 minutes or until golden on top and tender right through.

Average times Preparation — 25 minutes
Cooking — 50 minutes

PERSIMMON MOUSSE

1½ tablespoons gelatine
¾ cup boiling water
6 eggs separated
4 tablespoons castor sugar

2¼ cups stewed persimmons, puréed
¾ cup orange juice, approximately
3 tablespoons lemon juice
pinch salt

Dissolve gelatine in boiling water and set aside to cool. Beat egg yolks with sugar until pale and light.

Measure the persimmon purée and make it up to 3 cups with orange juice. Stir in lemon juice. Stir persimmon mixture into egg yolk mixture.

Beat egg whites with a pinch of salt until they form stiff peaks. Fold one-third of the egg whites into persimmon mixture using a rubber spatula. Fold the remaining egg whites into the mixture thoroughly but gently. Spoon into 6 individual glass bowls, cover and refrigerate until set.

The mousse may be served with unwhipped cream, however it is far more refreshing as it is.

Average times Preparation — 25 minutes
Setting — 4 hours

Do ahead Up to ½ day

Wine notes Persimmon Mousse could be accompanied by —
A: Lindemans Reserve Porphyry
E: and U: Château Lafaurie-Peyraguey (Sauternes)

FRUIT AND NUT CONFECTION

225 g shelled Brazil nuts, whole
225 g shelled almonds, whole
225 g shelled walnut halves
120 g dates, chopped
⅓ cup chopped mixed peel
½ cup chopped glacé cherries
120 g glacé pineapple, chopped
225 g glacé apricots, chopped
½ cup sultanas

½ cup raisins
¾ cup plain flour
½ teaspoon baking powder
½ teaspoon salt
¾ cup sugar
3 large eggs, beaten
1 teaspoon vanilla essence
¼ cup brandy

Combine nuts and fruits in a large bowl.

Sift flour with baking powder and salt, and add sugar. Add to fruits and nuts and mix very thoroughly.

Beat eggs and add vanilla and brandy. Stir into fruit mixture and blend well. This is a very stiff mixture.

Butter and line with buttered greaseproof paper or foil a 28 cm loaf pan and spoon mixture into it. Smooth top with a spatula and bake in 140°C (275°F) oven for approximately 2½ hours.

When cooked, remove from oven but leave in pan to cool for 10 minutes. Loosen edges with a knife and turn cake out on to a wire rack. Remove the paper immediately, and leave to cool. When the cake is cold wrap it in foil and store in the refrigerator.

Average times Preparation — 20 minutes
Cooking — 2½ hours
Cooling — 2½ hours

Wine notes Fruit and Nut Confection could be accompanied by a tawny port —
A: Lindemans Reserve Tawny Port Solera RF1
E: Taylor's Old Tawny Port
U: Christian Bros (Napa) Treasure Port

Do ahead Up to 3 weeks. Store in refrigerator wrapped in foil

MENU 9

The first course is similar to the scampi prepared at the famous Gritti Palace Hotel in Venice. The remaining courses can all be done ahead and, with pears at the peak of their season, this is one of the most delicious and refreshing sorbets you could have.

SKEWERED PRAWNS WITH LEMON BUTTER

30 green king prawns in the shell, heads removed
5 tablespoons olive oil
2 tablespoons olive oil, extra

5 tablespoons butter
¼ cup lemon juice
3 tablespoons fresh parsley, finely chopped

Soak 6 wooden skewers in water for 30 minutes. Thread prawns onto skewers, all facing the same way and fry in a heavy-based baking pan in 5 tablespoons oil over medium heat. Turn them over after 30 seconds on the second side.

Bake in same pan at 175°C (350°F) for 5 minutes (depending on size of prawns) or until just cooked.

Heat remaining oil with butter, juice and parsley until boiling. Arrange skewers on 6 warmed entrée plates, pour sauce over and serve at once with crusty bread.

Average times Soaking — 30 minutes
Preparation — 10 minutes
Cooking — 6 minutes

Wine notes Prawns need a crisp, Chablis-style white —
A: Peterson Family Chablis from the Hunter, bottled for Doug Lamb
E: Chablis Grand Cru les Blanchots (Domaine Laroche)
U: Byrd (Maryland) Seyval Blanc

Do ahead Up to cooking stage, ½ day

SHOULDER OF LAMB WITH DILL SAUCE

1¾–2 kg shoulder lamb
1 tablespoon salt
4 sprigs fresh dill

Sauce:

1 tablespoon plain flour
30 g butter
1 cup lamb stock, approximately
1 tablespoon white wine vinegar
1 teaspoon sugar
salt and freshly ground black pepper to taste
1 egg yolk
2 tablespoons freshly chopped dill

Pour 3½ litres boiling water over lamb in a large pan and simmer for 10 minutes. Skim. Add salt and dill. Cover pan and simmer for 1½ hours or until tender. Leave to cool in the stock. Skim off fat, strain and use some of the stock to make sauce.

To make sauce: cook flour in butter for 1 minute, gradually add 1 cup stock, vinegar, sugar, and seasoning. Whisk egg yolk and pour into the sauce, whisking. Return to pan to reheat carefully. If too thick, whisk in a little extra lamb stock. Stir in chopped dill, taste and adjust seasonings.

Carve lamb and serve with the sauce. Serve with vegetables in season or Steamed Julienne Vegetables (see next recipe).

Average times Preparation — 10 minutes
Cooking — 1¾ hours
Cooling — 3 hours

Wine notes Lamb with dill sauce needs a big, fruity red —
A: Amberton (Mudgee) Shiraz
E and U: Côtes du Rhône
(Guigal)

Do ahead Up to reheating lamb, ½ day

STEAMED JULIENNE VEGETABLES

200 g young carrots, cut in fine julienne 6 cm long
200 g young turnips, cut in fine julienne 6 cm long
200 g snow peas, or celery or chokos, cut in fine julienne 6 cm long

2 tablespoons butter
salt and freshly ground black pepper to taste

Prepare a steamer or pan with boiling water, place rack in it above the water. Alternatively, use a colander or a large sieve which will sit above water. Steam vegetables separately, because they all take different times to cook. Have the lid on but allow some of the steam to escape so green vegetables don't discolour. They will take 3 to 5 minutes. Take them out when *al dente* and refresh immediately in iced water to prevent further cooking.

Just before serving, heat butter in a frying pan until just changing colour, throw in all vegetables, toss them in butter with seasoning and serve. They should be only heated through, not recooked.

Average times Preparation — 20 minutes
Cooking — 15 minutes

Do ahead Julienne vegetables up to 2 hours before cooking

PEAR SORBET

Syrup:

1½ cups castor sugar
150 ml water

6 medium firm ripe pears, peeled, cored and
  diced coarsely
1–2 tablespoons lemon juice

Make syrup by stirring sugar and water together over low heat until sugar dissolves. Bring to boil and add pears. Put on lid and poach gently until pears are tender. Put pan in a bowl of iced water and leave to cool.

Mash pears in syrup with a fork and stir in lemon juice to taste. Churn until a good firm texture. Spoon into iced glasses and serve.

Average times Preparation — 10 minutes
                  Cooking — 15 minutes
                  Cooling — 1 hour

Do ahead Up to 1 day

Wine notes Pear Sorbet requires no wine

GINGER SLICE
Makes 24 to 30

120 g butter
1 teaspoon ground ginger
1 cup self raising flour
60 g sugar
salt

Icing:

2 tablespoons butter
3 teaspoons golden syrup
1 teaspoon ground ginger
4 tablespoons pure icing sugar

Using a food processor or an electric mixer, work the first 5 ingredients together. Press into a flat 18 cm × 27 cm pan and bake in 175°C (350°F) oven for about 15 minutes or until golden and cooked.

To make icing: in a small pan, melt butter with syrup and ginger and mix well. Take off heat and sift in icing sugar. Work to a smooth icing. Spread over warm base and leave to set. Cut into fingers.

Average times Preparation — 15 minutes
                  Cooking — 15 minutes
                  Cooling — 40 minutes

Do ahead Up to 5 days and store in airtight
             containers.

AUTUMN

MENU 10

A menu which is more suitable for a cool Autumn evening, beginning with a soup which, of course, should be done in advance and pigeons which heat through beautifully if you want to make them ahead. The dessert should be made in advance and can be accompanied by vanilla ice-cream or cream.

ZUCCHINI SOUP

1 large onion, chopped
2 cloves garlic, peeled and chopped
2 tablespoons butter
3 chicken cubes
3 cups boiling water

6 cups diced zucchini
½ teaspoon celery salt
freshly ground black pepper, to taste
¼ cup parsley leaves

Sauté onion and garlic in butter in pan until tender. Add remaining ingredients except parsley. Bring to boil and cook over medium heat 10 minutes, or until zucchini are tender.

Carefully pour into blender (if necessary, half at a time), add parsley, and blend at high speed until smooth. Return to pan to heat through and serve piping hot.

Average times Preparation — 10 minutes
Cooking — 15 minutes

Do ahead 1–2 days

Wine notes The soup calls for a fino
sherry —
A: Reynella Alicante Flor
E and U: Tio Pepe Sherry

PERUGIA PIGEONS

6 squab, weighing about 350 g each or 6 poussins (no. 5 chickens)
salt and freshly ground black pepper to taste
½ cup juniper berries
24 fresh sage leaves or 1 tablespoon dried leaves

4 tablespoons olive oil
3 cups dry red wine
1½ cups ripe black olives

Season the insides of birds. Place half the berries and sage inside birds and rub over with oil. Roast birds in hottest part of 180°C (375°F) oven for 25 minutes.

Remove birds and place on their sides in a heavy casserole dish. Pour over remaining ingredients, cover and simmer over low heat for a further 30 minutes or until the birds are tender. They should be moist and have just enough sauce to coat them when served.

Serve with baby boiled potatoes or hot buttered noodles and steamed broccoli florets.

Average times Preparation — 10 minutes
Cooking — 55 minutes

Do ahead Up to 1 day

Wine notes The pigeons call for a big, long-
finishing red —
A: Penfolds Grange Hermitage
E: Barolo (Marchesi di Barolo)
from a great year
U: Lytton Springs (Sonoma)
Zinfandel

LATTICE APPLE AND ALMOND TART
Serves 8 to 10

◆

Pastry:

1½ cups plain flour
½ cup self raising flour
½ cup castor sugar
pinch salt
180 g unsalted butter
1 egg, beaten and divided into two
1 extra yolk
1 tablespoon milk
1 teaspoon brandy
finely grated rind and juice of ½ lemon
¼ teaspoon vanilla essence
pinch ground cinnamon

Filling:

1 kg Granny Smith apples, peeled, cored,
    halved and sliced in 1 cm pieces
1 cup castor sugar
juice of 1 lemon
⅓ cup blanched, slivered almonds

◆

To make pastry: in a medium bowl, combine the two flours, sugar, and salt. Rub in butter with finger tips, make a well in the centre and add half the beaten egg and extra yolk, milk, brandy, rind, juice, vanilla and cinnamon. Stir together with a knife (it's important to keep hot hands out of mixture). Gather up pastry, flour lightly, flatten to 3 cm, and refrigerate in a plastic bag for at least 2 hours to chill well. This can be frozen and thawed to roll on the day it is needed.

To make filling: in a medium, heavy-based pan, combine apples, sugar and lemon and bring slowly to boil, stirring from time to time to prevent burning. Cook on low heat until apple slices are tender, cool.

To prepare pastry base: butter the base of a 23 cm spring form and dust with flour, shaking out excess flour. Roll one-third of the pastry to fit the base, press in with finger tips, trim off any excess. Prick all over and bake in centre of oven at 200°C (400°F) for 12 to 15 minutes or until golden. Cool. Roll remaining pastry into a long piece to line the sides of the spring form. Press long piece of pastry on to sides of pan and press down with a fork dipped in flour, pushing pastry about two-thirds of the way up the sides (it must be thin). Spoon apples into pan (they only half fill it). Cut lengths of pastry out of remaining pieces and make a lattice on top of apples. Add 1 tablespoon of water to the remaining beaten egg and paint over lattice and top of pastry. Scatter over almonds and bake in centre of oven at 200°C (400°F) for 35 to 40 minutes, or until cooked and golden. Cool before serving.

Average times Preparation — 35 minutes
Standing — 2 hours
Cooking — 50 to 60 minutes

Wine notes The apple tart needs a sweet
white with a long finish —
A: Lindemans Padthaway
    Auslese Rhine Riesling
E: Château Climens (Barsac) of
    a good year
U: Joseph Phelps (Napa) Late
    Harvest Johannisberg
    Riesling

Do ahead Up to 1 day

AUTUMN

MENU 11

This is an attractive luncheon or dinner menu, with the first and last courses needing to be made ahead, while the main course can be cooked while guests are at the table.

EGG-PLANT SALAD

---

2 large egg-plants weighing around 1 kg total
salt
2 cloves garlic, finely chopped
1 cup olive oil
1–2 tablespoons white wine vinegar, to taste
1–2 tablespoons lemon juice, to taste
salt and freshly ground black pepper to taste

Garnish:
2 medium tomatoes, cut into quarters and each quarter cut into 3
2 tablespoons finely chopped white onion or shallot
Greek ripe olives

Prick egg-plants all over with a roasting fork or knife and bake in foil on a baking tray in 220°C (450°F) oven for 1 hour, turning over once. Cool.

Cut in halves lengthwise and scrape out flesh with a fork or a small spatula, discarding the skin. Place in a colander over a bowl and sprinkle with 2 teaspoons of salt, mixing in by hand. Place a saucer on top to weigh down egg-plant for ½ hour. Wrap egg-plant in a clean tea-towel and wring out juices as thoroughly as possible. (The salting process is called disgorging and is to rid egg-plant of bitter juices.) Discard all juices.

Scrape egg-plant flesh into a medium bowl and beat in garlic, and oil in a thin steady stream using a wooden spatula (as though you were making a French mayonnaise). If oil is added too fast, the egg-plant won't accommodate all of it. Beat in remaining ingredients, tasting as you go.

Pile on to an oval platter, surround with tomatoes, scatter the centre with finely chopped onion or shallot and serve with olives and crusty Greek bread or pitta.

Average times Preparation — 20 minutes
Cooking — 1 hour
Standing — 30 minutes

Wine notes Egg-Plant Salad calls for a sparkling white —
A: Yalumba Brut de Brut Champagne
E: Château Moncontour (Vouvray)
U: Kornell (Napa) Sehr Trocken Champagne

Do ahead Up to garnishing, 3 days

SZECHUAN PRAWNS

1 kg green prawns, shelled and deveined
¾ teaspoon soda bicarbonate
2 teaspoons salt
½ teaspoon pepper
3 egg whites
3 cups peanut oil
2 tablespoon peanut oil, extra
12 peppercorns
2 tablespoons sesame oil
3 cloves garlic, finely minced
2–3 red chillies, finely chopped

Sauce:

1½ tablespoons cornflour
1 cup chicken stock
3 teaspoons sugar
3 teaspoons chilli oil
3 tablespoons light soy sauce
1½ tablespoons vinegar

3 tablespoons dry sherry
4 stalks fresh coriander, chopped

Place prawns in a medium bowl, add bicarbonate soda and mix well. Stir in salt, pepper, egg whites, mix well. Refrigerate 2 hours.

Mix sauce ingredients together.

Heat 3 cups of oil in a wok or frying pan, add half the prawns and stir to separate. When they change colour, drain and set aside. Repeat with remaining prawns. In same wok or pan, heat the remaining oil, add peppercorns, fry for 30 seconds, lift out with a slotted spoon and discard. Add sesame oil, garlic, chillies and prawns and stir well.

Mix sauce ingredients together. Add sauce and stir for 2 miniutes. Add sherry and coriander and serve.

Serve with rice.

Average times Preparation — 25 minutes
Standing — 2 hours
Cooking — 10 minutes

Wine notes Szechuan Prawns, with spicy flavours, need an aromatic white
A: Leasingham (Clare) Rhine Riesling Bin 7
E: Liebfraumilch (Blue Nun)
U: Christian Bros (Napa) Johannisberg Riesling

Do ahead Up to marinade stage, 2 hours

COEUR À LA CRÈME WITH TAMARILLO OR KIWI FRUIT SAUCE

375 g cream style cottage cheese
250 g cream cheese, softened
½ cup crème fraîche, see page 49
1 tablespoon icing sugar
½ cup thickened cream

Kiwi Fruit Sauce:

½ cup water
½ cup castor sugar
500 g ripe kiwi fruit, peeled and puréed
¼ cup orange juice

Tamarillo Sauce:

500 g tamarillos, skinned and sliced
¼ cup water
½ cup castor sugar
½ teaspoon finely grated orange zest
¼ cup orange juice

Cream the two cheeses together and fold in the crème fraîche. Line 6 coeur à la crème moulds with muslin and stand them on a small tray. Spoon mixture into moulds and level the tops. Refrigerate for 8 hours or overnight.

Pasta, Fig and Basil Salad

Wine:
Château Cissac (Cissac, Haut-Médoc)

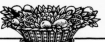

Bami Goreng

Unmould onto 6 dessert plates and carefully remove muslin. Sift icing sugar over the tops and serve with kiwi fruit or tamarillo sauce.

To make kiwi fruit sauce: bring water and sugar to the boil over medium heat, stirring until sugar dissolves. Boil 2 minutes and cool over iced water.

When syrup is cold, stir in kiwi fruit purée and orange juice and refrigerate covered, until ready to use.

To make tamarillo sauce: cook tamarillos in water and sugar over medium heat, stirring until sugar dissolves. Reduce heat to low and leave to stew gently until tamarillos are tender.

Sieve sauce and return to pan. Add zest and juice and cook over medium heat until sauce reduces a little. Cool and refrigerate until ready to serve.

Note: to skin tamarillos, dip in boiling water for 30 seconds.

Average times	*Coeur à la crème —*
	Preparation — 10 minutes
	Standing — 8 hours
	Kiwi Fruit sauce —
	Preparation — 5 minutes
	Cooking — 5 minutes
	Cooling — 1 hour
	Tamarillo sauce —
	Preparation — 10 minutes
	Cooking — 15 minutes
	Cooling — 1 hour
Wine notes	Coeur à la crème with kiwi fruit,
	a sweet white with crisp acidity
	A: Leasingham Auslese Rhine
	Riesling
	E and U: Château Coutet
	(Barsac)

Do ahead *Coeur à la crème —*
Up to 1 day
Kiwi Fruit sauce —
Up to 5 days and keep refrigerated
Tamarillo sauce —
Up to 1 day

AUTUMN

MENU 12

This is one of my favourite menus for serving outdoors on a warm Autumn day or evening. Provided you follow the instructions carefully for the Hot Berry Soufflés, they will stay up long enough for you to carry them to your waiting guests.

ROCK MELONS STUFFED WITH CRAB SALAD

3 baby rock melons or cantaloups, halved and seeded
¾ kg freshly cooked blue swimmer crabs in shell *or* 2 × 210 g cans crab meat, drained and cartilage removed
1 Golden Delicious apple, diced finely with skin left on

1 cup finely chopped celery
¾ cup finely diced red and green peppers
¾ cup mayonnaise
¼ cup thickened cream
salt to taste
Worcestershire sauce to taste

6 small sprigs watercress to garnish

Place melon halves on tray, cover with plastic film and refrigerate until ready to fill. If using blue swimmer crabs, pick meat out of shells, removing all cartilage and stomach. Place crab meat in medium-sized bowl with all remaining ingredients except watercress, folding together gently with a rubber spatula. Taste and adjust seasoning if necessary. Just before serving, spoon mixture into prepared melon halves, garnish with watercress and serve with crisp dry toast and unsalted butter. The crab salad can be served in red mignonette lettuce cups instead of melon.

Average times Preparation — 25 minutes

Wine notes The melon and crab require a German-style white of Spaetlese standard —
A: Orlando (Barossa) Spaetlese Rhine Riesling
E: Graacher Himmelreich Spaetlese (Mosel)
U: Long (Napa) Johannisberg Riesling

Do ahead Prepare melons ½ day ahead. Make salad ½ day ahead, cover and refrigerate

HOW TO BUTTERFLY A LEG OF LAMB

Ask butcher not to cut and crack shank bone. Remove all fat from outside of leg. Remove the aitchbone.

Cut down line of thigh bone to knee. Scrape all the meat away from thigh bone, leaving it attached to leg, and remove thigh bone. (I also like to remove the kneecap.)

Sever meat and tendons from top end of shin bone to allow meat to open out, forming a 'butterfly' shape. Cut deep into leg almost through to the other side.

Cut away the pocket of fat in centre of leg at knee. Flatten meat as much as possible by banging it with a mallet. Some advocate that cutting deep slits into the thickest parts of the meat will ensure even cooking. I have found this to be unnecessary because different degrees of cooked meat are always welcome. Serve the thickest parts to those who prefer their meat rare.

BARBECUED BUTTERFLY LEG OF LAMB

1.5 kg leg of lamb, trimmed of fat with shank
    left whole

Marinade:

⅓ cup cider vinegar
¼ cup soy sauce
2 tablespoons peanut oil
3 cloves garlic, chopped
2 sprigs fresh thyme, or ½ teaspoon dried
    thyme

salt and pepper to taste
2 tablespoons dry white wine
1 cup beef or veal stock
1 tablespoon chopped parsley

Ask your butcher to butterfly a leg of lamb or see preceding recipe. Place meat in marinade at room temperature for 4 hours, or overnight in refrigerator, turning meat once. Drain meat, place in an oiled baking dish and reserve marinade. Bake in hottest part of 200°C (400°F) oven for 20 to 25 minutes depending on how well you like it done. Season well. Place lamb onto a warmed serving platter, reserving pan juices, and allow to rest for 10 minutes. Heat pan juice over medium heat, add wine and cook, stirring continuously for 2 minutes. Strain marinade into pan, add stock and cook over a high heat until reduced by half. Adjust seasoning and stir through parsley. Carve lamb in thin slices, running from top of leg towards shank, arrange on a serving platter, and serve sauce separately.

Serve with vegetables in season or Red Kidney Bean Salad (see next recipe).

Average times Preparation — 10 minutes
    Marinading — 4 hours
    Cooking — 25 minutes
    Resting — 10 minutes

Wine notes Lamb needs a Cabernet of
    medium weight —
    A: Brown Bros Koombahla
        Cabernet Sauvignon
    E: Château d'Angludet
        (Cantenac-Margaux, Haut-
        Médoc)
    U: Stag's Leap (Napa)
        Cabernet Sauvignon

RED KIDNEY BEAN SALAD

¾ cup parsley, finely chopped
¾ cup peas, cooked
¾ cup finely chopped celery
¾ cup finely chopped red and green pepper
¾ cup finely chopped spring onions
¾ cup corn kernels, drained
¾ cup finely diced carrot, cooked
300 g can red kidney beans, drained

Vinaigrette:

2 teaspoons French mustard
1 teaspoon salt
freshly ground black pepper
6 tablespoons olive oil
1½ tablespoons tarragon vinegar

Mix all salad ingredients together. Whisk vinaigrette ingredients together and adjust seasoning if necessary. Toss the vinaigrette 10 minutes before serving.

Average times Preparation — 20 minutes
    Cooking — 10 minutes

Do ahead Up to ½ day

HOT BERRY SOUFFLÉS
Makes 8 soufflés approximately

◆

4 egg yolks
5 tablespoons castor sugar
⅔ cup raspberry (or any other berry) purée,
  reduced down to ⅓ cup
8 egg whites
pinch salt
5 tablespoons castor sugar, extra

butter and castor sugar for soufflé dishes
icing sugar to dust

◆

Beat egg yolks and castor sugar until pale and fluffly and fold in half the reduced berry purée.

Beat egg whites with salt until they form soft peaks, then beat in extra castor sugar, 1 tablespoon at a time. Beat until mixture forms stiff peaks. Fold in remaining berry purée, then fold into yolk mixture. Spoon into 11 cm × 9 cm (1 cup) buttered and sugared soufflé dishes, level the tops with a spatula and run a finger around top edge.

Bake in hottest part of 200°C (400°F) oven for 11 minutes or until well risen and golden on top. Dust with icing sugar and serve at once.

Note: Cover and freeze the soufflés which are not wanted. Cook frozen soufflés when needed at 210°C (425°F) for 16 to 18 minutes or until well risen and golden on top.

Average times Preparation — 15 minutes
Cooking — 11 minutes

Wine notes With raspberry soufflés —
A: Evans Family Coonawarra
  Botrytis Cinerea Rhine
  Riesling
E: Château Coutet (Barsac) of a
  great year
U: Château St Jean (Sonoma)
  Late Harvest Johannisberg
  Riesling

Do ahead Mixture can be prepared up to
beating egg whites ½ day ahead

AUTUMN

MENU 13

A lovely Autumn dinner menu, with the main course requiring all last-minute attention. However, both the first and last courses can be prepared up to ½ day ahead.

FENNEL GRATINÉ

3 medium fennel bulbs, trimmed and cut lengthwise into 1 cm slices
salt

100 g butter, melted
freshly ground black pepper to taste
6 tablespoons freshly grated Parmesan cheese

Cook fennel in a pan of salted boiling water over high heat for 8 minutes. Drain and pat dry on paper towels. Brush a gratiné dish with one-third of the butter. Layer half the fennel in bottom and sprinkle with pepper, half the cheese and drizzle with half remaining butter. Repeat with remaining ingredients, drizzle with butter and bake in hottest part of 200°C (400°F) oven for 12 minutes, then place under a hot griller until top is nicely golden. Serve at once.

Average times Preparation — 10 minutes
Cooking — 22 minutes

Wine notes Fennel Gratiné needs a full-flavoured, fruity white —
A: Seppelt Reserve Bin Chardonnay
E: Châteauneuf-du-Pape Blanc (Chapoutier)
U: Pine Ridge (Napa) Chenin Blanc

Do ahead Up to oven stage, ½ day

DUCK IN RASPBERRY VINEGAR

3 × 1.5 kg ducks
salt and freshly ground black pepper to taste
3 oven bags
6 teaspoons plain flour
3 tablespoons finely chopped shallots
¼ cup raspberry vinegar
3 tablespoons demi glacé (beef stock reduced to ½ original volume)

¾ cup raspberry purée without seeds
1 tablespoon sugar (optional)
30 g butter, cut into 6 pieces

extra raspberries for garnish

Remove necks from ducks and pockets of fat from the back. Prick thoroughly all over and season insides generously. Flour oven bags with 2 teaspoons of flour each and seasoning and place 1 duck into each bag. Tie tops and prick once near the ties, so bags won't burst in oven. Cook on an oven rack in a baking dish in a 230°C (450°F) oven for 10 minutes, then reduce heat to 220°C (425°F) and continue to cook for 1¼ hours.

Remove ducks from oven bags, catching the juices in a tall jug. Place ducks back on rack and return to oven for a further 15 minutes or until tender. When ducks are cooked, set aside in a warm place to rest for 10 minutes before carving.

Remove fat from top of duck cooking juices and discard. Place baking dish over medium heat and sauté shallots until softened. Pour in vinegar and cook until reduced by 80 per cent watching that it does not burn. Stir in 2 cups of duck cooking juices and demi glacé and cook until reduced by half. Stir in raspberry purée and taste, adjusting seasoning if necessary. (If raspberries are not overly ripe you may need a little sugar.) Cook for 1 minute and keep warm.

Carve legs off duck and skin them. Skin duck breasts and carve in long slices from one end of duck to the other and arrange in a fan shape on 6 warmed dinner plates. Place duck legs below fan and keep warm while finishing sauce. (The wings are not used in this dish as there is very little meat on them.)

Bring sauce back to simmer and turn off heat. Swirl butter into sauce one piece at a time using a whisk. The sauce must not boil or it will thin.

Spoon a little sauce over duck breast slices and scatter with remaining raspberries. Serve at once.

Serve with steamed snow peaks and Potato Almond Croquettes (see next recipe).

Note: Raspberry vinegar is very easily made by placing ½ cup of fresh raspberries in a jar fitted with a plastic lid. Pour 1 cup white wine vinegar over raspberries and shake daily for 3 days or until vinegar is well flavoured and coloured. Strain off raspberries and use as needed.

Average times Preparation — 25 minutes
Cooking — 2 hours
Standing — 10 minutes

Wine notes Duck in Raspberry Vinegar needs a fruity red —
A: Thomas Fern Hill Estate Shiraz
E: Gigondas (Domaine Raspail-Ay)
U: Deer Park (Napa) Zinfandel

POTATO ALMOND CROQUETTES

500 g peeled and quartered potatoes boiled until tender
30 g butter, melted
1 egg

milk to bind
salt and pepper to taste
2 eggs, extra
1 cup flaked almonds, toasted lightly

Put potatoes through a potato ricer or push them through a sieve. Stir in melted butter and egg and mix thoroughly. Stir in just enough milk to make a stiff but creamy mixture and season to taste.

Roll mixture into 5 cm long croquettes using lightly floured hands. Beat extra eggs with a little seasoning in a shallow bowl. Dip croquettes one at a time into extra eggs and then into flaked almonds and stand on a buttered baking sheet. Bake in 220°C (450°F) oven for 10 minutes or until nicely golden. Serve at once.

Average times Preparation — 20 minutes
Cooking — 10 minutes

Do ahead Up to oven stage — ½ day

FRUIT BOWL RUBANE

Sugar Syrup:

1 cup water
½ cup sugar
1 vanilla bean, split in half lengthwise
⅓ cup kirsch

1 small pineapple, skinned, cored, cut into
   1 cm slices, each slice cut into 8 wedges
1 cup rock melon or cantaloup cut into 1½ cm
   cubes
1 box raspberries
1 cup sultana grapes
1 cup seeded water-melon balls

2 bananas peeled and sliced into 1 cm slices on
   the cross and sprinkled with the juice of ½
   lemon
1 box blueberries

Sponge Fingers:

5 55 g eggs, separated
⅔ cup castor sugar
1¾ cup plain flour, sifted
½ cup pure icing sugar, sieved
pinch salt
extra icing sugar

To make syrup: cook water, sugar and vanilla bean over low heat stirring until sugar dissolves. Remove vanilla bean, wash and dry and leave until thoroughly dried before putting away for future use. Stir in kirsch and set aside.

To arrange fruits: arrange in layers in a deep straight-sided glass bowl in the order in which fruits are listed, spooning a little of the syrup over each layer. Pour remaining syrup over layered fruits, cover with plastic film and refrigerate for at least ½ day. Serve with sponge fingers.

To make sponge fingers: beat egg yolks with two-thirds of castor sugar until pale and light. Fold in flour and icing sugar using a very light hand.

Beat egg whites with a pinch of salt until it forms firm peaks. Beat in the remaining castor sugar, 1 tablespoon at a time and continue to beat until stiff and glossy. Fold a quarter of the whites into yolk mixture, then fold in remaining whites keeping the mixture very light. Spoon into a large piping bag with a plain 2 cm piping tube.

Pipe 8 cm long fingers on buttered and floured baking trays, allowing enough space between each for spreading. Sieve extra icing sugar over sponge fingers and cook at 180°C (375°F) for 15 minutes or until golden. Cool on a wire rack and store in airtight containers until ready to use.

Average times *Fruit Bowl —*
Preparation — 35 minutes
Cooking — 5 minutes
Cooling — 20 minutes
Standing — 4 hours
Sponge Fingers —
Preparation — 15 minutes
Cooking — 15 minutes
Cooling — 10 minutes

Wine notes The fruit bowl requires no wine

Do ahead *Fruit Bowl —*
Up to ½ day
Sponge Fingers —
Up to 1 week, if stored in airtight containers

131

AUTUMN

MENU 14

The spicy soup which starts this menu is from the famous hotel in Dallas, Texas, Mansion on Turtle Creek and is one of their most popular soups. Followed by a simple pork and apple dish and finished with the best passionfruit soufflés, it's an ideal dinner party menu.

TORTILLA SOUP

3 × 20 cm thin corn tortillas
¾ cup peeled, chopped tomatoes
½ cup onions, chopped
1 tablespoon minced garlic
1 tablespoon maize oil

6 cups chicken stock
1 teaspoon ground cumin
½ teaspoon white pepper
½ large avocado, diced
½ cup coarsely grated cheddar cheese

Fry tortillas (according to directions on packet) and dry on paper towels. Purée tomatoes, onion and garlic together and cook in a stock pot in oil. Reduce mixture by one-quarter and pour in the chicken stock. Cook over low heat for ½ hour and add seasoning to taste.

Cut tortillas into julienne. Before serving, add diced avocado and tortillas. Serve into hot soup plates and pass cheese separately at the table.

Average times Preparation — 15 minutes
Cooking — 50 minutes

Wine notes Tortilla Soup needs a fino sherry
A: Reynella Alicante Flor
Sherry
E and U: Tio Pepe Sherry

Do ahead Prepare without tortillas and avocado up to 2 days ahead, adding them at the time of serving

PORK CHOPS WITH APPLES IN MUSTARD SAUCE

1.5 kg Golden Delicious apples
2 tablespoons butter
salt
6 pork loin chops, 2 cm thick, trimmed of all
fat

⅓ cup dry white wine
1½ cups thickened cream
1½ tablespoons Dijon mustard or to taste
freshly ground black pepper to taste

Peel and core the apples, quarter and slice them finely. (The slicing disc on a food processor is the quickest and most efficient way to do this.)

Choose a shallow ovenproof dish just large enough to hold pork chops side by side without crowding them. Lightly butter dish and spread apples in it. Bake at 220°C (450°F) for 15 minutes.

Salt chops and cook them in a frying pan in a little butter until nicely golden on each side, which will take about 7 to 8 minutes per side. Arrange chops over baked apples in dish. Pour wine into pan and let it reduce by half, stirring in all brown bits clinging to bottom and sides of pan. Pour reduced wine over chops.

Mix cream, mustard, salt and pepper and pour over chops and shake dish to let cream through to bed of apples. Cook 15 minutes at 220°C (450°F).

Serve with French beans.

Average times Preparation — 25 minutes
Cooking — 50 minutes

Do ahead Up to 2 hours

Wine notes The pork needs a big, fruity
white —
A: Sandalford Verdelho from
Western Australia
E: Château Coutet Sec (Barsac)
U: Morris (Contra Costa)
Chardonnay — Black
Mountain

PASSIONFRUIT SOUFFLÉS

25 g butter
castor sugar for dishes
1 cup castor sugar, extra
5 eggs, separated
2 extra egg whites
3 × 125 g cans passionfruit pulp, strained
3 teaspoons passionfruit seeds retained

1 tablespoon lemon juice
pinch of salt

icing sugar to dust
vanilla ice-cream to accompany

Butter and sprinkle with sugar 6 individual 1¼ cup soufflé dishes and place on a baking tray. Beat egg yolks with half the sugar until mixture ribbons. Stir in passionfruit juice, retained seeds and lemon juice. This much can be done ½ day ahead.

Beat egg whites with salt until stiff, gradually beat in remaining sugar until stiff. Fold one-third egg whites through yolk mixture, fold in remaining egg whites and spoon into prepared dishes.

Cook in hottest part of 200°C (400°F) oven for 17 minutes without opening door. Serve immediately, dusted with icing sugar and stand on a dinner plate, accompanied by vanilla ice-cream.

Average times Preparation — 25 minutes
Cooking — 17 minutes

Do ahead Basic soufflé mixture up to stirring
in lemon juice, ½ day

Wine notes With Passionfruit Soufflés —
A: Tyrrell's (Pokolbin) Semillon
Sauternes
E: Moulin Touchais (Anjou)
U: Château Ste Michel
(Washington) Johannisberg
Riesling Ice Wine

AUTUMN

MENU 15

The sauce to accompany the fettuccine is a delicious creamy vegetable sauce using virtually what-ever you can find in your pantry. But as a basis, this is the way I like to make it. And once you have mastered home-made pasta I doubt that you will ever buy it again. Followed by a delicious veal dish and the best lemon-flavoured cream caramels in the world you will enjoy this menu either at lunch or dinner.

FETTUCCINE WITH CREAMY VEGETABLE SAUCE

Pasta Dough recipe:
2 cups plain flour (approximately)
generous pinch salt
2 55 g eggs
2 teaspoons olive oil
cold water

Vegetable Sauce:
⅓ cup olive oil
1 medium white onion, finely chopped
1 medium carrot, finely chopped
1 small parsnip, finely chopped
2 sticks celery, sliced

1 medium egg-plant cut into medium dice
½ cup dry white wine
425 g can tomatoes
salt and freshly ground black pepper to taste
2 × 45 g cans flat anchovies
⅓ cup freshly grated Parmesan cheese
30 g butter, cut into 4 pieces
¼ cup freshly chopped oregano or 1 teaspoon
   dried, or parsley
extra freshly grated Parmesan cheese to serve
   at table

To make pasta: pile flour and salt on bench or table top and make a well in centre. Break eggs into well and add oil. With a fork, beat in eggs and oil, gradually incorporating flour into egg mixture. When this mixture is quite thick, dispense with fork and, using dough scraper, bring more flour into middle mixture. Working with both hands, knead mixture until it forms a ball. Add a little water if necessary. The dough should be kneaded until it feels like chamois leather, approximately 10 minutes. Alternatively, make in a food processor.
To make spinach tagliatelli: add 2 tablespoons cooked, *very* well drained and puréed spinach to dough instead of adding water.
   Rest the dough, wrapped in a damp tea towel, for 30 minutes or overnight if you like.
   Cut dough into quarters and feed one quarter at a time through a pasta machine, set on highest setting. (You may need a little more flour if the pasta is sticky.) Feed dough through machine several times on the first (thickest) setting. Then set machine on second thickest setting and feed pasta dough through once more. Continue this process, lowering setting each time until you reach thickness you desire. Finally, select shape of noodles you require on machine, and pass rolled pasta through it once more to cut it.
   Hang pasta over a rail and leave to dry, preferably overnight. Continue to repeat this process until you have rolled all pasta. Cut and hang it. Pasta keeps well if stored in an airtight container. However, it is much better if used within a day or two of being made. It can be cooked when it comes straight off the machine, but I like to dry it overnight as it's then much easier to handle.

To cook pasta: bring a large pan of salted water to the boil over high heat. When it reaches boiling point turn down heat and leave to simmer, with lid on until you are ready to cook pasta.
   Fresh pasta takes very little cooking time, so do not overcook it.

Return water to boil and when it is boiling rapidly add all pasta at once and stir with a wooden spoon. As soon as water returns to boil cook over high heat until pasta rises to surface and tastes *al dente*. Catch pasta with a pasta catcher or a sieve allowing most of cooking water to run off before pouring it into a large preheated bowl. Never strain pasta through a colander losing all the water.

To make sauce: in a large, heavy-based frying pan, heat oil and sauté onion over medium heat for 10 minutes, taking care that it does not burn. Add carrot and parsnip and sauté a further 5 minutes before adding celery and egg-plant. Stir and pour in white wine. Add tomatoes and their juice after first wringing them by hand into small pieces. Season to taste and simmer slowly for 1 hour. Chop anchovies roughly and stir into sauce with their oil. Stir in cheese and herbs and swirl in butter pieces to enrich sauce. Quickly spoon one-third of hot vegetable sauce into pasta and toss thoroughly with two spoons. Spoon remaining sauce over top of pasta and serve at once.

Average times *Pasta —*
Preparation — 20 minutes
Resting — 30 minutes
Rolling and cutting — 15 minutes
Drying — overnight
Cooking — 5 minutes approximately
Sauce —
Preparation — 15 minutes
Cooking — 1 hour 20 minutes

Do ahead *Pasta —*
1–2 days
Sauce —
Up to ½ day

Wine notes Pasta with vegetable sauce requires a big white —
A: Château Tahbilk (central Victoria) Marsanne
E: and U: Trebbiano d'Abruzzo (Valentini)

VEAL WITH CALF'S SWEETBREAD AND KIDNEY

6 × 125 g veal escalopes, flattened
salt and pepper, to taste
18 young spinach leaves, blanched and drained
2 calf's kidneys
500 g calf's sweetbreads, blanched, drained and skinned

125 g unsalted butter
3 tablespoons brandy
1½ cups veal stock, made from veal bones

Place half veal escalopes on a wooden board, slightly overlapping. Season and cover with half spinach leaves. Cut kidneys into four lengthwise, and remove all sinew. Lay half along centre of escalopes.

Cut prepared sweetbreads into four lengthwise and place half alongside kidneys. Prepare remaining ingredients the same way. Roll into two paupiettes (long firm rolls) and tie with string, very securely at several intervals.

In a heavy-based pan, heat butter. Seal veal on all sides over high heat, reduce heat and cook gently for approximately 20 minutes or until just done. Lift out of pan and keep warm.

Deglaze pan with brandy, pour in veal stock and reduce over medium heat until half the original volume is left. Taste and adjust seasoning if necessary.

Warm 6 plates and ladle a little of sauce on to each plate. Carefully remove string from veal and slice into 1 cm slices. Arrange slices in sauce and serve at once.

Serve with vegetables in season.

Average times Preparation — 35 minutes
Cooking — 35 minutes

Wine notes The strongly flavoured veal needs a full-flavoured Cabernet
A: Hardy's (McLaren Vale) Cabernet Sauvignon
E: Château Gruaud-Larose (St-Julien) of a great year
U: Freemark Abbey (Napa) Cabernet Bosché

Do ahead Prepare paupiettes up to cooking stage, up to ½ day ahead

LEMON CREAM CARAMELS

Caramel:

7 level tablespoons castor sugar
4 tablespoons water

Cream:

900 ml milk
zest of 2 lemons, removed with a vegetable
    peeler, with no pith
6 eggs
½ cup castor sugar

Prepare caramel by boiling castor sugar and water together until caramel colours. Pour into bottom of 6 × ½-cup custard cups. When set, butter sides of cups with unsalted butter.

Bring milk and zest very slowly to boil over low heat. Remove from heat and infuse for 10 minutes, then strain. Beat eggs and castor sugar until pale and light and whisk in hot milk gradually.

Strain mixture through a coffee strainer into custard cups and place in a dish of warm water which comes halfway up sides of cups.

Cook at 190°C (375°F) for about 45 minutes. Unmould after 10 minutes if serving hot, or chill and then unmould if serving cold.

Average times Preparation — 10 minutes
    Cooking — 55 minutes
    Infusing — 10 minutes
    Standing — 10 minutes

Wine notes Lemon Cream Caramels call for
    a late-picked, aromatic white —
    A: Orlando Spaetlese
      Frontignac
    E: Muscat de Beaumes de
      Venise (Jaboulet)
    U: Fetzer (Mendocino) Muscat
      Canelli

Do ahead If serving cold, up to 1 day

AUTUMN

MENU 16

◆

The entrée is a variation of one I tasted at an Adelaide restaurant some years ago and is full of delightful palate surprises. Followed by two old French classics which never fail to please, this is a beautifully colourful and inspiring menu for lunch or dinner.

TWO PEARS WITH A STILTON AND FRESH MINT DRESSING

◆

3 ripe but firm fleshed avocados
3 ripe pears (preferably Corella)
lemon juice to acidulate

Dressing:

1 cup olive oil
80 g Stilton
3 teaspoons to 1 tablespoon white wine vinegar
2 tablespoons finely chopped mint
freshly ground black pepper to taste

◆

Cut avocados in halves, remove stones and peel them. Cut pears in halves and core them, leaving on skins. With a very sharp knife cut each avocado half into thin slices almost through to the stem end like a fan. Place each half on an entrée plate, flatten slightly with your hand and squeeze over lemon juice. Slice pear halves (the length of pears) into thin slices all the way through pears, exactly the same thickness as avocados. Sprinkle lemon juice over them and insert one slice into each avocado fan slice skin side up.

To make dressing: in a food processor or a blender pour the oil, add the Stilton and blend until cheese is well incorporated into oil. Pour in enough vinegar to taste and add mint and black pepper. Just before serving, dress pears with enough dressing to cover them.

Average times Preparation — 25 minutes

Wine notes Two Pears with Stilton and Mint Dressing call for a richly aromatic white —
A: Orlando Eden Valley Traminer
E: Gewurtztraminer Vendage Tardive (Hugel) from Alsace
U: Grand Cru (Sonoma) Gewurtztraminer

Do ahead Dressing up to ½ day

NAVARIN OF LAMB

---

60 g butter
1.5 kg boned leg of lamb, cut into 75 g pieces
salt and freshly ground black pepper to taste
¼ teaspoon sugar
1½ tablespoons plain flour
3 cups beef stock
2 medium tomatoes, peeled and chopped coarsely

1 clove garlic, chopped finely
1 bouquet garni
12 pickling onions, skinned with 3 cm tops left on
12 baby potatoes, 'turned', see Introductory Notes
12 baby carrots, 'turned', see Introductory Notes
12 baby turnips, 'turned', see Introductory Notes
1 cup freshly podded peas

Heat butter in a large heavy casserole until foaming. Seal lamb on all sides until well browned. Season with salt and pepper and sugar. Spoon of all fat except for 1 tablespoon and discard. Sprinkle in flour and stir over medium heat for 2 minutes. Add stock which should just cover the meat. Add tomatoes, garlic and bouquet garni. Make sure the bouquet garni is submerged in stock. Cook in 150°C (300°F) oven for 1 hour. Cool and chill, preferably overnight.

Cook onions, carrots and turnips in separate pans of boiling salted water until *al dente*. Remove solidified fat from lamb and heat through until simmering. Stir in precooked vegetables and the peas and cook until peas are tender. Taste and adjust the seasoning and serve.

Average times Preparation — 60 minutes
Cooking — 1 hour 25 minutes
Chilling — overnight

Do ahead Up to cooking and adding vegetables, 1 day

Wine notes Navarin of lamb calls for a classic Cabernet, with berry fruit and astringency —
A: Lake's Folly (Pokolbin) Cabernet Sauvignon
E: Cos d'Estournel (St-Estèphe)
U: Robert Mondavi (Napa) Cabernet Reserve

RASPBERRY BAVAROIS

---

180 g raspberries
¾ cup castor sugar
½ cup water
2½ teaspoons gelatine

2 tablespoons Eau de Vie de Framboise
2 cups cream, lightly beaten

1 box raspberries to garnish

Purée berries in a food processor or blender. Dissolve castor sugar in water in a small pan over medium heat stirring until mixture boils. Remove from heat and whisk in gelatine. Cool for 5 minutes and stir into berry purée. Strain mixture through a sieve. Stir in liqueur. Fold cream into berry mixture and pour into a wetted savarin mould, cover and chill until set.

To unmould, pull mixture away from top edges of mould with fingers, dip into warm water and invert over a serving plate and shake out. Fill centre with fresh raspberries.

Average times Preparation — 15 minutes
Cooking — 5 minutes
Setting — 2–4 hours

Do ahead Up to ½ day

Wine notes Raspberry Bavarois calls for a luscious sweet white —
A: Peter Lehmann (Barossa) Semillon Sauternes
E: Château Rieussec (Sauternes)
U: Château St Jean (Sonoma) Late Harvest Johannisberg Riesling

AUTUMN

MENU 17

This quail salad was devised when I was confronted with a deep freeze clean out, and it was an instant success. Smoked quails can be substituted for roasted quails if you are fortunate enough to have a smoker. The next course, with goat cheese, is deceptively rich, but followed by flaming figs the menu is ideal for luncheon.

QUAIL SALAD

---

6 quails
60 g butter
12 curly endive leaves, washed, drained and crisped
12 mignonette lettuce leaves, washed, drained and crisped
6 baby Cos lettuce, washed, drained and crisped
1 medium carrot, peeled and cut into fine julienne
½ medium beetroot, boiled, skinned and cut into fine julienne
8 small white button mushrooms, sliced finely

2 medium tomatoes, skinned, seeded and cut into ½ cm strips
4 paper thin slices prosciutto crudo, cut into small squares

Dressing:

½ cup olive oil
1½ tablespoons red wine vinegar
salt and freshly ground black pepper to taste

6 quail eggs boiled, shelled and halved lengthwise

Roast quails in a heavy-based baking pan with the butter in 200°C (400°F) oven for 15 to 20 minutes or until the skins are crisp and browned and the quails are tender.

Arrange the three lettuces attractively on 6 large entrée plates and scatter over carrot, beetroot, mushrooms and tomatoes. Arrange prosciutto over salad.

To prepare dressing and serve: whisk all dressing ingredients together.

While quails are hot, carve off legs and wings and arrange on salad. Carve breasts into 2 to 3 thin slices and place attractively on top of salad. Arrange quail eggs over salad. Whisk dressing again and spoon over salads. Serve at once.

Average times Preparation — 35 minutes
Cooking — 20 minutes

Wine notes Quail Salad needs a lightly chilled, fruity, light to medium red —
A: Lindemans Padthaway Pinot Noir
E: Volnay Caillerets (Domaine Clerget)
U: Acacia (Napa) Pinot Noir

Do ahead Prepare vegetables and dressing up to ½ day

PASTA WITH GOAT CHEESE SAUCE

◆

3 large cloves garlic, peeled and chopped finely
2 tablespoons butter
2 tablespoons olive oil
1¼ cups walnuts, coarsely chopped
1 cup thickened cream
250 g soft goat cheese, skin left on and finely
    chopped

¼ cup freshly grated Parmesan cheese
375 g fine spaghetti
¾ cup tightly packed fresh basil leaves, finely
    sliced
salt and freshly ground black pepper to taste

◆

In a heavy-based pan, sauté the garlic in butter and oil over medium heat until softened. Add walnuts and cook until they are toasted and crisp. Set aside.

Mix together cream, goat cheese and Parmesan cheese.

Cook the pasta in 5 litres of salted water with 1 tablespoon of cooking oil until *al dente*. While pasta cooks, add basil to walnut mixture and season to taste. Strain pasta in a pasta catcher or sieve and pour into a large warmed serving dish. Toss with walnut mixture and then toss in cheese mixture. If sauce is too thick, add a little of the pasta cooking water. Serve at once.

Average times Preparation — 15 minutes
    Cooking — 20 minutes

Wine notes Pasta with Goat Cheese Sauce,
    continue with the red suggested
    for the first course

FLAMING FIGS

◆

18 firm ripe white figs, peeled
⅓ cup orange curaçao

⅓ cup brandy

◆

Prick figs thoroughly all over with a skewer and place in a large heavy-based frying pan with the curaçao and brandy. Warm through gently over medium heat and ignite as soon as liqueur and brandy are hot. Stir until flame dies and spoon into a glass serving dish. Serve warm or cold with cream.

Average times Preparation — 10 minutes
    Cooking — 5 minutes

Wine notes The figs are complemented by a
    sweet white —
    A: Petersons Hunter Valley
        Sauternes
    E: Gewurtztraminer Vendage
        Tardive (Hugel) from Alsace
    U: Château St Jean (Sonoma)
        Late Harvest Johannisberg
        Riesling

Do ahead If serving cold, up to 1 day

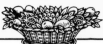

Perugia Pigeons

Wine:
Penfolds Grange Hermitage

Hot Berry Soufflés

Wine:
Chateau Lafaurie-Peyraguey (Sauternes)

AUTUMN

MENU 18

Three cold courses and all completely do-ahead make this an ideal luncheon menu for busy people who want to eat well. Serve the cake with coffee or if the menu is too long for a short lunch then omit it.

SWEETBREAD TERRINE

700 g sweetbreads (preferably veal)
2 tablespoons lemon juice
450 g veal and pork mince
225 g hardback pork fat, minced
2 rashers raw bacon (green), minced
1 large white onion, chopped finely
1 tablespoon salt
1 teaspoon fresh thyme or ½ teaspoon dried thyme leaves

300 ml thickened cream
2 eggs, beaten
125 g button mushrooms, sliced finely
1 tablespoon green peppercorns, rinsed and drained
125 g ghee

baby cornichons (French dill cucumbers) and fresh dill to garnish

Soak sweetbreads in salted water for 3 hours. Rinse and place in medium-sized pan with just enough water to cover, plus lemon juice. Simmer gently 10 minutes, drain, skin under running cold water.

Combine veal pork mince, pork fat, bacon, onion, salt and thyme. Fold in cream and eggs, mushrooms and peppercorns. Spoon half the mixture into a buttered 24 cm terrine, layer sweetbreads on top and cover with remaining mixture. Bake at 175°C (350°F) for 1½ hours covered very tightly with a layer of foil and a lid.

Remove from oven and weigh down until cold. Remove weights and refrigerate overnight.

Serve sliced and garnished with baby cornichons (French dill cucumbers) and wisps of fresh dill.

Average times Soaking — 3 hours
Preparation — 30 minutes
Cooking — 1 hour 40 minutes
Cooling — overnight

Wine notes Sweetbread Terrine calls for a late-picked aromatic white —
A: Orlando (Barossa) Spaetlese Rhine Riesling
E: Steinberger Riesling Spaetlese from the Rheingau
U: Ventana (Monterey) Johannisberg Riesling

Do ahead At least 1 day and up to 2 days

SALT DUCK IN CIDER WITH ORANGE SALAD

3 × 1.6 kg ducks

Brine Solution:

700 g *gros sel*
8 cups water

4 cups cider
2 onions, stuck with 4 cloves
2 bay leaves
6 peppercorns

Orange Salad:

6 oranges, preferably navel
2 medium odourless onions
1 large red pepper, skinned and seeded
¾ cup black olives

Salad Dressing:

5 tablespoons fine olive oil
2 tablespoons orange juice
salt and freshly ground black pepper, to taste
1 clove garlic, finely chopped

pickled walnuts and gherkins to serve

To cook duck: remove fat from back openings of ducks and discard.

Make brine solution by dissolving salt in water and cooling it. Put ducks in this for 1½ days. They should be covered. Turn them over each ½ day.

Pour off brine and discard. Place ducks on their sides in a heavy heat proof casserole. Pour over cider, add onions, cloves, bay leaves and peppercorns. Cover and bring slowly to a simmer for 1 hour or until tender. Cool in cider and refrigerate.

Carve legs and wings off ducks and remove wing tips. Carve breasts into long thin slices and arrange on a platter with legs and wings. Serve cold with pickled walnuts and gherkins and orange salad.

To make salad: using a very sharp knife, skin oranges removing all rind and pith and catching juices in a bowl. Cut them into segments, discarding membranes, slice onions finely, pressing out rings, and cut red pepper into julienne. Arrange attractively in a bowl, scatter over olives and dress at the last moment.

To make dressing: whisk all the ingredients together until thoroughly incorporated.

Average times *Duck —*
Standing — 1½ days
Preparation — 20 minutes
Cooking — 1 hour
Cooling — preferably over-
night
Salad Dressing —
Preparation — 20 minutes

Wine notes With Salt Duck in Cider, a full-
flavoured Chardonnay —
A: Tisdall Mt Helen
Chardonnay from central
Victoria
E: Chassagne-Montrachet
(Louis Latour)
U: Mount Eden (Santa Clara)
Chardonnay

Do ahead *Duck —*
At least 1 day and up to 3 days

ALMOND PISTACHIO CAKE

Syrup:

2 tablespoons orange and lemon zest, cut into
   fine julienne
½ cup water
2 tablespoons sugar

500 g blanched almonds
125 g pistachios, blanched

1 cup castor sugar
½ cup dry white wine, (approximately — use
   less rather than more)
pinch salt
6 eggs, separated

icing sugar to dust

Blanch orange and lemon zest in boiling water for 30 seconds and drain. Bring water and sugar to the boil stirring constantly until sugar dissolves. Boil 5 minutes, add orange and lemon zests and simmer for a further 5 minutes. Set aside and leave to cool.

Place almonds and pistachios into a food processor and grind several seconds. With the machine still running add castor sugar and just enough wine to keep machine running. Add a pinch of salt to egg yolks and add them to the mixture and process a further 2 seconds. (Alternatively, mince the almonds and pistachios, mix in sugar and wine with a wooden spoon and add yolks with salt.)

Fold syrup and orange and lemon zests into mixture. Whip egg whites with a few grains of salt until they are firm. Fold one-third of the whites into almond pistachio mixture using a very light hand. Fold remaining whites into mixture in the same manner.

Spoon into a well buttered 23 cm cake pan and cook in a water bath, which comes half way up sides of cake pan, in centre of 200°C (400°F) oven for 15 minutes. Reduce oven to 190°C (375°F) for a further 25 minutes or until well risen, golden on top and firm to touch. Cool in cake pan for 20 minutes before turning out to finish cooling on a rack. Dust liberally with sifted icing sugar and accompany with unwhipped cream.

Average times Preparation — 30 minutes
                Cooking — 50 minutes
                Cooling — 30 minutes

Wine notes Almond Pistachio Cake needs a
              fortified sweet wine —
              A: Baileys Show Tokay from
                  northern Victoria
              E and U: Boal Madeira
                    (Henriques &
                    Henriques)

Do ahead Up to 3 days

AUTUMN

MENU 19

The perfect menu for a warm Autumn lunch or dinner, which is totally do-ahead. Another prize for busy cooks.

SPINACH ORANGE SOUP

50 g butter
2 medium white onions, chopped
2 bunches fresh spinach weighing about 600 g
    total, stalks removed, or young silverbeet
    and washed very thoroughly in several
    changes of water and chopped roughly
2 medium potatoes, peeled and cubed
3 cups chicken stock

orange rind (with no white pith), removed
    with a vegetable peeler
6 black peppercorns (rind and peppercorns tied
    in muslin)
¼ teaspoon grated nutmeg
salt to taste
6 tablespoons whipped cream

rind of ½ orange, cut into julienne and
    blanched to garnish

In a large saucepan, heat butter over medium heat and cook onions for 5 minutes or until soft, stirring from time to time. Add all the other ingredients, except cream and orange julienne, bring to boil and simmer for 30 minutes over medium heat without a lid. Cool over a basin of cold water. Remove muslin bag and discard.

Purée soup, reheat if serving hot, taste and adjust seasonings. Serve with 1 tablespoon of cream on each serving topped with orange match sticks.

Note: If you wish to serve this soup cold, after puréeing stir in ½ cup of cream, taste and adjust seasonings and chill very thoroughly. Serve with orange rinds scattered over the top.

Average times Preparation — 25 minutes
Cooking — 40 minutes
Cooling — 10 minutes
Chilling — preferably over-
night

Do ahead At least 1 day

Wine notes The soup needs no wine

VEAL AND HAM PIE
Begin 1 day ahead

Chicken Stock:

3 chicken carcasses
1 onion
1 clove
1 piece celery
1 piece carrot
6 black peppercorns

Flaky Pastry:

1½ cups plain flour
½ teaspoon salt
150 g butter
150 ml iced water
lemon juice

Egg Glaze:

1 egg beaten with pinch salt

Filling (Make 1 day ahead):

750 g lean shoulder of veal, cut in chunky
    cubes
200 g lean ham, sliced thickly
1 onion, finely chopped
1 tablespoon parsley, finely chopped
finely grated zest of 1 lemon
salt and pepper
1 tablespoon brandy
1 cup good jellied chicken stock plus ½ cup
    extra
1 teaspoon fresh sage leaves, chopped roughly
    (or ½ teaspoon dried)

To make jellied stock: put chicken carcasses in just enough cold water to cover. Add remaining ingredients. Bring to boil, then simmer uncovered for 40 minutes. Strain into a clean pan and simmer, uncovered for a further 20 minutes or until reduced by one-third. Refrigerate, preferably overnight, lift off fat and measure stock.

To make pastry: sift flour and salt. Work butter into a pliable condition and divide into 4 pieces. Rub one portion into flour, then add water and 3 drops of lemon juice and/or extra water. The dough and butter must both be the same consistency. Turn on to a lightly floured board and knead to a good, even consistency. Roll into a rectangle approximately 18 cm × 38 cm. Spread the second portion of butter over two-thirds of surface, keeping it 2.5 cm from outer edges. Sprinkle lightly with flour and fold into three, unbuttered end first. Press open ends lightly with rolling pin, then turn pastry 90 degrees. Roll out pastry again to the same size rectangle as before and repeat the process. Continue this way until all butter is used. Wrap in greaseproof paper and refrigerate for 30 minutes.

To make pie: butter a deep 5-cup pie dish and arrange veal, ham, onion, parsley, rind and seasonings and herbs in layers until dish is filled, doming the top slightly. Add brandy to measured stock and pour in 1 cup, retaining the extra ½ cup for later.

Roll chilled pastry to thickness of a 10 cent coin, cut a long strip 3 cm wide and stick down around top edge of dish using a little egg glaze. Moisten strip with water. Drape pastry over top of pie and trim it to same size as outer side of strip of pastry underneath. Pinch two layers together between thumb and finger and brush generously with glaze, but don't get it on the cut edges of the pastry or it won't rise.

Make a hole in centre of the top. Cut remaining pastry into decorations, stick down with egg glaze, glaze tops not edges, and chill for ½ hour. Glaze once more and cook at 220°C (425°F) for 30 to 40 minutes. Wrap pie in double layer of wet greaseproof paper, return to oven and lower temperature to 180°C (360°F) for another hour or until meat is tender when tested with a skewer through central hole in pastry. When cooked, place a funnel in the hole, pour in remaining stock and leave until cold, preferably overnight. Serve cold.

Note: If pastry dough gets too warm during the making, chill until more workable.
Accompany the pie with a green mixed salad.

Average times Preparation — 1 hour 10 minutes
Cooking — 2 hours 40 minutes (includes stock)
Chilling — 2 × 30 minutes
Cooling — overnight

Wine notes The pie needs a chilled rosé —
A: Anglesey (Angle Vale) Dry Rosé
E: Tavel Rosé (Rhône)
U: Heitz (Napa) Grignolino Rosé

Do ahead Stock, 1 day. Pastry up to rolling stage, 1 day. Completed pie, 1 day

BAVAROIS WITH CHANTILLY CREAM AND BLACKBERRY SAUCE

Chantilly Cream:

1 cup thickened cream, chilled
¾ teaspoon vanilla sugar

Blackberry Sauce:

1 box blackberries or any other ripe berries, or
  125 g frozen berries
⅓ cup castor sugar
lemon juice to taste

Bavarian Cream:

2 cups milk
1 vanilla bean, split lengthwise
5 teaspoons gelatine
3 tablespoons cold water
1½ tablespoons eau de vie de framboise
6 egg yolks
⅔ cup castor sugar

To make Chantilly cream: whip cream and sugar together until it forms just firm peaks. (In hot weather, chill the bowl.) Reserve half the quantity for decoration and refrigerate covered.

To make blackberry sauce: blend fruit (if using frozen berries or fruit defrost first, catching juices) and castor sugar together in a blender or food processor until smooth. Stir in lemon juice to taste.

To make Bavarian cream: bring milk and vanilla bean slowly to the boil in a pan over low heat. Turn off heat, cover and leave to infuse for 10 minutes. Mix together gelatine, cold water and liqueur in a small bowl. In a medium bowl, beat egg yolks and castor sugar until mixture ribbons (when you lift the beater above the mixture it should leave a ribbon pattern on top). Remove vanilla bean from hot milk, wash and dry on paper towel. Reserve for making vanilla sugar. Beating constantly, pour hot milk on to yolk mixture slowly. Return mixture to the same pan and cook slowly over low heat, stirring constantly, until mixture thickens and coats the back of a wooden spoon. Immediately remove from the heat and stir in gelatine mixture. Cool in a basin of cold water, stirring from time to time. If you do accidentally cook sauce and it curdles, blend until it is smooth again, and return to recipe as though nothing had gone wrong.

To make Bavarois: using a rubber spatula, very carefully fold half the Chantilly cream into the Bavarian cream. Rinse a 6-cup metal mould with cold water then sprinkle ¼ cup castor sugar into it, distributing it evenly around the inside. This will help when turning out the Bavarian cream.

Cover base of mould with a thin layer of the blackberry sauce. (Use any left-over sauce to spoon around Bavarian cream at serving time.) Very carefully pour Bavarian cream mixture into prepared mould, cover with plastic film and leave to set in the refrigerator for a minimum of 2 hours or longer in hot weather.

To unmould, dip mould into warm water for a few seconds, then invert and shake out on a serving dish. Using a forcing bag fitted with a star tube, decorate Bavarian cream with reserved Chantilly cream, and spoon remaining blackberry sauce around base.

Average times Preparation — 40 minutes
Cooking — 15 minutes
Standing — 10 minutes
Cooling — 20 minutes
Setting — 2 hours

Wine notes The Bavarois calls for a sweet
white —
A: St Leonards (Rutherglen)
  Late Harvest Semillon
E: Château Coutet (Barsac) of a
  good year
U: Château Bethune (Napa)
  Late Harvest Semillon

Do ahead Sauce 1 day. Bavarois and
Chantilly cream, ½ day

146

AUTUMN

MENU 20

The first course is from a famous chef in the north of Italy, Angelo Paracucchi, whose influence on my work is evident throughout these menus. It's a real prize; one to be used over and over again. In fact, served as a main course it's an excellent luncheon dish simply followed by fresh fruit. The Florentine shoulder of lamb is the kind of roast which came from the Ecumenical Council in Florence in 1430. It is followed by a zabaglione from the Gritti Palace Hotel in Venice and it's one of the best in the business.

SOUFFLÉ GNOCCHI

1¼ cups plain flour, sifted
2 teaspoons salt
1 cup cold water
125 g butter, cut into small pieces
6 55 g eggs
½ cup finely grated Parmesan cheese

2 cups béchamel sauce (see page 65)
½ cup thin cream
½ cup finely grated Parmesan cheese, extra
30 g butter

extra finely grated Parmesan cheese for serving

Combine flour and salt. In a medium, heavy pan, heat water and butter until boiling. Immediately (so the mixture doesn't reduce) pour in flour and salt. Stir with a wooden spoon over medium heat until mixture forms a ball, leaving sides of pan. Reduce heat and cook slowly for 5 minutes stirring with wooden spoon. Cool for 10 minutes.

Place mixture in a food processor and with machine running mix in 1 egg at a time, working well between each addition. (This can be done by hand, beating eggs in 1 at a time, using a wooden spoon.) Beat in ½ cup Parmesan cheese and cool. Pile one-third of mixture into a large piping bag fitted with a 1 cm plain tube.

Have ready a large pan of rapidly boiling salted water and a sharp thin-bladed knife. Rest piping bag on edge of pan, holding it in your second hand, that is, your less dextrous hand. Squeeze bag and at the same time, using knife, cut off 4 cm lengths of mixture with your master hand. This must be done extremely quickly or else the first gnocchi will be cooked before the last ones are in water. Only ever attempt to cook one-third of the mixture at a time. When gnocchi have risen to the surface and feel resilient to the touch, they are done (about 1½ to 2 minutes). Lift out with a skimmer into a large bowl of cold water to prevent further cooking. Repeat with remaining mixture.

Drain gnocchi and place on a tray lined with a clean tea towel, cover and refrigerate until ready to use. This much can be done in the morning for the evening, or you may proceed with the recipe without refrigerating. Arrange gnocchi in a single layer in a large buttered gratiné dish or lasagne dish. Pour over béchamel sauce, which has been thinned with cream, scatter with extra Parmesan cheese and dob with butter over the top. Bake in the centre of 220°C (425°F) oven for 12 to 15 minutes or until the gnocchi have expanded and the sauce is bubbling. Serve at once, and pass extra Parmesan cheese at the table.

Average times Preparation — 20 minutes
Cooking — 30 minutes
Cooling — 10 minutes

Do ahead Up to 2 days, covered and refrigerated

Wine notes Soufflé Gnocchi is rich and flavoursome, so needs a full-flavoured, wooded white —
A: Tyrrell's (Pokolbin) Wood Matured Semillon
E and U: Frascati Superiore ('Villa Portziana')

FLORENTINE SHOULDER OF LAMB

◆

3 cloves garlic, peeled and cut into slivers
2–2.5 kg shoulder of lamb, boned out

a few branches of fresh rosemary or fennel
salt and freshly ground black pepper

◆

Stick garlic into meat, using a sharp knife to insert. Roll meat and tie it with string at 2 cm intervals, running the branches of rosemary or fennel along meat and hold in place with string. Season generously with salt and pepper.

Cook in a lightly oiled baking dish in 180°C (350°F) oven. During cooking, keep basting meat with its own juices. You can add potatoes or other vegetables to cook around lamb. Cook lamb 1¼ to 1½ hours or until done the way you like it. Rest 10 minutes before removing strings and herbs. Carve into 1½ cm slices.

Serve fried egg-plant slices with the lamb.

Average times Preparation — 10 minutes
Cooking — 1¼ hours
Standing — 10 minutes

Do ahead Up to oven stage, 1 day

Wine notes Florentine Lamb requires a fruity astringent red —
A: Petaluma Coonawarra Shiraz Cabernet
E and U: Tignanello (Antinori) from Tuscany

ZABAGLIONE

◆

2½ teaspoons gelatine
1 tablespoon hot water
9 egg yolks

½ cup castor sugar
½ cup Marsala

◆

Dissolve the gelatine in hot water. Put with all the remaining ingredients into zabaglione pan or alternatively a large pyrex bowl set over a pan of simmering water. The water must not touch the mixture. Whisk mixture constantly until it thickens and triples in volume, approximately 15 minutes. Remove from hot water and continue to beat until it is nearly cool. (You can hasten cooling process by beating over iced water.)

Spoon into individual glasses, cover and refrigerate until set.

Average times Preparation — 5 minutes
Cooking — 15 minutes
Cooling — 20 minutes
Chilling — 2 hours

Do ahead Up to 2 hours before serving

Wine notes Zabaglione, with its Marsala flavour, needs a light Marsala, or a fortified, sweet white —
A: Coolawin Estates Old Liqueur Sweet White
E and U: Marsala Garibaldi Dolce (Diego Rallo & Figli) from Sicily

WINTER

AUTHORS NOTE
Every recipe is designed to serve six unless stated otherwise.

WINTER

MENU 1

———◆———

This is an easily executed menu for lunch or dinner and the pears were one of my family's favourite desserts.

THIN SPAGHETTI WITH EGG-PLANT

———◆———

500 g egg-plants
salt
3 tablespoons olive oil, to sauté
2 cloves garlic, finely chopped
2 tablespoons finely chopped Italian parsley

425 g can peeled table tomatoes
¼ teaspoon hot chilli, finely chopped, or to
    taste
olive oil for frying
375 g fine spaghetti

———◆———

Peel the egg-plants and cut them lengthwise in slices 2 cm thick. Spread out in a single layer and salt them liberally. Leave to disgorge for 30 minutes.

In a medium pan sauté garlic in olive oil over medium heat until garlic begins to colour lightly. Stir in parsley, tomatoes, chilli and salt to taste and cook uncovered for 25 minutes stirring from time to time.

Pour enough oil into a large heavy frying pan to come 2½ cm up the side and heat until very hot. Pat the egg-plant slices dry on paper towel and fry them in a single layer a few at a time until nicely golden on both sides. Drain on crumpled paper and repeat with remaining slices. Cut the fried egg-plants into long slices approximately 1 cm wide. Add to tomato sauce and cook for a further 3 minutes. Taste and adjust the seasoning.

Bring a large pan of salted water to the boil. When it has reached a rapid, rolling boil stir in pasta and cook until it is *al dente*.

Have a large warmed serving bowl ready with one-third of sauce in it. Catch pasta and drop into bowl. Toss thoroughly. Pour in remaining sauce, toss again and serve at once.

Average times Preparation — 15 minutes
              Standing — 30 minutes
              Cooking — 55 minutes

Wine notes Spaghetti with egg-plant needs a
            medium-bodied red —
            A: Lindemans Nyrang Hermi-
               tage
            E and U: Montepulciano
                   d'Abruzzo (Valentini)

Do ahead Sauce up to ½ day

CHICKEN IN CINNAMON SAUCE

3 tablespoons olive oil
2 × 1.4 kg chickens. Cut each into 10 serving size pieces, discarding wing tips and backs of chickens
2 cloves garlic, finely chopped
1 large white onion, finely chopped

500 g ripe tomatoes, peeled and chopped
3 cloves tied in muslin
2 teaspoons ground cinnamon
salt and freshly ground black pepper to taste
1 cup water

Heat oil in a flame-proof casserole over high heat. Fry several chicken pieces at a time stirring until golden all over. Lift out with a slotted spoon, set aside and repeat with remaining chicken pieces.

Reduce heat and return all the chicken pieces to casserole. Stir in garlic and onion and cook stirring until softened. Add tomatoes, cloves, cinnamon, salt and pepper to taste and pour in water. Stir, cover and simmer for 35 minutes or until the chicken is cooked.

If the sauce is too thin lift out chicken pieces, place on a warm serving platter and set aside in a warm place. Reduce sauce over medium high heat stirring with a wooden spatula until it is a good consistency. Spoon over chicken and serve.

Accompany the chicken with a green salad.

Average times Preparation — 25 minutes
                 Cooking — 1 hour

Do ahead At least 1 day and up to 2 days

Wine notes The Chicken in Cinnamon Sauce would be complemented by continuing the red from the first course

PERFECT BROWN PEARS

2 tablespoons golden syrup
1 cup water
6 medium Beurre Bosc pears
2 pinches mixed ground spice
¼ teaspoon ground ginger
4 navel oranges, skinned and sliced finely
2 tablespoons slivered almonds, toasted

Chantilly Cream:
300 ml thickened cream
pure icing sugar sifted, to taste
vanilla essence to taste

Bring golden syrup and water to boil. Split pears lengthwise leaving the stems attached to one of each half. Using a teaspoon scoop out cores. Lie pears skin side down in a baking dish and pour over the boiling syrup. Sprinkle over spice and ginger and cook in 175°C (350°F) oven for 1 hour or until tender, basting from time to time.

Cool pears, basting them occasionally with syrup to prevent them from drying out. Arrange pears around edge of an oval serving dish with stalk ends facing outwards. Fill centre with orange slices and sprinkle almonds over them.

To make Chantilly cream: beat cream with enough icing sugar and vanilla essence to taste until cream stands in soft peaks. Spoon cream into the 12 hollowed-out pears, cover and chill until ready to serve.

Average times Preparation — 20 minutes
                 Cooking — 50 minutes
                 Cooling — 2 hours

Do ahead Up to Chantilly cream stage, 1 day

Wine notes The Perfect Brown Pears are complemented by a sweet white —
A: Mt Pleasant Sauternes
E and U: Château Doisy-Védrines (Barsac) of a good year

WINTER

MENU 2

---◆---

A delightfully easy and attractive family menu suitable for day or night.

CREAM OF WHITE ONION SOUP

---◆---

60 g butter
6 medium white onions, sliced
1 tablespoon plain flour
300 ml water
salt, pepper to taste
750 ml milk

finely chopped parsley to garnish
1 egg yolk, beaten, or 1 tablespoon cream
(optional)

---◆---

Heat butter and when sizzling, add onions and cook stirring for 3 minutes, without allowing them to colour. Stir in flour, then add water, still stirring. Reduce heat and season with salt and pepper. Cook for 10 minutes to reduce, stirring from time to time. Stir in milk and simmer very gently for 15 minutes or until onions are soft. To serve, sprinkle top with chopped parsley.

This soup can be puréed but is very good as it is. It may be enriched by adding 1 beaten egg yolk or 1 tablespoon of cream at the last moment.

Average times Preparation — 10 minutes
Cooking — 30 minutes

Wine notes Onion soup needs a medium sherry —
A: Lindemans Reserve BinZ898A Amontillado Sherry
E and U: Dry Sack Sherry

Do ahead Up to 1 day

RACK OF LAMB WITH BLACK CURRANT SAUCE

---◆---

6 × 4-cutlet racks of lamb, very well trimmed and French boned
salt and fresh ground black pepper to taste

Black Currant Sauce:
300 ml reduced veal stock
250 g black currant jelly
1½ teaspoons potato flour
1 tablespoon port
250 g black currants in syrup, drained

---◆---

Roast racks of lamb in hottest part of 200°C (400°F) oven for 20 to 25 minutes, turning after first 10 minutes and salting only after browned. Turn again after 10 minutes and season second side. Remove from oven and keep warm for 10 minutes before serving.

To make sauce: heat veal stock in medium pan, add jelly and mash with a potato masher. Blend flour and port and thicken sauce. Add currants and heat through.

Spoon sauce onto 6 warmed dinner plates and stand racks of lamb in sauce.

Serve steamed or roasted vegetables in season with the lamb.

Average times	Preparation — 5 minutes	**Do ahead** Sauce, up to 1 day
	Cooking — 25 minutes	
Wine notes	Lamb requires a full-flavoured	
	Cabernet —	
	A: Enterprise Cabernet	
	Sauvignon, from Clare	
	E: Chateau Pichon-Longueville	
	(Pauillac)	
	U: Heitz (Napa) Cabernet	
	Sauvignon — Bella Oaks	

TRIFLE

one half of a 20 cm plain sponge (Genoise)
60 ml Madeira or medium sherry
6 macaroons
60 g raspberry jam or 1 box fresh raspberries
thick pastry cream (see below)
1 cup cream

Thick Pastry Cream:

700 ml milk
4 egg yolks
5 tablespoons castor sugar
6 tablespoons plain flour
1 teaspoon cornflour

Garnish:

¼ cup slivered almonds, toasted
6 crystallized violets (see page 191)

Break sponge into large pieces and place in a clear glass (1 litre) serving bowl. Pour madeira or sherry over sponge. Break the macaroons over top and stand for ¼ hour, while making the pastry cream.

To make pastry cream: heat milk. Mix egg yolks, castor sugar and two flours together in a medium bowl. Pour hot milk over them, whisking. Return to pan and cook, whisking constantly until thickened and smooth. Make very sure flour is thoroughly cooked in the cream — taste to test. Cool over cold water, whisking. This prevents a skin forming.

To assemble trifle: spoon jam or raspberries over sponge and macaroons.

When pastry cream is slightly cooled, pour over trifle. Whip cream until it forms ribbons and spread over cooled pastry cream. Cover with plastic film until ready to serve.

Garnish with slivered almonds and crystallized violets.

Average times	Preparation — 15 minutes	**Wine notes** The trifle is complemented by a
	Cooking — 10 minutes	fortified sweet white —
	Standing — 15 minutes	A: Baileys Show Tokay from
	Cooling — 1 hour	northern Victoria
		E and U: Rainwater Madeira
Do ahead Up to garnishing, 1 day		(Leacock)

WINTER

MENU 3

An excellent menu for family entertaining beginning with a rich shellfish soup, followed by a Scandinavian-inspired lamb dish which is an old favourite. The potato straw cake to accompany the lamb is so good that you will find yourself using it over and over again.

SHELLFISH SOUP

30 g butter
1 medium white onion, sliced
1 tablespoon tomato purée
1 clove garlic, crushed
salt and pepper to taste
1 teaspoon sugar
1 fresh bouquet garni
1 tablespoon plain flour

½ cup dry white wine
2 cups fish stock
500 g scallops, cleaned
500 g green prawns, shelled, deveined and cut
  in two
125 g white button mushrooms, sliced finely
1 teaspoon lemon juice

freshly snipped dill to garnish

In a stock pot, heat butter and sauté onion until golden. Add tomato purée, garlic, salt, pepper, sugar and bouquet garni. Simmer 5 minutes and add flour and stir 2 minutes. Pour in wine and stock and cook (it's a fairly thick mixture) for 20 minutes. Remove bouquet garni and add scallops, prawns and mushrooms and simmer for 2 minutes. Stir in lemon juice. (Do not boil the soup after adding the shellfish).

Serve in warm soup bowls and scatter with freshly snipped dill.

Average times Preparation — 20 minutes
Cooking — 35 minutes

Wine notes Shellfish Soup calls for a fresh,
acid white —
A: Brown Bros (north-eastern
  Victoria) Sauvignon Blanc
E: Sancerre Clos de la Poussie of
  a good year
U: St Clement (Napa)
  Sauvignon Blanc

Do ahead Up to cooking fish and mushrooms, 1 day

COFFEE BASTED LAMB

2 cloves garlic, peeled and cut into slivers
1.75 kg leg of lamb, well trimmed of fat
1 tablespoon peanut oil
2 teaspoons salt
1 teaspoon dry mustard
1 cup veal or chicken stock

1 cup very strong milk coffee
1 tablespoon plain flour
½ cup cream
salt and freshly ground black pepper to taste
2 tablespoons red currant jelly

Using a sharp knife, insert garlic slivers into lamb near the bone in several places. Rub oil all over lamb. Mix salt and mustard together and rub well into lamb.

Put lamb in a heavy, dry baking dish and roast in hottest part of 210°C (420°F) oven for 10 minutes. Turn lamb, baste with stock and return to the oven for a further 20 minutes. Turn the lamb again and baste with coffee. Leave lamb to cook until the way you like it, approximately another 10 minutes for medium-rare lamb.

When lamb is cooked, place on a warm serving dish and keep warm while resting for 10 minutes.

To make sauce: place baking dish over low heat and whisk in flour. Cook for 2 minutes. Whisk in cream and red currant jelly. When jelly has melted, taste and adjust seasoning. Cook over low heat for 10 minutes whisking from time to time. Strain sauce and serve with lamb.

Serve with Potato Straw Cake (see next recipe).

Average time Preparation — 15 minutes	**Wine notes** Lamb in coffee, with its gamy
Cooking — 40 to 60 minutes	flavour, needs a robust red —
Resting — 10 minutes	A: Robson (Pokolbin) Shiraz
	E: Côte-Rôtie (Jasmin)
Do ahead Prepare lamb up to oven stage, up	U: Sierra Vista (El Dorado)
to ½ day ahead	Zinfandel

POTATO STRAW CAKE

750 g old potatoes, peeled and washed	salt and pepper to taste
125 g butter	

Coarsely grate potatoes and cover with cold water. Drain and wash again to remove starch. Drain in a colander, spread them out in a clean tea-towel and roll up, pressing out as much moisture as possible.

This much can be done up to 1 hour in advance. In a heavy 22 cm frying pan, heat 75 g of butter over a medium heat until golden. Add potatoes and pack down with back of a fork. Sprinkle with salt and pepper and put half remaining butter in small pieces on the top. Cover with a lid and cook over low to medium heat for 15 minutes. With a spatula, lift up one side to see if cake is golden and set underneath. When it is, slip cake onto a large flat lid, pizza tray or back of an oven tray. Turn lid upside down over frying pan, so cake lands uncooked side down in frying pan. Cut remaining butter into small pieces and place around sides of cake, allowing it to melt and run under it.

Average times Preparation — 10 minutes
Cooking — 35 minutes

PEASANT GIRL

2½ cups ginger nut biscuits, finely ground	2 teaspoons lemon zest, finely grated
90 g butter, melted	4 cups stewed apple slices
1½ cups thick cream, lightly beaten	6 tablespoons coarsely grated dark chocolate

Mix ground biscuits with melted butter. Mix cream and lemon zest together. Spoon biscuit mixture into base of 6 glass bowls and layer apples over them. Top with cream and grated chocolate, cover and chill until ready to serve.

Average times Preparation — 20 minutes	**Wine notes** Peasant Girl needs a fortified,
	sweet white —
	A: Morris (Rutherglen) Liqueur
	Tokay
	E: Malmsey Madeira (Henriques
	& Henriques)
	U: Cresta Blanca (Mendocino)
Do ahead Up to ½ day	Triple Cream Sherry

WINTER

MENU 4

If you are ever lucky enough to be able to pick your own field mushrooms then this is the ideal starter. I once made it with a 20 cm mushroom and cut it into wedges before serving. Followed by two easily executed dishes which are warming and delicious you'll find this menu excellent for family Winter entertaining.

STUFFED MUSHROOMS

½ cup fresh white breadcrumbs
½ cup finely chopped ham or bacon
½ cup finely grated Parmesan cheese
1 clove garlic, finely chopped
¼ cup finely chopped parsley

stalks of 12 medium open mushrooms, finely chopped
salt and freshly ground black pepper to taste
caps of 12 medium open mushrooms
2 tablespoons olive oil

Make stuffing by mixing breadcrumbs, ham or bacon, cheese, garlic, parsley, mushroom stalks and seasonings. Place mushroom caps upside down in a single layer in lightly buttered ovenproof dish. Pile filling into mushroom caps dividing it equally between them. Drizzle olive oil over tops, cover dish with lid or foil and cook at 200°C (400°F) oven for 20 to 25 minutes.

Average times Preparation — 20 minutes
Cooking — 20 minutes

Wine notes Stuffed Mushrooms need a chilled light red or rosé —
A: Idyll Blush Rosé from the Geelong district of Victoria
E: Tavel Rosé
U: Concannon (Alameda) Zinfandel Rosé

Do ahead Up to oven stage, ½ day

DEVILLED LAMB CHOPS

12 chump chops, trimmed of all fat
2 × 425 g cans peeled tomato pieces
2 sticks celery, sliced roughly
2 medium onions, cut in thin slices
3 teaspoons French mustard
1½ tablespoons brown sugar
2 cloves garlic, crushed

1½ tablespoons Worcestershire sauce
1½ tablespoons lemon juice
3 tablespoons sherry
1 tablespoon fresh rosemary leaves

6 tiny rosemary sprigs to garnish

Arrange chops in a heavy casserole dish. Place in hottest part of 200°C (400°F) oven for 25 minutes. Pour off fat and discard it. Heat the tomato pieces in a pan, stir in all the other ingredients except rosemary sprigs and pour over lamb. Cover casserole and return to oven for

20 to 35 minutes or until lamb is tender. Garnish with fresh rosemary sprigs.
Serve with steamed or boiled potatoes and a mixed green salad.

Average times Preparation — 10 minutes
Cooking — 60 minutes

Do ahead At least 1 day and up to 3 days

Wine notes Devilled Lamb Chops require a
fruity Cabernet —
A: Rouge Homme
(Coonawarra) Cabernet
Sauvignon
E: Château La Dominique (St-
Émilion) of a great year
U: Beaulieu (Napa) Cabernet
Sauvignon — Rutherford

RHUBARB PIE

◆

Pastry:

1 cup plain flour
pinch salt
90 g butter chilled, cut into 6 pieces
1–2 tablespoons iced water

Filling:

5 tablespoons sugar
2 cups water
2 bunches rhubarb, washed and cut into 5 cm
lengths

Sauce:

rhubarb cooking syrup
1 tablespoon cornflour

Egg Wash:

1 egg yolk
pinch salt

◆

To make pastry: sift flour and salt and rub butter into it using fingertips until mixture resembles oatmeal. Stir in enough iced water to bring mixture to a ball. Knead dough lightly on a lightly floured board. Flatten to 3 cm, wrap in waxed paper and refrigerate for 30 minutes. Alternatively, make in a food processor.

To make filling: bring sugar and water to boil in a large stainless steel pan, stirring to dissolve sugar. Add rhubarb and cook gently until it is tender. Drain rhubarb in a colander, catching syrup in a medium stainless steel pan.

To make sauce: cool 1 tablespoon of rhubarb cooking syrup and mix with cornflour. Whisk into remaining syrup and cook over medium heat whisking until mixture thickens. Cook slowly for 3 minutes and keep warm until ready to serve.

To assemble pie: spoon drained rhubarb into a 23 cm pie plate. Butter top edge of pie plate.
Roll chilled pastry to fit top of pie plate and place over rhubarb and trim off excess pastry. Whisk egg yolk and salt together and paint over pastry. Prick all over with a skewer.
Cook for 25 to 35 minutes in 220°C (425°F) oven or until the pastry is golden and cooked. Serve pie hot with sauce in a jug and a bowl of whipped cream.

Average times Preparation — 20 minutes
Standing — 30 minutes
Cooking — 40 minutes

Do ahead Prepare pastry up to 1 day

Wine notes Rhubarb Pie needs no wine

WINTER

MENU 5

The salmon roulade recipe was given to me by an Adelaide friend and I've used it successfully for many years, often changing the filling. The main course was devised when I had a bottle of fine vintage port opened and, wanting to do justice to it while it was still in its prime, I tossed it into the oxtail. This is the result which I know you will enjoy. The ice-cream recipe was first published in *Bon Appetit*, written by me in 1982. It's an excellent end to a lovely winter's menu.

SMOKED SALMON ROULADE
Serves 8

60 g butter
90 g flour
salt and white pepper to taste
¾ teaspoon sugar
2 cups milk
4 eggs separated
pinch salt

Filling:
1 cup whipped cream
375 g smoked salmon pieces, chopped
2 tablespoons finely chopped fresh dill
salt and white pepper to taste

Butter a 28 cm × 38 cm Swiss roll pan and flour it lightly. Heat butter in a medium-sized pan and stir in flour, seasonings and sugar. Add milk and bring to boil whisking over high heat. Boil for 2 minutes, take off heat and beat in egg yolks, one at a time. Leave to cool. Whisk egg whites with a pinch of salt until they form stiff peaks and fold into egg yolk mixture using a very light hand. Pour into prepared pan and level with a spatula.

Bake in hottest part of 180°C (350°F) oven for 40 minutes or until puffed and golden. Place a clean tea-towel over a cake rack and turn roulade out onto it. With assistance of tea-towel roll up lengthwise and leave to cool on rack with tea-towel rolled up around it.

Fold all the filling ingredients together and taste. When roulade is quite cold, unroll it and spread with prepared filling. Roll up again, trim ends and place on a serving dish. Serve cut in 2 cm slices.

Average times Preparation — 25 minutes
Cooking — 50 minutes
Cooling — 30 minutes

Do ahead Make roulade up to 1 day ahead.
Fill up to ½ day ahead

Wine notes Smoked Salmon Roulade calls
for a spicy white —
A: Montrose (Mudgee)
Traminer Riesling
E: Gewurtztraminer (Trimbach)
from Alsace
U: Phelps (Napa)
Gewurtztraminer

OX TAIL IN PORT

3 ox tails, jointed
2 onions, peeled and sliced
80 ml peanut oil
2 fresh bouquet garni
600 ml beef stock
750 ml bottle port
salt and fresh ground black pepper

pinch of mace
2 strips of orange rind (not pith)
2 carrots, peeled and diced coarsely
2 turnips, peeled and diced coarsely
2½ tablespoons plain flour
500 g shelled, green peas
freshly chopped parsley

Remove as much fat as possible from the ox tails. Soften onions in hot oil in heavy flameproof casserole. Lift out with a slotted spoon and seal tail joints over high heat until nicely browned.

Add bouquet garni, seasoning, stock and port. Bring to simmer, cover and cook for 3 to 4 hours or until nearly done. Add carrots and turnips, cover and cook until tender.

Using a bulb baster, draw off fat. Mix flour with a little extra stock or water and stir into casserole, cook over medium heat until thickened and taste to make sure flour is thoroughly cooked. Adjust seasoning.

Boil the fresh green peas until just tender. Spoon ox tail into centre of a serving platter, surround with peas, scatter parsley over tail joints and serve with crusty French bread.

Note: I have often made this recipe using a pressure cooker. Proceed exactly the same way but cook for only 45 minutes before adding the 2 root vegetables. They will take about 3 minutes at pressure, then remove lid (after cooling, of course), test both vegetables and ox tail for tenderness and thicken sauce, after removing fat, in the same way as before.

Average times	Preparation — 30 minutes Cooking — 3–4 hours — pressure cooker 45 minutes Standing — preferably overnight	E: Côte-Rôtie (Guigal) of a good year U: Shenandoah (Amador) Zinfandel
Wine notes	Ox Tail in Port needs a robust red — A: Baileys Hermitage from north-eastern Victoria	**Do ahead** Meats which give off a lot of fat are best made the day before, so the fat has a chance to congeal in the refrigerator and can simply be lifted off using a small palette knife. Do not cook root vegetables though until the day you need the ox tail

LEMON-GINGER ICE-CREAM
Makes 1 litre

600 ml thickened cream pared rind 3 medium lemons (no pith) ¾ cup castor sugar	6 egg yolks ¾ cup lemon juice ½ cup finely chopped preserved ginger in syrup, drained

Combine cream and lemon rind in a heavy medium pan and bring slowly to the boil. Remove from heat, cover and set aside for 10 minutes.

Beat castor sugar and egg yolks in a large bowl until pale and mixture forms ribbons when beaters are lifted above it. Strain cream into yolk mixture whisking constantly and discard lemon rind. Return mixture to pan and place over low heat, whisking constantly until mixture is thick enough to coat back of wooden spoon. Do not boil or mixture will curdle. (If curdling occurs, immediately transfer to a blender or food processor and mix at high speed until smooth). Transfer to a bowl set over ice and cool completely, either by whisking or with a circle of greaseproof paper set directly on top of cream to prevent a skin forming.

Stir lemon juice and ginger into cooled cream and refrigerate until thoroughly chilled, at least 1 hour. Transfer mixture to an ice-cream churn and process according to manufacturer's instructions. Turn into a plastic container, cover and freeze until ready to use. Let soften slightly before serving.

Average times	Preparation — 10 minutes Cooking — 15 minutes Standing — 10 minutes Cooling — 1½ hours Freezing — 2 hours (after churning)	**Do ahead** At least ½ day, preferably overnight **Wine notes** Lemon-Ginger Ice-Cream requires no wine

WINTER

MENU 6

The first course needs to be made in advance, as does the second, which is a charming beef dish from the south of France. I first tasted it with friends whilst sitting on a terrace surrounded by olive groves and bougainvillea on the Côte d'Azur in the early 1970s. It was one of my catering business' most fashionable dishes in Melbourne during those years. Pears are complemented by something hot like ginger or pepper. This is a lovely way to prepare them and is very different.

AVOCADO MOUSSE

---

3 teaspoons gelatine
¾ cup hot water
2 large ripe avocados, puréed
lemon juice, to taste
cayenne pepper to taste

salt to taste
2 cups thickened cream, whipped lightly

sliced lemon or fresh shellfish, to garnish

Stir gelatine and water together until gelatine dissolves. Cool slightly. Stir avocado purée, lemon juice and seasonings together in a large bowl. Stir in cooled gelatine and fold in cream. Pour into 4-cup wetted mould. Cover with plastic film and refrigerate overnight or until set.

To unmould, pull mixture away from top edge of mould with fingers, dip mould in warm water, invert over serving plate and shake out. Garnish with decorated and sliced lemons or fresh shell fish and serve.

Average times Preparation — 20 minutes
Setting — 4 hours

Wine notes Avocado Mousse needs a fruity
white —
A: Leasingham Traminer
Riesling from Clare
E: Deidesheimer Kieselberg
Riesling Spaetlese
(Rheinpfalz)
U: Freemark Abbey (Napa)
Johannisberg Riesling

Do ahead Up to ½ day

ESTOUFFADE OF BEEF ARLESIENNE

---

3 tablespoons olive oil
250 g lean smoked bacon, in the piece
1 kg buttock steak, cut into 2 cm cubes
3 tablespoons plain flour
1½ cups dry white wine
1½ cups water

5 medium white onions, skinned and quartered
salt and freshly ground black pepper to taste
1 fresh bouquet garni
5 cloves garlic, skinned and bruised, tied in muslin
6 large tomatoes, skinned and quartered
1 cup black olives

Heat oil in a cast-iron casserole. Skin bacon and cut into 2 cm cubes and brown in hot oil rendering as much fat as possible. Stir until bacon is nicely golden and lift out with a slotted spoon. Set aside.

Brown beef in hot oil and bacon fat, stirring until it is well sealed on all sides. (If the casserole is too small, brown half the beef at a time.) Return bacon to casserole and stir in flour. Pour in wine and water and stir until well incorporated. Add onions and seasoning, bouquet garni and garlic. Cover and cook in 200°C (400°F) oven for 45 minutes. Stir in tomatoes and olives and continue to cook until meat is tender. Remove garlic and bouquet garni and serve.

Accompany with a green salad.

Average times	Preparation — 20 minutes Cooking — 1 hour 20 minutes	**Wine notes**	The beef needs a strong red — A: Henschke Mt Edelstone Shiraz E: Domaine de Mont-Redon Châteauneuf-du-Pape U: Roudon-Smith (Santa Cruz) Zinfandel
Do ahead	Up to 2 days		

PEARS IN SAUTERNES WITH CRÈME ANGLAISE SPIKED WITH GREEN PEPPERCORNS

6 ripe, yellow pears preferably with stalks
juice 1 lemon
1 bottle Sauternes

Crème Anglaise:

300 ml milk
1 vanilla bean, split lengthwise
3 egg yolks
2 tablespoons castor sugar
1 tablespoon green peppercorns, washed and drained

Peel pears and cover with cold water and lemon juice. Bring bottle of Sauternes gently to a simmer in a pan (not aluminium) just large enough to hold 6 pears standing upright. Place pears upright in simmering Sauternes and discard acidulated water. Cover pears and cook gently for 30 minutes or until tender. Cool in Sauternes.

To make Crème Anglaise: bring milk and vanilla bean slowly to boil in a medium-sized pan. Whisk egg yolks and castor sugar together until pale and light. Remove vanilla bean from milk, wash and dry it and reserve for making vanilla sugar. Pour hot milk over egg yolks, whisking constantly. Return mixture to milk pan and cook over medium heat, whisking until sauce thickens enough to coat the back of a wooden spatula. Do not let the mixture boil.

Cool over a bowl of iced water, whisking from time to time, or set a circle of greaseproof paper immediately on top of sauce to prevent a skin forming. When sauce is cold, stir in green peppercorns.

Spoon a sea of sauce into centre of 6 flat dessert plates and stand a pear in each. Serve any remaining sauce separately in a jug at table.

Average times	Preparation — 10 minutes Cooking — 40 minutes Cooling — 2 hours	**Wine notes**	Pears spiked with peppercorns call for a rich sweet white — A: Orlando (Barossa) Auslese Semillon E: Château Rieussec (Sauternes) U: Phelps (Napa) Late Harvest Johannisberg Riesling
Do ahead	Up to 1 day but do not stir peppercorns into sauce until 1 to 2 hours before serving or sauce becomes too hot		

WINTER

MENU 7

———◆———

This is good family mid-Winter fare for lunch or dinner, with two do-ahead dishes, leaving only the pudding to be cooked at the last minute.

CREAM OF GREEN PEA SOUP

———◆———

45 g butter
2 large white onions, coarsely chopped
400 g frozen peas
5 cups chicken or veal stock

salt and pepper to taste

1 tablespoon finely chopped fresh mint to garnish

———◆———

Heat butter in a large pan and cook onions stirring over medium heat until softened, but do not let them brown. Add peas and stir over high heat for 2 minutes, add stock and seasoning and simmer with lid off for 30 minutes. Cool soup over cold water and purée, preferably in a blender. Return to pan and heat through, adjust seasoning. Serve and garnish with fresh mint. A little thickened cream may be stirred through the soup at the last minute if wanted.

Average times Preparation — 10 minutes
Cooking — 40 minutes
Cooling — 10 minutes

Wine notes The soup is complemented by a
fino sherry —
A: Seppelt Show Fino Sherry
E and U: Ynocente Sherry
(Valdespino)

Do ahead 1–2 days

STEAK AND KIDNEY PIE

1 large onion, chopped
1.5 kg lean beef, cut into 2½ cm cubes
100 g butter
375 g button mushrooms, quartered
1 ox kidney, skinned, cleaned and sliced
2 cups water or beef stock made with 2 beef cubes
1 tablespoon chopped parsley

salt and pepper to taste
4 rashers bacon, rind removed and fried till crisp, crumbled coarsely
1 sheet pre-rolled puff pastry

Egg Glaze:

1 egg
pinch of salt

Cook onion and beef in a heavy pan with butter until golden brown. Add mushrooms and kidney and cook, stirring for 2 minutes. Add water or stock and parsley and cook slowly on low heat until tender. Season to taste.

Pour into a buttered pie dish, place cooked bacon on top and leave to cool. Top with a layer of puff pastry; trim and stick down. Decorate with offcuts of pastry. Beat egg and salt together and brush over pastry. Bake in 220°C (425°F) oven for 20 to 25 minutes or until pastry has risen and is golden. Serve piping hot.

Accompany the pie with a green salad.

Average times Preparation — 25 minutes
Cooking — 60 minutes

Do ahead Filling up to oven stage, 1 day.
Completed pie, up to ½ day

Wine notes Steak and Kidney Pie is complemented by a hearty red —
A: Lindemans Hunter River Burgundy
E: Côtes du Rhône (Guigal)
U: Foppiano (Sonoma) Petite Syrah

BREAD AND BUTTER PUDDING

8 thin slices white bread, without crusts
⅓ cup sultanas
45 g unsalted butter, softened
3 tablespoon soft brown sugar
2½ cups milk

vanilla bean, split lengthwise
3 eggs, beaten
freshly grated nutmeg

ice-cream and cream to serve

Stamp bread in pretty shapes (I like to make heart shapes). Scatter sultanas in base of a buttered lasagne or gratiné dish. Butter bread and place butter-side up, side by side or slightly overlapping, on top of sultanas. Sprinkle sugar over top. Slowly heat milk with vanilla bean and when just boiling remove from heat and leave to infuse with lid on for 10 minutes. Remove vanilla bean, wash and dry it thoroughly and reserve for making vanilla sugar. Pour hot milk on to beaten eggs and strain mixture into prepared dish. Grate nutmeg over top and set dish aside for 30 minutes to allow bread to soak up flavours.

Bake in 180°C (350°F) oven for 35 to 40 minutes or until set and golden brown on top. Serve at once, with ice-cream and cream.

Average times Preparation — 15 minutes
Cooking — 45 minutes
Standing — 40 minutes

Do ahead Up to oven stage, ½ hour ahead

Wine notes Bread and Butter Pudding needs an aromatic sweet white —
A: Mt Pleasant Sauternes
E and U: Muscat de Beaumes de Venise (Cave des Vignerons de Beaumes de Venise)

163

WINTER

MENU 8

Beginning with two do-ahead courses this menu leaves you free to pay attention to a classical French recipe which I've adapted for the busy cook.

CRAB PÂTÉ

Béchamel Sauce:

30 g butter
1 tablespoon plain flour
1 cup milk, approximately
salt and pepper to taste

2 teaspoons gelatine powder
¼ cup dry white wine

30 g butter, extra
1 small white onion, chopped finely
½ large red capsicum, seeded and chopped finely
¼ teaspoon sugar
¾ teaspoon hot chilli sauce
250 g frozen, Alaskan crab, *or* 250 g canned crab after draining (keep juice)

To make béchamel sauce: heat butter in a small pan and cook flour in it for 2 minutes, whisking. Measure crab juices and pour in milk to measure 1 cup. Pour into roux and cook over medium heat whisking until thickened. Cook over low heat for 5 minutes — season to taste.

To make pâté: stir gelatine into wine and heat over hot water to melt and set aside. Heat butter in a small frying pan and sauté onion until soft. Add capsicum, stir and cook over medium heat with lid on for 2 minutes. Add béchamel sauce with sugar, chilli sauce and gelatine mixture. Stir over high heat until it boils.

Pour into a medium bowl and fold through crab, keeping legs in chunky pieces. Taste and adjust seasoning. Cool to blood temperature over a bowl of cold water stirring from time to time.

Rinse a 2½ cup mould with cold water and pour mixture into it. Cover with plastic wrap and refrigerate until set, about 4 hours or overnight.

To serve, dip mould in warm water, pull mixture away from top sides of mould, invert over a serving plate and shake out. Serve with salad greens and sliced cucumbers.

Average times Preparation — 20 minutes
Cooking — 25 minutes
Setting — 4 hours

Wine notes Crab Pâté needs a white wine with high acidity —
A: Lindemans Hunter River Reserve Bin Chablis
E: Chablis 1er Cru Fourchame (Regnard)
U: Wente (Alameda) Grey Riesling

Do ahead ½ day at least

VEAL GOULASH

———◆———

60 g butter
1.5 kg stewing veal (from shoulder) cut in large
   pieces about 5 cm
8 pickling onions, peeled
1 tablespoon paprika
4 medium tomatoes, quartered

1 medium green pepper, seeded and cut into
   2½ cm dice
salt
1 cup light sour cream
2 tablespoons capers (optional)

———◆———

In a heavy, flameproof casserole, heat butter until it foams, drop in veal pieces and seal them on all sides. Lift out and sauté pickling onions until just golden.

Stir in paprika, then tomatoes, green pepper and salt to taste. Cover and cook over very low heat until meat is tender, about 35 to 40 minutes. Stir through sour cream and serve hot, with capers scattered over top if desired. Accompany with fluffy dried boiled potato quarters.

Average times Preparation — 15 minutes
Cooking — 55 minutes

Do ahead Make 1 day ahead but do not add
sour cream or it may ferment

Wine notes Veal Goulash is traditionally
served with the hearty
Hungarian red Bikaver (Bull's
Blood) —
A: Allandale (Pokolbin) Shiraz
E and U: Egri Bikaver

TARTE TATIN (APPLE TART)

———◆———

375 g packet puff pastry
7 medium Granny Smith apples
1 cup castor sugar

1 teaspoon cinnamon
60 g unsalted butter

———◆———

Choose a 24 cm heavy-based frying pan and wrap handle in several sheets of foil if it is not heatproof.

On a lightly floured board, roll pastry to a circle a little larger than frying pan rim. Place frying pan upside down on pastry and cut around it with a sharp knife. Leave pastry to rest while you prepare apples, or refrigerate on board if weather is very hot.

Peel apples, halve them and remove cores. Cut each half into 4 pieces and drop into a large bowl. Sprinkle with sugar and cinnamon.

In frying pan, melt butter and pour over sliced apples, mixing well. Without wiping out frying pan, make rings of apples in base of frying pan, and fill in all gaps. (The base becomes the top of tart.) Pour remaining apples pieces over top and level them.

Carefully place circle of pastry over apples. Place frying pan in hottest part of 180°C (350°F) oven and bake for 35 minutes or until pastry has risen and is golden. Take frying pan from oven, and over medium heat cook for 2 to 3 minutes. Turn heat down to low and continue to cook, caramelizing juices in the tart, for 10 minutes. Do not let catch or top of tart with be spoiled.

Run a spatula around edge, invert on a large pizza tray or flat saucepan lid, then slide onto a serving dish. The crust will form the base of tart and caramelized apples will cover top. Serve warm or cold. This tart may be accompanied by thick or thin cream.

Average times Preparation — 30 minutes
(with ready made puff pastry)
— 20 minutes
(with pre-rolled pastry)
Cooking — 45 minutes
Do ahead Can be made in advance if serving
cold but is never as good as when
served straight from pan

Wine notes Tarte Tartin needs a long-
finishing sweet white —
A: Mitchelton Coonawarra
Botrytis Rhine Riesling
E: Château Coutet (Barsac)
U: Jekel (Monterey) Late Har-
vest Johannisberg Riesling

WINTER

MENU 9

A beautiful dinner party menu with a first course which requires not only dexterity but very careful watching at the last minute. I have unashamedly pinched the idea from a famous restaurateur in Munich. Finishing with a classic French dessert, I've changed the Summer fruit, which is usually apricots or plums, to apples and pears, which are ideal cooked this way. The chocolate pastilles were originally called Aussie chocolates for a demonstration which I gave overseas to illustrate the versatility of our Australian dried fruit industry. They are very easy and will always be a great hit.

PLATE COOKED SALMON TROUT WITH HERB BEURRE BLANC

Beurre Blanc:
See Lime Beurre Blanc in Stuffed Trout with Julienne Vegetables, page 95 substitute lemon juice for lime juice

600–700 g very thin slices salmon trout or rainbow trout (no skin)

6 baby white button mushrooms, finely sliced through the stalk to garnish
18 fresh tarragon leaves to garnish

Make Beurre Blanc as instructed on page 95 and keep warm. Keep the tarragon to garnish the sauce.

Dip the fish slices into hot sauce and arrange, not overlapping, on 6 large heatproof entrée plates. Cook under a hot grill on lowest level until fish turns opaque. You must watch it very carefully because sauce will curdle if it is over-heated.

Scatter with mushrooms and strew with tarragon. Serve at once.

Average times Preparation — 15 minutes
Cooking sauce — 10 minutes
Fish — 1 to 2 minutes

Wine notes Salmon trout's richness needs a top quality Chardonnay with fresh acidity —
A: Seville Estate Chardonnay from the Yarra Valley in Victoria
E: Corton-Charlemagne (Louis Latour)
U: Robert Mondavi (Napa) Reserve Chardonnay

ROAST FILLET OF BEEF WITH POT POURRI OF VEGETABLES

2 × 700 g fillets of beef, skinned and trimmed
thoroughly
60 g butter
salt and freshly ground black pepper to taste
1 cup beef stock
6 young carrots, peeled and cut into 4 cm
lengths
3 young medium turnips, peeled and cut into
2 cm dice
6 medium pink eye potatoes, peeled and cut
into 2 cm dice

750 g stringless beans, topped and tailed and
left whole *or* Italian ribbon beans or snake
beans cut into 8 cm lengths
1 cup shelled peas
60 g butter

¼ cup freshly chopped parsley to garnish

Smear beef with butter and place in a heavy baking dish. Roast in hottest part of 200°C (400°F) oven for 10 minutes, turn over fillet and season generously. Return to oven for another 10 minutes, turn again and season second side. Cook for another 10 minutes for medium-rare beef. Remove to a platter and keep warm while resting for 10 minutes.

Spoon off all remaining fat in baking dish except for 1 tablespoon. Place over high heat and scrape up all caramelized juices on bottom of pan, using a whisk. Pour in stock and cook, whisking from time to time until sauce has reduced by half. Taste and adjust seasoning if necessary and set aside to keep warm.

Cook vegetables separately by either steaming or boiling in salted water until *al dente*. Drain thoroughly and set aside.

Carve fillet into 2 cm thick slices and arrange slightly overlapping down centre of a warmed serving platter. Arrange vegetables in groups, keeping colours separate around beef. Butter vegetables with extra butter and spoon sauce over beef. Garnish with parsley and serve at once.

Average times Preparation — 25 minutes
Cooking — 30 minutes
Standing — 10 minutes

Wine notes The beef needs a full-flavoured
red —
A: Barry (Clare) Jud's Hill
Merlot Cabernet Sauvignon
E: Château Latour à Pomerol of
a great year
U: Clos du Val (Napa) Merlot

APPLE AND PEAR CLAFOUTI

6 eggs	juice of 1 lemon
1½ cups thickened cream	1 tablespoon soft brown sugar
1½ tablespoons pure icing sugar, sifted	½ teaspoon cinnamon
3 tablespoons kirsch	2 tablespoons butter
3 Granny Smith apples	3 tablespoons icing sugar, extra
3 ripe pears	

Butter a 6-cup china or glass gratiné dish. In a medium bowl, beat eggs with cream, icing sugar and kirsch. Peel apples and pears, halve and core them and slice into 1 cm thick slices. Place in buttered dish, pour over lemon juice and mix well to prevent browning. Scatter over brown sugar, cinnamon and again toss fruit well.

Pour over egg cream mixture. Dot top of the dish with butter, wipe around the sides and top of dish and place in hottest part of 170°C (360°F) oven for 30 minutes or until golden on top, puffed up and set around sides and still a little creamy in centre. Dust top with icing sugar and serve warm accompanied with ice-cream.

Average times Preparation — 10 minutes
Cooking — 30 minutes

Wine notes With the clafouti —
A: Orlando (Barossa) Semillon Auslese
E: Château Climens (Barsac) of a good year
U: Phelps (Napa) Late Harvest Johannisberg Riesling

CHOCOLATE PASTILLES
Makes 36

375 g dark chocolate, chopped into small pieces	36 flaked almonds, toasted
36 small dried apricots or 18 halves	36 seedless raisins
36 slivers angelica	36 sultanas
18 glacé cherries, halved	

In a small pan, melt chocolate over a pan of hot water. Stir from time to time with a wooden spoon. It will take about 10 minutes. Do not let water underneath boil. Meanwhile, cover 3 oven trays with greaseproof paper sticking it down at the corners with a little butter so it won't slip. When chocolate is smooth, use a teaspoon to drop it, 1 teaspoonful at a time onto the trays, leaving room to spread. Smooth chocolate over with back of teaspoon, making the circles about 4 cm in diameter. Working quickly, stick 1 piece of each fruit and almond into each chocolate and leave to set in refrigerator. Carefully, remove each pastille with a spatula and store in an airtight container in a cool place. Serve with coffee.

Average times Preparation — 20 minutes
Cooking — 10 minutes

Wine notes Chocolate Pastilles need a liqueur muscat —
A: Baileys (Glenrowan) Award Muscat
E: Muscat de Frontignan Vin de Liqueur
U: Novitiate (Santa Clara) Black Muscat

Do ahead Up to 4 days, if stored in a cool place and kept airtight

WINTER

MENU 10

This entrée is one of my favourites and has proved very popular at all my cooking classes. Originally from a famous hotel in Dallas, I sometimes serve it at lunch with poached Moreton Bay bugs, still warm from the poaching stock. The casseroled veal chops were served at every top boardroom table in Melbourne during the 1960s and 1970s and are just as popular today as they were then. Followed by one of the richest and best chocolate desserts in the business, this is an ideal menu for mid-winter entertaining and it's mostly do-ahead. The Turkish Delight is a nice cleansing finish to the menu and should be served with coffee.

WARM SPINACH, MUSHROOM AND BACON SALAD

---

400 g fresh young spinach
3 rashers lean streaky bacon, rinds removed

Dressing:

1 egg
1 tablespoon Dijon mustard
1 tablespoon red wine vinegar

salt and freshly ground black pepper to taste
1 cup peanut oil

Garnish:

¾ cup white button mushrooms, finely sliced
1 medium carrot, cut into fine julienne, blanched

Remove roots from spinach, shred leaves from stems and wash leaves in as many changes of water as is necessary to remove all sand and soil. Dry and tear into bite-size pieces. Keep airtight until ready to use. Just before serving, pile into a large salad bowl.

Fry the bacon in a heavy-based pan over medium heat, turning at least once. As fat is rendered from bacon, pour it off to allow bacon to cook as crisply as possible. Drain on crumpled paper towel, cool and chop coarsely.

To make dressing: in a small pan, whisk all dressing ingredients together except oil. Bring slowly to boil, slowly whisking in oil. As soon as mixture boils, remove from heat and pour over prepared salad. Add bacon and mushrooms, toss very well and pile up on individual warm salad plates. Garnish with mushrooms and carrot and serve at once.

Average times Preparation — 20 minutes
Cooking — 5 minutes

Wine notes Warm Spinach, Mushroom and Bacon salad does not need a wine, although one could serve a fruity, light to medium red —
A: Château François (Pokolbin) Shiraz Pinot
E and U: Freisa del Piemonte (Marchesi di Barolo)

Do ahead Prepare spinach, keep airtight and refrigerate to keep crisp. Bring to room temperature 1 hour before serving

CASSEROLED VEAL CHOPS WITH BABY ONIONS

16–24 baby onions, peeled with 2 cm tops left
   on
125 g butter
1 teaspoon sugar
salt and freshly ground black pepper to taste

18 small potatoes, peeled
12 veal chops, trimmed of excess fat
⅔–1 cup veal stock
3 tablespoons finely chopped parsley

In a small heavy frying pan sauté onions in 30 g of butter, tossing them until golden on all sides. Pour in ⅓ cup of water, the sugar and seasoning. Cover and simmer until onions are almost cooked through and water is absorbed. Set aside.

Heat another 30 g of butter in a small heavy frying pan and toss potatoes in it over high heat until they are golden on all sides, reduce heat and continue to cook until tender.

Heat remaining butter in a heavy casserole and brown chops quickly on both sides over high heat. Season well, cover casserole and simmer gently for 20 minutes. Add onions and stock and simmer for 10 minutes. Add potatoes, adjust seasoning and sprinkle with parsley.

Serve with a green vegetable.

Average times Preparation — 20 minutes
             Cooking — 1 hour

Wine notes The veal requires a shift to a
            heavier red —
            A: Tyrrell's Old Winery
                Cabernet Merlot
            E and U: Châteauneuf-du-Pape
                    Domaine de Vieux
                    Telegraphe

Do ahead Up to 1 day

FROZEN CHOCOLATE PRUNE TORTE

Crust:

125 g chocolate flavoured biscuits, crushed
   finely
60 g butter, melted

Filling:

1 tablespoon brandy
6 stoned prunes, cut into quarters
125 g dark chocolate, cut into small pieces
2 teaspoons instant coffee powder

3 egg yolks
vanilla essence, to taste
4 egg whites
1½ tablespoons castor sugar
¾ cup cream, whipped

100 g dark chocolate cut into small pieces to
   garnish

To make crust: mix crushed biscuits with melted butter in a medium bowl and pat into an 18 cm spring form. Stamp down with a straight sided glass and bake in centre of 175°C (350°F) oven for 10 minutes. Cool.

To make filling: pour brandy over prunes and leave to macerate. Bring a pan of water to a simmer and remove from heat. Place chocolate and coffee in a large heatproof bowl and place over hot water until melted. Stir and cool slightly.

Beat in egg yolks, one at a time, and add vanilla. Beat egg whites until they form soft peaks, beat in castor sugar and continue to beat until mixture forms stiff peaks. Fold one-third of the whites into chocolate mixture using a rubber spatula, then fold in remaining egg whites. Fold in whipped cream and the macerated prunes. Pour into prepared crust. Cover with foil and freeze, preferably overnight.

To prepare garnish: melt chocolate over hot water without heating it and stir with a wooden spoon. Using a spatula spread evenly on back of a baking tray. It's important that you use the back of the tray and that the tray is perfectly flat. Leave chocolate to set softly. It must not be solid.

Mark chocolate into 8 cm strips, the length of the baking tray. Using pastry spatula, grip the blade at both ends and exert more pressure at one end than the other. Drag across top of chocolate towards you to prevent tray slipping. The chocolate should roll and gather into tiny pleats at the end where you're exerting more pressure. The thickness of the curl depends on the pressure exerted on spatula so that the harder you press the thicker the curl will be. Place curls in single layers on a tray and put into freezer until ready to use.

To serve torte: remove spring form sides and place torte with base still attached to it on a serving platter. Arrange chocolate curls in a rosette on top of torte and place on bottom shelf of refrigerator for approximately ½ an hour before serving.

Average times Preparation — 35 minutes
Cooking — 20 minutes
Freezing — preferably overnight

Wine notes Frozen Chocolate Prune Torte requires a fortified muscat —
A: Lindemans Reserve Old Liqueur Muscat Solera No. 1625
E: Muscat de Frontignan Vin de Liqueur
U: Novitiate (Santa Clara) Black Muscat

Do ahead Up to 3 weeks in advance. Chocolate curls should be frozen on the tray until rock hard then stored in an airtight container and frozen until needed.

TURKISH DELIGHT

450 g sugar
30 g gelatine
300 ml water
1 teaspoon citric acid

green food colouring
1 teaspoon peppermint essence
30 g cornflour
30 g icing sugar

Put sugar and gelatine in a pan, add water and heat until boiling, stirring all the time. Boil 5 minutes, stirring constantly. Remove from heat and add citric acid, colouring and flavouring. Pour into a wetted shallow 18 cm × 27 cm pan and leave overnight to set. In hot weather, set in the refrigerator.

When set, dip pan into lukewarm water. Turn out on to greaseproof paper. Mix cornflour and icing sugar together and spread onto greaseproof paper, slightly larger than pan. Coat Turkish Delight thoroughly with icing sugar and cornflour and cut into squares. Store in an airtight container.

Average times Preparation — 15 minutes
Cooking — 7 minutes
Setting — overnight

Do ahead Up to 5 days in advance and stored in airtight containers

WINTER

MENU 11

The Mediterranean-inspired main dish is easy, though it requires last minute cooking for the beef. Followed by a do-ahead dessert which is famous all over the world because of its light melt-in-the-mouth quality and with an entrée of delightfully easy Hot Prawn and Snow Pea Salad, this is a delightful mid-Winter dinner menu.

HOT PRAWN AND SNOW PEA SALAD

24–36 green king prawns depending on size, shelled, tails left intact and deveined
375 g snow peas topped, tailed and strung
12 snake beans, topped and tailed and cut into 6 cm lengths
250 g baby white button mushrooms, sliced finely

juice of 1 or 2 lemons depending on taste
salt and freshly ground black pepper to taste
125 g butter
12 baby cos lettuce leaves, washed, drained and crisped

6 wisps fresh Italian parsley to garnish

Cook prawns in a pan of simmering salted water for 1½ minutes. Remove with a slotted spoon, set aside and keep warm. Return to boil and blanch snow peas (no lid) for 1 minute. Lift out with a slotted spoon and set aside to keep warm. Poach snake beans in same simmering water until *al dente*, approximately 3 minutes. Drain and set aside to keep warm.

Cook mushrooms with some lemon juice and seasoning in the butter in a large heavy pan over high heat stirring constantly for 2 to 3 minutes.

Arrange lettuce leaves on 6 warmed dinner plates. Scatter snow peas and snake beans over top and arrange prawns over the top. Spoon mushroom mixture over salads and garnish each with a wisp of parsley.

Average times Preparation — 35 minutes
Cooking — 10 minutes

Wine notes The prawn salad needs a flavoursome, white burgundy-style wine —
A: Mt Horrocks Semillon from Watervale
E: Meursault Genevrières of a good year
U: Jekel (Monterey) Private Reserve Chardonnay

FILLET OF BEEF MONÉGASQUE

Monégasque Sauce:

1 tablespoon olive oil
2 large white onions, chopped finely
750 g ripe tomatoes, skinned, seeded and chopped roughly
1 fresh bouquet garni
3 tablespoons veal or beef stock
1 teaspoon brown sugar
1 tablespoon white wine vinegar
½ lemon, sliced thickly

salt and freshly ground black pepper to taste
1 teaspoon potato flour
3 tablespoons water

2 tablespoons olive oil
1.5 kg fillet of beef, very well trimmed and skinned
salt and pepper to taste

6 black olives, pitted and cut in halves lengthwise to garnish

(top) Navarin of Lamb
(lower) Veal Rib Chops with Leeks

Wine:
Lake's Folly (Pokolbin) Cabernet Sauvignon

Quail Salad

Wine:
Lindemans Padthaway Pinot Noir

To make sauce: heat olive oil in a large pan, stir in onions and cook until softened over medium heat. Add tomatoes, stir and cook 2 minutes. Add bouquet garni, stock, sugar, vinegar, lemon and seasoning to taste. Simmer the sauce covered, for 30 minutes over medium heat stirring from time to time. Remove bouquet garni and lemon slices and put sauce through a mouli (food mill).

Return sauce to pan, bring back to a simmer and cook a further 5 minutes with the lid off. Mix potato flour and water together and stir into sauce. Simmer for 2 minutes or until thickened. Set aside and keep warm.

To cook beef: heat oil in a large heavy baking pan and seal beef on both sides with a very high heat. Season liberally and place in 200°C (400°F) oven for 25 minutes for medium-rare beef. Set aside and keep warm to rest for 10 minutes before serving.

To serve: cut beef into equal size thick pieces and place on 6 warmed dinner plates. Spoon sauce over top of beef and garnish with the half olives. Serve at once with boiled potatoes.

Average times Preparation — 30 minutes
Cooking — 1 hour
Standing — 10 minutes

Do ahead Sauce up to ½ day

Wine notes The beef needs a big, spicy Shiraz —
A: Birk's Wendouree Shiraz
E and U: Cornas (Clape)

CHOCOLATE ROULADE

◆

6 eggs, separated
6 tablespoons castor sugar
180 g dark chocolate, broken into small pieces
1 tablespoon water
pinch salt

Filling:
300 ml thickened cream, beaten to soft peaks

Garnish:
¼ cup flaked almonds, toasted
1 tablespoon pure icing sugar

◆

Line a 26 cm × 30 cm Swiss roll pan with a double layer of greaseproof paper. Brush paper with melted butter and sprinkle with plain flour, knocking out any excess.

In a medium bowl, beat egg yolks and castor sugar until pale and thick. Melt chocolate and water together over a pan of hot water until smooth. Cool slightly and stir into egg yolk mixture.

Beat egg whites with salt until they form stiff peaks. Fold one-third into chocolate mixture gently but thoroughly, using a rubber spatula. Fold remaining egg whites into chocolate mixture and spoon into prepared pan and level with a spatula.

Cook in hottest part of 200°C (400°F) oven for 12 to 15 minutes or until well risen and crust has formed. Slide the paper and cake out of pan on to a cooling rack covered with a clean tea-towel. Cool for 10 minutes, carefully remove paper and roll up roulade carefully in the tea-towel and leave until quite cool.

Unroll roulade and spread with whipped cream. Roll up carefully again with the aid of the tea-towel. Trim off ends, lift off tea-towel and rack and place on a serving platter. Scatter with almonds and sift icing sugar over the top.

Average times Preparation — 30 minutes
Cooking — 15 minutes
Cooling — 45 minutes

Do ahead Roulade up to 3 days. Fill roulade up to 3 hours before serving

Wine notes Chocolate Roulade requires a muscat —
A: Bullers (Rutherglen) Liqueur Muscat
E: Grand Roussillon
U: Novitiate (Santa Clara) Black Muscat

WINTER

MENU 12

The first course, which was taught to me in Italy, could also be served as an accompaniment to any lamb or veal dish. Followed by one of the easiest kidney dishes imaginable and a decadently rich ice-cream, it's a superb Winter lunch or dinner menu.

EGG-PLANT CAKES WITH FRESH TOMATO SAUCE

1 kg egg-plants
3 cups milk
60 g butter
½ cup olive oil
1 teaspoon fresh marjoram leaves, chopped, or
  ½ teaspoon dried
2 tablespoons béchamel sauce, see page 65
2 tablespoons finely grated Parmesan cheese
1 tablespoon butter, melted
freshly grated nutmeg, to taste
½ teaspoon salt
pinch white pepper to taste
2 eggs, beaten

Fresh Tomato Sauce:
1 tablespoon olive oil
1 white onion, diced
500 g ripe tomatoes, peeled, seeded and
  chopped
sugar to taste (optional)
salt and freshly ground black pepper to taste
½ cup dry white wine

extra marjoram leaves to garnish

Peel egg-plants and cut into 3 cm cubes. Place in a large bowl, pour over milk, cover and stand for 2 hours. Pour off milk and discard.

In a large, heavy frying pan, heat butter and oil and fry egg-plant cubes with marjoram for about 15 minutes over low heat, stirring from time to time. Do not let them take on any colour. When all juices have evaporated, purée in batches in a blender or food processor. Transfer to a large bowl and stir in béchamel sauce, cheese, melted butter, seasonings and eggs.

Butter 6 ½-cup moulds and spoon mixture into them. Place two layers of paper in bottom of a baking dish (this is to ensure even baking), stand moulds on paper and pour in enough warm water to come half way up sides of moulds. Bake in centre of 200°C (400°F) oven for 40 minutes or until set. Insert a knife in centre: it should come out clean.

To make tomato sauce: in a medium pan, heat oil, add onion and cook over low heat for 10 minutes. Add tomatoes, a few grains of sugar if tomatoes are not overly ripe, seasonings and wine. Cook, stirring from time to time, until reduced and a good consistency. Taste and adjust seasonings. Pass through a mouli (food mill) or a coarse strainer and serve while hot.

To serve: spoon a sea of fresh tomato sauce on to each plate, and unmould cakes into the centre. Place a leaf of marjoram on each and serve hot.

Average times *Cakes —*
Preparation — 20 minutes
Standing — 2 hours
Cooking — 55 minutes
Sauce —
Preparation — 10 minutes
Cooking — 40 minutes

Do ahead *Cakes —*
Up to oven stage, 2 hours
Sauce —
Up to 1 day and heat through
gently

Wine notes Egg-plant cakes need a light red —
A: Tyrrell's Old Winery Pinot Noir
E and U: Moulin-à-Vent Beaujolais (Louis Latour)

DEVILLED KIDNEYS

12 lamb's kidneys
12 rashers of middle bacon
¾ cup tomato ketchup

3–4 tablespoons Worcestershire sauce
3 tablespoons parsley, finely chopped

Skin kidneys, cut in halves lengthwise and remove white core. Cut rinds off bacon and each rasher in half. Wrap each half kidney in a piece of bacon and pack tightly into a small ovenproof dish.

Bake in 200°C (400°F) oven for 25 to 35 minutes, depending on size of kidneys.

Draw the fat off cooking juices with a bulb baster, or blot with kitchen paper. Stir tomato ketchup and Worcestershire sauce into juices, heat through in oven for 5 minutes and serve with parsley, scattered over the top.

Serve the kidneys with a green salad.

Average times Preparation — 20 minutes
Cooking — 35 minutes

Wine notes Devilled Kidneys call for a full-flavoured red —
A: McWilliam's Claret, from Hanwood
E: Saint-Joseph (Trollat)
U: Mt Veeder (Napa) Cabernet Sauvignon

Do ahead Up to oven stage, ½ day

DRIED APRICOT ICE-CREAM

250 g dried apricots, chopped finely
½ cup water
3 tablespoons lemon juice

600 ml thickened cream
1 cup castor sugar

Soak apricots in water and lemon juice for 4 hours or overnight. Stir cream and castor sugar together and pour over apricots, mixing well.

Churn, then spoon into a wetted 6-cup mould, cover and freeze until firm. Unmould by dipping in warm water, invert over a serving dish and shake out. Return to freezer to firm before serving. Serve with coconut biscuits (see next recipe).

Average times Preparation — 15 minutes
Standing — 4 hours
Freezing — 4 hours or over-night

Wine notes Dried Apricot Ice-Cream is complemented by a long-finishing sweet white —
A: Lindemans Padthaway Auslese Rhine Riesling
E: Nederburg Edelkeur from South Africa
U: Château St Jean (Sonoma) Late Harvest Johannisberg Riesling

Do ahead Up to 3 days

COCONUT BISCUITS
Makes 30 approximately

90 g unsalted butter
1 cup sugar
2 eggs, 60 g, beaten
vanilla essence to taste

⅓ cup cornflour
⅔ cup desiccated coconut
1¼ cups plain flour, sifted
30 almonds in skins (approximately)

Beat butter and sugar until pale and fluffy. Add eggs and flavouring. Fold in dry ingredients and place in teaspoonfuls on a lightly buttered oven slide, leaving plenty of space between the biscuits to spread. Top each with an almond and bake in 175°C (350°F) oven for 25 minutes or until golden. Store in airtight containers.

Average times Preparation — 20 minutes
Cooking — 25 minutes

Do ahead Up to 1 week and store in airtight containers

WINTER

MENU 13

A do-ahead soup using a highly underrated vegetable followed by a delicious Greek moussaka which can be made ahead. This menu is finished with one of the best orange soufflés I have ever eaten. It's from Rogues Restaurant in Sydney.

TURNIP SOUP

30 g butter	salt and white pepper to taste
6 young turnips, peeled and sliced	6 cups boiling water
½ teaspoon sugar	1 egg yolk
	1 tablespoon cream

Heat butter in a large pan and slowly cook turnips, stirring from time to time, for 5 minutes. Stir in sugar, salt and pepper. Pour in boiling water and let soup simmer till turnips are soft. Pass through a mouli or sieve.

Beat egg yolk in the cream and add to soup to bind it, just before serving, but do not let it boil.

Average times Preparation — 10 minutes
Cooking — 30 minutes

Wine notes Turnip Soup needs a fino sherry —
A: Yalumba Chiquita Sherry
E and U: Ynocente Sherry
(Valdespino)

Do ahead At least 1 day and up to 3 days but only add egg yolk and cream at time of serving

ARTICHOKE MOUSSAKA

10–12 globe artichokes	*Mornay Sauce:*
½ lemon	
juice of 1 lemon	60 g butter
1 teaspoon salt	3 tablespoons plain flour
¾ cup fine white breadcrumbs	3 cups milk
3 tablespoons olive oil	3 tablespoons Parmesan cheese
1 medium onion, finely chopped	3 eggs, lightly beaten
500 g minced beef or lamb	salt and pepper to taste
½ cup red wine	
freshly ground black pepper to taste	
1 tablespoon finely chopped parsely	

To prepare artichokes: break off stems close to base and remove tough outer leaves. Cut top third of leaves off each and trim bases. Immediately rub over with ½ lemon. Put artichokes in a bowl of cold water with juice of 1 lemon.

Bring enough water to boil with salt and the ½ lemon to cover artichokes. Drain artichokes and cook over medium heat for 20 minutes or until tender. Drain in a colander and leave to cool slightly.

Butter a gratiné dish and sprinkle breadcrumbs over base. Cut artichokes into 4 and place in gratiné dish.

Heat oil in a medium heavy pan and fry onion until transparent, stirring from time to time. Stir in minced meat and cook until golden. Pour in wine and cook for 5 minutes. Season and stir in the parsley and 1 cup of hot water. Simmer over medium heat until water has evaporated. Spoon meat mixture over artichokes.

To make mornay sauce: heat butter in a medium pan and whisk in flour, cooking for 2 minutes over medium heat. Whisk in milk gradually and cook until sauce boils and thickens, whisking constantly. Reduce heat and leave to cook for 5 minutes. Remove from heat and cool slightly before whisking in cheese, eggs, and seasoning.

Pour mornay sauce over artichokes and cook in 175°C (350°F) oven for approximately 30 minutes or until golden and bubbling. Serve at once.

Average times Preparation — 15 minutes
Cooking — 1½ hours

Wine notes Moussaka needs a full-flavoured
red —
A: Capel Vale Shiraz from
Western Australia
E: Barbera d'Asti (Francoli)
U: Martini (Napa) Barbera

Do ahead Up to ½ day

ORANGE SOUFFLÉ

⅓ cup castor sugar
⅓ cup water
7 large oranges
½ cup castor sugar, extra
6 eggs, separated

1½ tablespoons Grand Marnier or other
orange liqueur
3 tablespoons castor sugar, extra

icing sugar to dust

Butter and sugar 6 × 300 ml (1¼ cups approximately) soufflé dishes and stand on a baking tray.

Make a syrup by boiling the castor sugar with the ⅓ cup water. Finely grate the zest of 1½ oranges and drop into hot sugar syrup to blanch for 3 to 4 minutes. Squeeze the juice of all oranges, pour into a pan and reduce over high heat by half its original volume. Stir in ½ cup castor sugar. Drain orange zest from syrup and add to mixture, discarding syrup. Cool mixture, add egg yolks and whisk. Pour in orange-flavoured liqueur and whisk well.

Beat egg whites until they form firm peaks, beat in 3 tablespoons castor sugar, 1 tablespoon at a time, and beat until it forms a meringue. Fold gently into orange mixture using rubber spatula. Spoon into prepared soufflé dishes and bake in hottest part of 210°C (425°F) oven for 12 to 15 minutes approximately or until risen and golden on top. Serve at once, dusted with icing sugar.

Average times Preparation — 30 minutes
Cooking — 35 minutes

Wine notes Orange Soufflé needs a crisp,
sweet white —
A: Petaluma Coonawarra
Botrytis Cinerea Rhine Ries-
ling
E: Château Coutet (Barsac)
U: Phelps (Napa) Late Harvest
Johannisberg Riesling

Do ahead Base mixture up to egg white stage,
up to ½ day

WINTER

MENU 14

If you must cook oysters, then this is one way of doing them. Inspired by the Adelaide Hilton's Grange Restaurant this is a special start to a mid-Winter dinner. Followed by a hearty do-ahead dish, finished with a delightfully light fruit dessert, and followed by Florentines to serve with coffee, this is a menu which everyone will enjoy.

GRATINÉ OYSTERS WITH GREEN PEPPERCORNS

---

6 dozen oysters in shells
3 shallots, very finely chopped
1 cup dry white wine
½ cup thick cream

1 teaspoon crushed green peppercorns
¾ cup Hollandaise sauce, see below
3 tablespoons whipped cream
6 lemon halves to garnish

Poach oysters with shallots in dry white wine for 1 minute and remove with a slotted spoon. Add cream and crushed green peppercorns to the poaching pan and reduce to half its original volume. Cool. Mix with Hollandaise sauce and fold in whipped cream.

Arrange a dozen oyster shells on each of 6 large plates and warm in 190°C (375°F) oven. Place poached oysters in warmed oyster shells, coat with sauce and glaze under a hot griller.

Serve with lemon halves.

INSTANT HOLLANDAISE SAUCE

---

4 egg yolks
250 g butter

lemon juice to taste
white pepper to taste

Work egg yolks on high speed in a blender or food processor for 2 minutes. Bring butter to the boil and discard any white froth on top. Pour boiling 'golden oil' slowly on to yolks with machine on high. Add lemon juice and pepper to taste.
Note: Hollandaise sauce can be kept warm by standing in a warm water bath but it must not be re-heated or it will curdle.

Average times Preparation — 20 minutes
Cooking — 10 minutes

Wine notes The oysters need a crisp, acid white —
A: Tyrrell's (Pokolbin) Pinot Riesling Vat 63
E: Chablis 1er Cru Fourchame (Regnard)
U: Concannon Santa Maria Valley Chardonnay

VENISON CHASSEUR

1½ tablespoons oil
1½ tablespoons butter
1.25 kg lean venison from the buttock, cut into
4 cm cubes
2 medium white onions, chopped coarsely
1½ tablespoons plain flour
2 cups beef stock
¾ cup dry white wine
2 cloves garlic, crushed

3 shallots, finely chopped
3 teaspoons tomato purée
1 bouquet garni (consisting of 2 small pieces of
celery tied around 1 bay leaf, 1 sprig of
parsley and 1 sprig of thyme)
salt and freshly ground black pepper to taste
300 g white button mushrooms, quartered
2 tablespoons finely chopped fresh parsley

Heat oil and butter in a heavy-based flameproof casserole and stir in venison, a few pieces at a time so that they brown and seal equally all over. Lift out with a slotted spoon and reserve. Repeat with the remaining venison until it is all well sealed. Lift out with a slotted spoon and reserve. Stir in onions and sauté over medium heat until golden brown. Stir in flour and cook over low heat stirring constantly for 2 minutes. Return venison to casserole and pour in stock, wine, garlic, shallots, tomato purée, bouquet garni and salt and pepper. Stir well and bring the mixture slowly to a simmer.

Cover and cook gently in centre of 175°C (350°F) oven for 1½ to 2 hours until venison is tender. Stir from time to time throughout the cooking to prevent casserole from sticking. If it gets a little dry, add stock or water.

Fifteen minutes before venison is finally cooked stir in mushrooms. Cover casserole and continue to cook. Discard bouquet garni and adjust seasoning if necessary. Sprinkle with finely chopped parsley and serve with a potato or rice dish.

Average times Preparation — 25 minutes
Cooking — 1¾ hours

Wine notes Venison needs a big red —
A: Redbank Marong Shiraz,
from the Western District
of Victoria
E: Côte-Rôtie (Jasmin)
U: Shenandoah (Armador)
Zinfandel

Do ahead At least 1 day and up to 2 days

FRESH FRUIT COMPOTE

Syrup:

1½ cups water
¾ cup castor sugar

5 red-skinned apples
juice of 1 lemon
4 ripe pears
1½ cups dark grapes, or ¾ cup raisins

In a medium pan, bring water and sugar to boil, stirring, over a high heat. Boil rapidly for 5 minutes. Peel apples, reserving peel and slice them quickly. Pour half the lemon juice over them and drop into hot syrup with apple peel. Poach over a medium heat for 5 minutes. Remove apple slices with a slotted spoon to a glass serving dish.

Peel, core and slice the pears thickly, pour over remaining lemon juice and poach 4 minutes in sugar syrup. Remove with a slotted spoon and add to the apples. Poach grapes or raisins (the grapes may be seeded first if you wish), until just tender then lift out with a slotted spoon. Cool syrup and strain it over fruits, discarding apple skins. By now syrup will be a beautiful rose colour. Serve with lightly whipped cream.

Average times Preparation — 15 minutes
Cooking — 20 minutes
Cooling — 1½ hours

Wine notes The fruit compote requires no wine

Do ahead Up to 3 days

FLORENTINES
Makes 12 biscuits

30 g almonds, chopped finely
30 g walnuts, chopped finely
45 g mixed citrus peel, chopped finely
30 g sultanas, chopped finely
½ cup plain flour
1 cup brown sugar
60 g butter, softened

Icing:

120 g dark chocolate, chopped

Mix nuts and fruits with flour and sugar and mix in butter until mixture comes together. Divide into 12 portions and place on greased trays (about 4 to a tray to allow for spreading), flatten out a little and bake for 6 to 8 minutes in 200°C (400°F) oven till golden.

Cool on tray for a minute or two, but remove before they become too brittle.

To make icing: melt chocolate gently over hot water, and spread on undersides of Florentines. Leave to set before storing in an airtight container.

Average times Preparation — 20 minutes
Cooking — 8 minutes
Cooling — 20 minutes

Wine notes Florentines need a rich, fortified wine —
A: Seppelt Para Liqueur Port
E and U: Pedro Ximenez Solera
Superior Sherry
(Valdespino)

Do ahead Up to 1 week, store in a cool place and keep airtight

WINTER

MENU 15

A Chinese-inspired first course which must be prepared at the last minute begins this menu. It is followed by a superb chicken dish which I learnt while working at Leith's Restaurant in London in the early 1970s. Finishing with rich crêpes, it's a menu which requires quite a lot of preparation on the day it is served.

SAUTÉ PRAWNS WITH WALNUTS

2 egg whites
¾ teaspoon monosodium glutamate
2 teaspoons sesame oil
salt and finely ground white pepper to taste
2 tablespoons cornflour
375 g fresh royal red prawns, peeled and deveined
2 tablespoons peanut oil
3 cm piece of green root ginger, peeled and cut into fine slices

2 medium carrots, peeled and sliced 1 cm thick
90 g drained bamboo shoots, sliced
10 small spring onions, peeled and cut into 2 cm lengths
¾ cup walnut halves
¾ cup fresh green peas
12 tiny white button mushrooms
1 teaspoon cornflour, extra
¾ cup chicken stock
few drops tabasco sauce

Whisk egg whites, monosodium glutamate, sesame oil, salt, pepper and cornflour together and dip prawns into the mixture. Prepare a pan of boiling water and keep it simmering. Drop the coated prawns into boiling water for 5 seconds a few at a time, and drain thoroughly, then dry on paper towel.

Pour peanut oil into a wok or heavy-based frying pan and heat until hot. Stir in the ginger, carrot, bamboo shoots and the spring onions and stir fry until *al dente*. Add the prawns, walnuts, peas and mushrooms. Mix extra cornflour with a little of the chicken stock and when smooth add all the stock and a few drops of tabasco sauce. Pour this over vegetables and heat through until sauce is opaque and cooked through. Serve at once.

Average times Preparation — 15 minutes
Cooking — 15 minutes

Wine notes Sauté prawns with spicy flavours call for an aromatic white with clean acidity —
A: Petaluma Rhine Riesling
E: Scharzhofberger (Egon Müller) from the Saar
U: Trefethen (Napa) Johannisberg Riesling

STUFFED CHICKEN BREASTS

3 × 1.5 kg chickens. (Use breasts and thighs only. Keep drumsticks for another recipe like Honey-Glazed Chicken Wings.)
45 g butter

Filling:
6 chicken thighs
150 g ham off the bone
1 tablespoon finely chopped parsley
1 tablespoon finely chopped tarragon
1 egg white
salt and fresh ground black pepper to taste
½ cup cream, approximately, chilled
45 g butter

Mushroom Sauce:
60 g butter
3 tablespoons flour
2 cups chicken stock (made from carcasses)
½ cup dry white wine
1 cup cream
salt and pepper to taste

150 g white button mushrooms, sliced finely

freshly chopped parsley and tarragon to garnish

Remove breasts from chickens and set aside. Dismember the carcasses and separate thighs and drumsticks. Freeze drumsticks for another recipe. Make a stock from wing tips, skin and carcasses and cook for 30 minutes. Remove fat and cool.

To prepare filling: remove flesh from thighs and put with the ham through a mincer fitted with a coarse disc or grind in food processor. Add herbs, seasoning and egg white. Mix thoroughly but handle it gently, don't pack it down. Add only enough cream to make mixture moist. Chill mixture, covered, for 30 minutes.

Put into a piping bag fitted with a 2 cm plain nozzle. Cut a pocket in each breast and force in stuffing. Flatten fillets (at the back of the breasts) with a meat mallet and fold over stuffing. Melt butter in a heavy pan and when it foams seal breasts on both sides but do not let the tops brown.

Cook breasts top side up in 240°C (450°F) oven for about 10 minutes or until puffed and white on top and brown underneath. Do not turn over.

To make sauce: melt butter and cook in flour for 2 minutes. Add cooled stock and whisking constantly, cook until sauce thickens. Add wine. Lower heat and continue to cook until a good consistency. Add cream, seasonings and mushrooms and cook for 10 minutes over low heat.

Add the breasts to the hot sauce and cook them for 5 minutes.

Serve on a platter and coat with a little sauce. Sprinkle over the herbs and pass remaining sauce in a sauce boat.

Serve with steamed carrot batons and broccoli florets.

Average times Preparation — 50 minutes
Cooking — (including stock) 1 hour
Chilling — 30 minutes

Wine notes Chicken calls for a light to medium red —
A: Seville Estate (Yarra Valley) Pinot Noir
E: Pommard les Rugiens (Domaine Clerget)
U: Sokol Blosser (Oregon) Pinot Noir

Do ahead Stock and filling of breasts, preferably 1 day. Sauce and cooking of breasts, up to ½ day. Reheat breasts in sauce in moderate oven, covered, until just warmed through

CRÊPES PRALINE

Praline:
½ cup unblanched almonds
⅓ cup castor sugar

Praline Butter:
90 g butter
½ cup castor sugar
3 tablespoons crushed praline
rum to taste

Batter:
½ cup plain flour
pinch salt
1 teaspoon sugar
1 whole egg and 1 yolk
300 ml milk
1 tablespoon melted butter or peanut oil

peanut oil
pure icing sugar

To make praline: put the almonds and castor sugar in a small heavy pan and heat gently. When sugar is golden, stir carefully with a metal spoon. When praline has reached a dark but not burnt colour, turn out on to an oiled pan to set. When it is set, crush with a rolling pin or put it in pieces in a food processor or blender. Store in an airtight container until ready to use.

To make praline butter: cream butter, beat in castor sugar a little at a time, and when white and fluffy mix in the crushed praline and flavour well with rum. Do not make too moist.

To make crêpes: sift flour with a pinch of salt into a bowl. Add the sugar. Make a well in centre and drop in whole egg and extra yolk. Add a little of the milk, and whisk in slowly, incorporating the flour. Add the rest of milk whisking well, but do not over-work batter or it will need to rest for a longer period. Alternatively, make batter in a food processor. Add butter or oil and whisk until there are no lumps in the batter. Rest for 30 minutes.

Heat an 18 cm crêpe pan with a little peanut oil. Tip off any spare oil and pour in just enough batter to cover the bottom of pan. Tip off any excess batter. Cook over high heat until crêpe is set on top, turn over and cook second side which never takes as long to cook as first side. As each crêpe is cooked, pile them on top of each other and leave wrapped in a clean tea-towel until needed. Make at least 13. Never use the first one made.

To assemble the crêpes; spread the inside of each crêpe (the spotted side) with the praline butter, roll-up and place in a lightly buttered shallow dish. Warm through in 175°C (350°F) oven and serve immediately, dusted with sifted icing sugar.

Average times Preparation — 35 minutes
Cooking — 35 minutes
Standing — 30 minutes

Wine notes Crêpes Praline call for a sweet
white —
A: Tyrell's (Pokolbin) Semillon
Sauternes
E and U: Château Lafaurie-
Peyraguey (Sauternes)

Do ahead 1 day — up to heating through in
oven

WINTER

MENU 16

Jerusalem artichokes are not used nearly enough, simply because they require so much peeling which is rather laborious. This entrée makes it all worthwhile, especially as it can be done ½ day ahead. It is followed by a rack of lamb and a decadently rich chocolate cake which everyone loves — hence its name! A superb mid-Winter menu for busy people as only the lamb and vegetable require last minute cooking.

JERUSALEM ARTICHOKES IN TOMATO AND HAM SAUCE

---

1 kg Jerusalem artichokes
juice 1 lemon
3 tablespoons olive oil
200 g white onions, chopped coarsely

500 g tomatoes, cored, skinned and chopped coarsely
250 g leg ham, cut into julienne
2 tablespoons freshly chopped parsley

Peel artichokes and acidulate in just enough cold water to cover with the lemon juice.

Heat oil in a large heavy frying pan and cook onions until softened. They must not brown. Drain artichokes and cut in halves. Stir in tomatoes and artichokes and cook over low heat for 45 minutes or until artichokes are tender.

Add ham and stir gently until heated through. Serve hot with parsley scattered over the top.

Average times Standing — 30 minutes
Preparation — 30 minutes
Cooking — 55 minutes
Do ahead Up to ½ day and heat through gently

Wine notes The entrée calls for a rosé —
A: Reynella Cabernet Rosé
E: Cabernet d'Anjou
U: Heitz (Napa) Grignolino Rosé

RACK OF LAMB PROVENÇALE

---

3 cloves garlic, crushed
1½ cups finely chopped parsley
180 g butter

salt and freshly ground black pepper
6 racks of lamb, each with 4 cutlets, French boned and trimmed of most fat

---

Make a paste with garlic, parsley, butter, salt and pepper. Spread on skin side of racks. Lie racks, parsley side up, in a roasting dish and bake in centre of oven at 200°C (400°F) for approximately 25 to 30 minutes, or until it is cooked the way you like it. Rest 10 minutes in a warm oven before serving.

Serve with Glazed Carrots (see next recipe).

Average times Preparation — 15 minutes
Cooking — 30 minutes
Standing — 10 minutes

Wine notes Rack of lamb needs a rich Cabernet —
A: Mitchelton (central Victoria) Cabernet Sauvignon
E: Château Gloria (St-Julien) of a good year
U: Inglenook (Napa) Cabernet Sauvignon — Limited Cask

Do ahead Up to oven stage, ½ day

GLAZED CARROTS

500 g young, small carrots   45 g butter
½ cup water   1 tablespoon dark brown sugar

Scrape carrots, leaving 2 cm tops on. (Split in half lengthwise if too large.) Put into a shallow dish and pour water around them. Dot with butter and sprinkle with sugar. Cook uncovered in 200°C (400°F) oven for 30 minutes approximately, or until water has evaporated and carrots are *al dente*.

Average times Preparation — 10 minutes   **Do ahead** Up to oven stage without water, ½
Cooking — 30 minutes   day

LOVERS' CHOCOLATE CAKE

⅓ cup prunes, stoned and chopped   200 g chopped dark chocolate, melted
¼ cup Drambuie   scant ¾ cup plain flour, sifted
3 eggs, separated   ¾ cup pecan or walnut pieces, chopped
⅔ cup castor sugar   roughly
125 g unsalted butter, softened   pinch salt

Soak prunes in Drambuie. Beat egg yolks and castor sugar until pale and light. Whisk butter into warm chocolate and fold into yolk mixture. Fold in flour, pecans or walnuts, prunes and Drambuie with a rubber spatula. Beat whites with salt until firm but glossy and fold into chocolate mixture. Pour into a buttered 20 cm cake pan and bake in centre of 200°C (400°C) oven for exactly 24 minutes. Cool in pan. Serve dusted with icing sugar and accompany with crème fraîche, see page 49.

Average times Preparation — 20 minutes   **Do ahead** Up to 1 day
Cooking — 24 minutes
Cooling — 30 minutes

Wine notes Chocolate cake requires a
muscat —
A: Seppelt Rutherglen Muscat
E and U: Grand Roussillon

WINTER

MENU 17

This is a soup I grew up on as a child and have always adored. I always make a lot because each day it is heated it improves and thickens so much, that it is almost a meal in itself. Followed by an easy lamb dish and a very attractive pear dessert, it's a menu I've designed so that you are free to do the last minute fiddling with the pears without worrying about the other courses.

SPLIT PEA SOUP

200 g split peas, green or yellow
1.5 litres water
1 kg bacon bones or ham bone
salt and freshly ground black pepper, to taste
1 medium carrot, peeled and chopped roughly

1 medium turnip, peeled and chopped roughly
1 medium onion, peeled and chopped roughly
1 stick celery, coarsely chopped
2 teaspoons fresh mint, chopped
1 tablespoon plain flour
fried bread croûtons

Wash peas and soak overnight. Bring to boil in a large pan with water, ham or bacon bones and seasoning. Add vegetables and simmer till tender, about 1½ hours. Remove the bones, retaining meat. Purée with mint in a food processor or blender.

Return to pan along with any meat from the bones and bring to boil. Add flour blended smoothly with a little cold water, stir until boiling, cook 3 minutes, cool and refrigerate for 1–2 days before re-heating and serving with croûtons of fried bread.

Average times Preparation — 15 minutes
Soaking — overnight
Cooking — 1½ hours

Wine notes The soup needs a nutty
sherry —
A: Lindemans Reserve Bin
Z898A Amontillado
E and U: Dry Sack Sherry

Do ahead At least 1 day and up to 5 days. It will keep satisfactorily up to 5 days in the refrigerator, provided you heat it every day to boiling point and let simmer, stirring to prevent sticking, for at least 5 minutes

SAUTÉ LAMB CHOPS

100 g butter
12 small lamb chops, well trimmed of fat
2 medium white onions, chopped finely
6 shallots, chopped finely
5 cloves garlic, chopped finely
6 tablespoons plain flour
2 fresh bouquet garni
300 ml dry white wine

4 cups veal stock
2 tablespoons tomato paste
salt and freshly ground black pepper to taste
4 medium carrots, sliced in ½ cm slices
500 g shelled fresh green peas

finely chopped fresh parsley to garnish

In a large heavy-based casserole, heat butter until it foams. Add enough chops to just cover base of pan without crowding it and brown them well. Turn over and brown the other sides. Lift out chops and keep warm. Repeat browning process with remaining chops and return them all to the pan.

Add onions, shallots and garlic and stir well until they begin to take on a little golden colour. Stir in flour and cook for 2 minutes stirring. Add bouquet garni, wine, stock, tomato paste and seasonings and stir well. Cover and simmer for 35 minutes stirring from time to time so that sauce does not burn. Remove the bouquet garni and discard.

Bring carrots to boil in cold salted water and simmer until *al dente*. Strain and keep warm. Cook peas in boiling salted water, uncovered for 4 to 5 minutes or until tender. Drain and keep warm.

Spoon chops into centre of a heated serving platter and spoon vegetables around them. Spoon just enough sauce over top of meat to moisten it and pour the rest into a sauce boat to be passed at the table. Garnish with finely chopped parsley and serve at once.

Average times Preparation — 30 minutes
Cooking — 1 hour

Wine notes Sauté Lamb Chops call for a soft, long red —
A: Tisdall Cabernet Merlot, from northern Victoria
E: Château Rouget (Pomerol)
U: Sterling (Napa) Merlot

Do ahead Up to 1 day except vegetables which must be cooked at the last minute

CHOCOLATE-COATED PEARS
Make in morning for evening meal

◆

3 cups water
¾ cup sugar
rind of 2 oranges, removed with a vegetable peeler, without pith
6 pears

100 g dark chocolate, chopped
¼ cup vegetable oil
6 small fresh garden leaves, like citrus or camellia

◆

Bring sugar and water to the boil, stirring all the time until sugar dissolves. Add rind and simmer uncovered until reduced by one-third.

Peel pears and poach them whole in sugar syrup until tender. Drain and place on a foil-covered tray in the freezer until very cold, but not frozen.

Melt chocolate in a small pan over a pan filled with hot water. Stir from time to time with a wooden spoon. As soon as the chocolate has melted, spread chocolate evenly over the tops of the leaves, but not on sides and place on a small tray. Sit in refrigerator or freezer if it is very hot.

Remove chocolate pan from hot water and reheat water if necessary. Stir in oil and place back over the hot water. Stir until a good smooth consistency.

Dip pears into chocolate to cover completely. If chocolate is not deep enough, spoon it over the pears. Stand them upright on a foil-lined tray and set in refrigerator. Serve accompanied with a small biscuit or cream.

Average times Preparation — 20 minutes
Cooking — 30 minutes
Chilling — 2 hours

Wine notes Chocolate-Coated Pears call for a chilled, light muscat —
A: Seppelt Rutherglen Muscat
E and U: Muscat de Beaumes de Venise (Cave des Vignerons de Beaumes de Venise)

Do ahead At least ½ day

Chocolate Desserts:
(left) Dolce Torinese
(top right) Frozen Chocolate Prune Torte
(lower right) Chocolate-Coated Pears

Wine:
Morris (Rutherglen) Liqueur Muscat

(left) Dried Apricot Ice-Cream
(centre) Strawberry Ice-Cream
(below) Coconut Biscuits

WINTER

MENU 18

Two easy old favourites begin this menu which is followed by an Italian dessert which takes some days of planning. Almost the hardest part about the dessert is finding two moulds which fit adequately inside each other. If it's height you are looking for, then I suggest you try two jugs, one of course must be much smaller than the other. And violets picked from your own garden and crystallized at home are far superior to bought ones. It's a lovely menu for any Winter occasion.

WATERCRESS SOUP

---

5 cups veal or chicken stock	salt and pepper
1 bunch watercress (keep the youngest leaves for garnish)	1 cup cream
125 g butter	¼ cup small watercress leaves, to garnish
½ cup plain flour	

Using a deep stock pot, bring stock to the boil and drop in the roughly chopped watercress. Cook it uncovered, preferably not in aluminium which tends to spoil colour of green vegetables.

Meanwhile prepare the roux by melting butter in a small pan and stirring in flour. Cook the roux for 2 minutes, stirring all the time. Cool.

Ladle some of the hot stock on to the roux and whisk. Scrape all the roux into the watercress and stock, add salt and pepper and cook over low heat for 20 minutes, stirring from time to time. Cool soup a little and either blend or pass through a mouli (food mill).

Reheat soup and stir in cream, adjust seasoning and garnish with watercress leaves on top.

Average times Preparation — 10 minutes
Cooking — 30 minutes
Cooling — 10 minutes

Wine notes Watercress Soup is complemented by a nutty sherry —
A: Lindemans Reserve Bin
Z898A Amontillado Sherry
E and U: Dry Sack Sherry

Do ahead Preferably 1 to 2 days

PORK FILLETS IN CIDER WITH APPLES

6 medium pork fillets
1–2 tablespoons peanut oil
60 g butter
2 small onions, finely chopped
2 Golden Delicious apples, quartered and sliced
2 cups stock
300 ml cider
salt and pepper
30 g butter, softened

Garnish:
4 Golden Delicious apples, cored and sliced
60 g butter, extra

Brown pork fillets in a sauté pan in oil and butter. Take them out and reserve. Sauté onion and apple for a few minutes but do not let them take on any colour. Return fillets to pan and add stock and cider. Season with salt and pepper, cover pan and simmer for 25 minutes or until fillets are tender.

Lift out fillets, slice diagonally and keep them warm. Strain pan juices and return to pan and reduce a little if necessary. Whisk in softened butter, piece by piece, until it is well incorporated into sauce. Test for seasoning and adjust if necessary.

Fry apple slices reserved for the garnish in butter, until softened. Arrange sliced fillets attractively in a serving dish, spoon some of the sauce over the top and pass rest in a sauce boat. Arrange apple slices around dish.

Serve with steamed snake beans.

Average times Preparation — 10 minutes
Cooking — 45 minutes

Wine notes Pork in cider is complemented by a full-flavoured, aromatic white —
A: Wolf Blass Rhine Riesling
E: Riesling (Hugel) of a good year from Alsace
U: Martini (Napa) Johannisberg Riesling

VANILLA SPUMONI FILLED WITH ORANGE SORBET

Serves 12 or more
Make 2 days ahead

Vanilla Spumoni:

sugar syrup made from ½ cup sugar and 1 cup
  water, boiled then chilled
8 egg yolks
vanilla essence, to taste
2 cups thickened cream, whipped

Orange Sorbet:

sugar syrup made from ¾ cup castor sugar and
  ¾ cup water, boiled then chilled
1 cup orange juice
juice ½ lemon

pure icing sugar to dust
20 chocolate leaves
tear-drop cachous, to decorate
10 crystallized violets, to decorate (see next
  recipe)

To make vanilla spumoni: whisk sugar syrup, egg yolks and vanilla together. Cook in a double saucepan whisking constantly until thickened. Whisk mixture over a bowl of ice or cold water until cold. Fold in whipped cream, pour into a mould which has been rinsed out with cold water. Place a similar shaped mould, but smaller, inside, cover and freeze.

To make sorbet: mix sugar syrup and citrus juices together and churn until firm. Remove the inner mould from the spumoni by pouring warm water into it, then empty. Spoon churned sorbet into cavity and level the top. Cover and leave to set overnight.

To serve, dip the mould into warm (not hot) water and invert on a flat plate and shake out. If it shows any signs of melting return to freezer to firm. Dust spumoni with icing sugar and stick chocolate leaves upright around base and cap. Arrange crystallized violets around centre with tear-drop cachous. To serve, cut in halves through the diameter and lift off the top half. Cut into wedges like a cake. Serves 12 or more and can be made with any flavours you wish.

Average times Preparation — 1 hour
Cooling — 30 minutes
Setting —
  Spumoni — overnight
  Orange Sorbet —
  overnight

Do ahead At least 2 days

Wine notes Vanilla Spumoni with Orange
Sorbet requires no wine

CRYSTALLIZED VIOLETS

violets which have been picked in the sun
egg white

sieved pure icing sugar
safflower oil for oiling tray

The violets must have a fresh musk flavour so the flowers must be fresh and if possible, picked in the sun!

Whip egg white so it is soft but not stiff. Trim stems of violets to 1 cm. Dip each head into the egg white then the sugar. Shake off excess sugar and place upright on a very lightly oiled tray. Dry all day or overnight.

Note: Rose petals can be crystallized the same way.

Do ahead Up to 1 week but store in an airtight container and away from
light

WINTER

MENU 19

◆

Sorrel is another vegetable which is not used nearly enough and goes beautifully with eggs. This starter is easy and can be done up to ½ day ahead. The Coq au Vin is from my Cordon Bleu days in Paris and is followed by a dessert which takes some time and dexterity; but if you wish to take a short cut then by all means use pre-rolled puff pastry. However, this recipe for puff pastry is one of the easiest and once mastered you will find that you use it over and over again. The apples can be substituted for pears if you wish.

SORREL STUFFED EGGS

◆

1 bunch sorrel, leaves stripped off stems and washed thoroughly
8 large fresh eggs, hard boiled and halved lengthwise
⅓ cup thick cream

1 tablespoon sour cream
¼ teaspoon anchovy paste
salt and freshly ground black pepper to taste

6 sprigs watercress to garnish

◆

Reserve the 6 best sorrel leaves. Steam remaining leaves in a colander over boiling water (not touching) or in a steamer for 8 minutes. Purée and measure ⅓ cup.

Remove yolks from eggs and reserve the best 12 whites. Sieve yolks into a bowl and stir through the sorrel purée, thick cream, sour cream and anchovy paste with salt and pepper to taste. Spoon mixture into a pastry bag fitted with a large star tube and pipe into reserved whites. Chill eggs, covered for 1 hour to firm.

Arrange eggs on the reserved sorrel leaves on 6 entrée plates and garnish them with sprigs of watercress.

Average times Preparation — 25 minutes
Cooking — 8 minutes
Chilling — 1 hour

Wine notes Sorrel Stuffed Eggs need a flavoursome sherry —
A: Seppelt Show Amontillado
E and U: Tio Diego Sherry
(Valdespino)

Do ahead Up to ½ day

COQ AU VIN

2 × 1.5 kg chickens, each cut into drumsticks, thighs, wings and the breasts cut into 4 pieces each (that is 20 pieces altogether). Reserve the neck, wing tips and backs for stock
½ teaspoon salt
2 black peppercorns
100 g butter
2 white onions, chopped coarsely
3 tablespoons plain flour
2 shallots, chopped finely
3 cloves garlic, crushed and chopped finely
3 tablespoons tomato paste

2½ cups dry red wine, preferably a burgundy style
2 chicken stock cubes
salt and freshly ground black pepper to taste
fresh bouquet garni
1 teaspoon sugar
300 g baby pickling onions, peeled
200 g streaky bacon in the piece, skinned and cut into 1 cm dice
300 g white button mushrooms cut into quarters
½ cup chicken stock made from the reserved chicken pieces
2 tablespoons cognac

Pour 2 cups water over chicken backs, necks and wing tips. Add ½ teaspoon salt and 2 black peppercorns. Simmer for 25 minutes and strain. Remove fat with a bulb baster and return to pan to reduce to ½ cup. Cool.

Heat ⅔ of butter in a heavy-based pan over high heat and sauté a few chicken pieces at a time until golden brown on both sides. Remove with a slotted spoon and set aside. Seal remaining chicken pieces in the same way.

Stir in chopped onions and cook over medium heat stirring until softened. Stir in flour and brown, stirring for 2 minutes. Add shallots, garlic, tomato paste, wine, stock cubes, salt, pepper, bouquet garni, sugar and chicken pieces and stir well. Bring to a simmer and cook gently for 20 to 25 minutes or until the chicken is almost tender. Lift the chicken out and set aside.

Bring pickling onions to the boil with just enough cold water to cover and simmer gently until almost tender. Drain and set aside.

Bring bacon pieces to the boil with just enough cold water to cover and simmer gently for 2 minutes. Drain thoroughly. Heat the remaining butter in another heavy-based pan and sauté until well rendered and golden. Lift out with a slotted spoon and set aside with chicken. In the same pan, brown pickling onions, shaking the pan until they are almost tender. Lift out with a slotted spoon and set aside with chicken and bacon pieces.

In the same pan sauté mushrooms stirring constantly until lightly browned for 2 minutes. (If there isn't enough fat in the pan add a little extra butter).

Strain sauce into a large clean pan. Place pan in which you made the sauce over high heat and pour in stock, scraping base of pan and bring to boil. Add to strained sauce and whisk. Bring sauce to a gentle simmer, cover and simmer for 5 minutes. Put chicken pieces into hot sauce with bacon and pickling onions and stir in the cognac. Heat until warmed through.

Spoon chicken pieces onto a large warmed serving platter and pour over sauce. Accompany with hot fluffy rice or hot buttered noodles.

Average times Preparation — 45 minutes
Cooking — 1 hour 40 minutes

Wine notes Coq au Vin requires a burgundy-style, full-flavoured red —
A: d'Arenberg (McLaren Vale) Gold Medal Burgundy
E: Gevrey-Chambertin Clos de la Justice (Bourée)
U: Frick (Monterey) Pinot Noir

Do ahead Up to 1 day, but do not overcook chicken

APPLES IN PASTRY

───────◆───────

6 medium Golden Delicious apples, cored with
an apple corer

Quick puff pastry:
180 g butter, chilled
1½ cups plain flour
¼ teaspoon salt
200 g light sour cream

Filling:
12 raisins, finely chopped
1 tablespoon walnuts, finely chopped
1 tablespoon crushed macaroons
1 tablespoon clear honey

Syrup:
½ cup sugar
2 cups water
2 cups sweet white wine

Egg glaze:
1 egg yolk
2 tablespoons cream

───────◆───────

To make puff pastry: cut butter into 10 pieces and place in bowl with flour and salt. Process quickly until the butter is coarsely chopped into flour. Add sour cream and process a few seconds longer until mixture forms a ball. Immediately turn off the machine. Flatten dough and wrap in plastic. Refrigerate for 1 hour.

On a lightly floured board roll dough into a rectangle, keeping all edges as straight as possible measuring approximately 15 cm × 35 cm. Fold into thirds (like a book) making a smaller rectangle. Rotate the dough 90 degrees. Repeat rolling and folding process once more and press two finger marks into dough. (This represents two turns). Cover and refrigerate for 30 minutes. Repeat rolling and turning process once more, marking dough with four fingerprints after you have completed four turns. Chill a further 30 minutes and make two more turns. Wrap and chill until ready to use.

To stuff and cook apples: wedge a small piece of foil in the base of each apple to keep stuffing in place. Mix stuffing ingredients together and stuff into apple hollows. Stir syrup ingredients together in a pan which is just large enough to hold the 6 apples standing, stirring until sugar dissolves.

When mixture is boiling, stand apples in pan, cover and simmer slowly until almost tender. Very carefully lift out of the hot stock and set aside to drain and cool. When apples are cold, cut pastry in halves and return one-half to the refrigerator. Roll pastry on a lightly floured board into a rectangle. Cut into three. Stand an apple on each of the 3 pieces and gather up one corner at a time, pressing down the folds as if you were gift wrapping a parcel. When all 4 corners are gathered around the top end of the apple pinch the folds together. Do the same with remaining pastry and apples.

Whisk egg yolk and cream together and paint over pastry. Place on a well-buttered baking sheet and refrigerate for 30 minutes.

Bake in centre of 180°C (350°F) oven until pastry is cooked and golden, about 15 minutes. Serve at once with Fromage Blanc (see next recipe).

Average times Pastry —
Preparation — 25 minutes
Chilling — 2½ hours
Apples —
Preparation — 25 minutes
Cooking — 30 minutes
Resting — 30 minutes

Do ahead Pastry, up to 3 days. Can be frozen for up to 3 months. Apples up to oven stage, ½ day in advance

Wine notes With Apples in Pastry —
A: Orlando (Barossa) Auslese Semillon
E: Bonnezeaux Château Les Gauliers (Anjou)
U: San Martin (Santa Clara) Late Harvest Johannisberg Riesling

FROMAGE BLANC

250 g Neufchâtel cheese, at room temperature
½ cup natural full fat yoghurt, at room temperature

½ cup thickened cream, at room temperature

Whisk all the ingredients together, cover and refrigerate until ready to use.

Average times Preparation — 5 minutes   **Do ahead** Up to 2 days

INDEX

Warm Squid Salad with Pink
    Peppercorns 44
Watercress Soup 189
Whipped Cream Sorrel Sauce 90
Whisky Figs 54
Whitebait Mousse 32
White Onion Soup, Cream of 152
Whiting Duglère 83

Y

Yoghurt, Frozen Pudding 105

Z

Zabaglione 148
Zucchini Soup 121
Zucchini, Stuffed 65